THE SINGING VOICE

THE
SINGING VOICE

ROBERT RUSHMORE

*"Why is life different when
the singing stops?"*
JAMES REEVES

ILLUSTRATED WITH PHOTOGRAPHS

AND DRAWINGS

DODD, MEAD & COMPANY

NEW YORK

Grateful acknowledgement is made to the following for permission to reprint the material indicated:

C. M. Bowra for quotation from *PRIMITIVE SONG*, published by Weidenfeld & Nicholson, 1962. Copyright 1962 by C. M. Bowra.

Friedrich S. Brodnitz for quotation from *KEEP YOUR VOICE HEALTHY*, published by Harper & Row, Copyright 1953 by Friedrich S. Brodnitz.

E. P. Dutton & Co., Inc. for two drawings by Gluyas Williams from *PEOPLE OF NOTE* by Laurence McKinney, Copyright 1939, 1940 by Laurence McKinney. Renewal Copyright 1967 by Laurence McKinney. Reprinted by permission of E. P. Dutton & Co., Inc.

Harper & Row for quotation from two books by L. de Hegermann-Lindencrone, *IN THE COURTS OF MEMORY*, Copyright 1912 by Harper & Brothers and *THE SUNNY SIDE OF DIPLOMATIC LIFE*, Copyright 1914, by Harper & Brothers.

Mrs. Gerard Hoffnung for three drawings by Gerard Hoffnung from *THE HOFFNUNG MUSIC FESTIVAL*, Copyright 1956 by Gerard Hoffnung.

Houghton Mifflin Company for quotation from *MEN, WOMEN AND TENORS* by Frances Alda, Copyright 1937 by Frances Alda.

The Macmillan Company for quotation from *HOW TO SING* by Lilli Lehmann, Copyright 1924 by The Macmillan Company.

Methuen & Co., Ltd., for quotation from *THE TEACHING OF ELISABETH SCHUMANN* by Elizabeth Puritz, published 1956.

National Association of Teachers of Singing for editorial "Whither?" by Karl Trump, President, published in *The NATS Bulletin*, Vol. XXVI, No. 3 February/March 1970, p. 1. Permission to reprint granted by the author and the editor of *The NATS Bulletin*.

The New-York Historical Society for quotation from *LIFE OF EMMA THURSBY* by Richard Gipson, Copyright 1940 by the New-York Historical Society and Richard McCandless Gipson.

Opera for quotation from book review by Rupert Bruce Lockhart of *ANATOMY OF A VOICE*, April, 1966.

Oxford University Press for quotation from *A NATURAL APPROACH TO SINGING* by Judith Litante, Copyright 1959 by Judith Litante.

Punch for quotation of "Schwaltztenor" by M. W. Branch, Copyright by *Punch*, London.

G. Schirmer, Inc. for quotation from *SINGING* by Herbert Witherspoon, Copyright 1925 by G. Schirmer, Inc.

Charles Scribner's Sons for quotations of pages 148-51 and 446 from *OF LENA GEYER* by Marcia Davenport, Copyright 1936 by Marcia Davenport. Renewal Copyright 1964. Reprinted by permission of Charles Scribner's Sons.

Marziale Sisca for eight caricatures by Enrico Caruso, from *CARICATURES BY CARUSO*, published by La Follia di New York, Copyright 1951, by Marziale Sisca.

Most of the information in the lists of biographical facts about singers was obtained from *A CONCISE BIOGRAPHICAL DICTIONARY OF SINGERS* by K. J. Kutsch and Leo Riemens published by the Chilton Book Company, 1969.

ISBN 0-396-06243-1
Library of Congress Catalog Card Number: 70-135211

*Printed in the United States of America
by The Cornwall Press, Inc., Cornwall, N. Y.*

FOR
KATE MAXWELL
AND
ALL WHO LOVE THE SINGING VOICE

ACKNOWLEDGMENTS

The highly encouraging interest of two people in particular made this book possible. I had mentioned the idea of *The Singing Voice* to Frank Merkling, editor of *Opera News,* whose character I had always judged to be purposeful but gentle until he all but held me up for a series of articles based on the subject that appeared in the magazine during the season of 1966-67. I would have lapsed back into lethargy but for another forceful personality, William Cole, writer, anthologist, and free lance editor who declared that now the articles were written a book must follow and found various means of making me apply myself. It is impossible to thank both of them adequately.

I have been absorbed by the singing voice since childhood, but the first person who enabled me to write about it was Mary Ellis Peltz, former editor of *Opera News,* now archivist of the Metropolitan Opera Company to whom I have always been deeply grateful. In connection with this book Gerald Fitzgerald, currently an editor of *Opera News,* has been most helpful and encouraging. George Martin also read the manuscript and made many helpful suggestions and corrections. My thanks to Allen Klots, Jr., editor of this book, for his enthusiasm happily tempered by a most careful attention to organization and detail.

In New York I have worked in the Music Division (old and

new) of the New York Public Library as well as in the New York
Society Library. In London I have found valuable research material in the British Museum and also the London Library. To
the staffs of these institutions my sincere thanks.

I am most grateful to two lovers of singing, Vivian Liff and
George Stuart, who threw open to me not only their extraordinary
pictorial and record collections but the hospitality of their house
as well. George Selden Thompson has been extremely enthusiastic
and encouraging about this project as was, in earlier years, John
Richardson. I am grateful to William Seward for delightful and
instructive evenings spent at his studio, also editorial advice.

Neighbors through the long New England winters during which
this book was written and revised made its publication possible
perhaps more than they realized. I speak particularly of James and
Rosalie Becker, George and Katherine Dirgo, and Maurice and
Ida Lambert who gave succor and rescue at times when it was
very much needed, as did Jack and Antonia Grumbach.

Finally my family has put up with endless discourses on the
subject of the singing voice together with a great many playings
of recordings. Of them I would like to thank particularly my step-
son, Thomas Urquhart, who has put me in touch with literature
or other materials pertaining to the singing voice, and my wife,
who has painstakingly read the book. Caroline Urquhart has been
of great assistance in making the index.

A NOTE TO THE READER

After reading the manuscript of this book my wife put it down and said in an outraged tone, "But you haven't mentioned Tito Gobbi!" A good friend riding a couple of pre-dinner drinks began excitedly to make *lists* of his favorite vocalists to whom I had not referred. An outside reader for a publishing house snuffled and snorted his way through the manuscript and gracefully mixing his metaphors complained that I had not fashioned a work "with the ring of authority and the hallmark of sterling."

This book, however, was only conceived as a loose, informal survey of some of the varying aspects of the subject of the singing voice. The author has no degree in music of any kind, has never sung professionally and can make no scholastic nor academic claims to authority over his subject other than those bestowed by extensive vocal training plus a pair of ears. Though I have struggled for objectivity in commenting on some of the battles that so fiercely rage over the fields of vocalism, the book by its very nature is a subjective one. When, for instance, the need to mention a singer with a certain type of voice has come up, naturally I have chosen my favorite to the possible exclusion of a reader's beloved. The discussions of pop singers are limited because it seems to me that they belong more properly in a book about stage personalities rather than one dealing with the singing voice per se. Finally the reader will note that artists heard mainly in New York and London are mentioned—for the simple reason that these cities have been home bases for the author during his lifetime.

For all sins of omission or favoritism, I humbly ask the reader's indulgence. Volume after volume could be written about the singing voice and the subject not exhausted nor the treatment ever be wholly authoritative. This book is offered as a highly personal review of the singing voice by one voice-lover to the thousands and thousands who share this love—in the hope that it will interest, perhaps stir, but not outrage.

INTRODUCTION:

VOCAL SPELLS

THE FAIR SINGER

To make a final conquest of all me,
  Love did compose so sweet an enemy,
In whom both beauties to my death agree,
  Joining themselves in fatal harmony:
That while she with her eyes my heart doth bind,
She with her voice might captivate my mind.

I could have fled from one but singly fair:
  My disentangled soul itself might save,
Breaking the curléd trammels of her hair:
  But how should I avoid to be her slave,
Whose subtle art invisibly can wreathe
My fetters of the very air I breathe?

It had been easy fighting in some plain
  Where victory might hang in equal choice;
But all resistance against her is vain,
  Who has the advantage both of eyes and voice:
And all my forces needs must be undone,
She having gainéd both the wind and sun.

—*Andrew Marvell*

On from the loudspeakers they came—the voices of Pinza, Ella
Fitzgerald, Bjoerling, Piaf. Seated in a living room with a spread-
ing oak tree illuminated outside the windows, we asked for more,
more! the way people do in the intensity of an addiction. Now the
one choosing the records, as though the appropriate time had at
last arrived (all the other singers having been no more than a
preparation for this one) lowered the needle and at the first sound
of the voice a sigh, a sense of being blessed went through all who
were in the room.

"Casta Diva, Casta Diva . . ."

sang Rosa Ponselle, this aria which as one writer has said "begins
so like the quivering of moonbeams on the water." Once again, as
many times before, we were in the thrall of this unique singing
voice, silent, fascinated—lost.

That the singing voice is one of the most potent weavers of
spells over mankind cannot be a startling fact to anyone. Yet in
the variety of responses it can evoke from people the singing voice
is astonishing. Human beings react to vocal sounds with passionate
adoration, disgust, amazement, anger, indifference or total boredom. Take, for example, the period in English history when in
late winter, 1727, riots began to break out in and around the
King's Theatre, London. Demonstrations occurred frequently
among the common mobs of that hurly-burly era but in this case
it was the aristocrats—the Countess of Burlington, Sir Robert
Walpole—who were proving themselves to be every bit as animal
as the members of the lower orders. And what was the issue that
had aroused such violence? Not as might be supposed, differences
over religion, or politics, or affairs of state. Far simpler, it was
whether one opera singer called Francesca Cuzzoni was preferable
to another named Faustina Bordoni. The controversy which at one
moment seemed almost to threaten England with civil war raged
over the merits of a pair of sopranos. In the end revolution was

averted by the management offering the proud, stingy Cuzzoni one less guinea for her next season's appearances than Faustina, an arrangement that vanity would not permit. Ambrose Phillips, a poet of the time, wrote Cuzzoni's exit lines:

> Tuneful mischief, vocal spell,
> To this island bid farewell;
> Leave us as we ought to be
> Leave the Britons rough and free.

In our own time partisanship of a favorite singer continues with unabated vehemence and even violence. Not very long ago Rudolf Bing had to eliminate solo curtain calls for a while at the Metropolitan Opera House, because they incited rival fans to excess in cheering their favorites. Nor are these passions stirred up only by operatic voices. Let a critic write that the latest Beatles record is a failure or that the new Barbra Streisand release is second-rate and he will be flooded with abusive letters denouncing him as "arrogant," "rude," "prejudiced," "silly," "vicious," "inelegant," "coarse," or "shoddy" to take a random sampling from letters published in the record magazines, *Stereo Review* and *High Fidelity*.

Why, we ask ourselves, does the singing voice have this extraordinary power to turn human beings into maniacs? Why do fans of singers suffer hardships, go without sleep, practice extremes of economies, risk bodily injury (and inflict it) to be present at a performance of their idols? What stirs up the urge that exceeds anything musical to possess some object, some trifling scrap * that has somehow been connected with a favorite singer?

As we progress in this survey of the singing voice the reader will soon realize that little about it can be discussed in a truly

---

* Nellie Melba records in her memoirs that on her last night of singing in Russia, attempting to sign programs after the performance, she had her pencil snatched from her, which was then "bitten to pieces with a single crunch of strong, white teeth" and distributed by a young man "to his chosen friends" who received them with reverence.

scientific way. The singing voice is so closely linked with inconsistent human behavior itself that much has to be adduced or hypothesized with no really provable conclusions. Nevertheless the fact seems inescapable that the vocal spell is partly a sexual one and usually, though not always, a singer will have a greater attraction to listeners of the opposite sex. The squeals of female teeny-boppers just awakened to puberty are provoked most frequently by a male singer—or what passes for a male. In reverse, one reads this comment from a masculine reviewer of popular music on the singing of Peggy Lee: "For a male listener it could be and still can be stupefyingly sexual." Among older women it is noticeable that the manly tones of a baritone or a bass are what stir up flutters of response particularly when the voices come from big, manly-looking physiques.

Let it not be thought, however, that the fascination of the singing voice is exclusively sexual. Another kind of spell that singers cast over mankind is in banishing cares and allaying melancholy or sadness. The mercurial Saul was calmed by the beautiful playing and singing of David, "the sweet singer of Israel." Perhaps more extraordinary was the soothing power of Carlo Broschi, called Farinelli, a castrated Italian vocalist, who became the most influential figure in the court of the Spanish King Philip V, from his ability to sing away the monarch's melancholic madness.

How understand this comforting, soothing spell that the singing voice can exert? The explanation may well be a very simple one. Along with our sexual drives, one of our strongest urges is to be taken care of, to go back to the sheltered, irresponsible condition we knew as infants. What accomplishes this return more swiftly than the sound of a singing voice returning us to a time when a lullaby close to our ears meant safety . . . warmth . . . contentment?

* * * *

From some people the singing voice draws entirely different reactions. These may range from diffidence through discomfort to downright desperation. "I have sat through an Italian opera," complained Charles Lamb, "till for sheer pain and inexplicable anguish, I have rushed out into the noisiest places of the crowded streets to solace myself."

A violent dislike of singing—particularly the operatic kind— has always been a fecund source for humorists. Jiggs is forever trying to get out of going to the opera with Maggie who believes it confers social status upon herself. She also sings as well—excruciatingly. In top form, Mark Twain describes going to a performance of *Lohengrin* in *A Tramp Abroad*. "There were circumstances that made it necessary for me to stay through the four hours to the end . . . yet at times the pain was so exquisite I could hardly keep the tears back. At those times, as the howlings and wailings and shriekings of the singers and the ragings and roarings and explosions of the vast orchestra rose higher and higher and wilder and wilder and fiercer and fiercer, I could have cried . . ."

Again we have to ask why should there be some so indifferent or even hostile to the beauties of the singing voice? And again we can only turn to speculation for an answer. Perhaps it lies in the nature of music itself which divides up roughly into the kind that is sung and the kind that is played. In the great masterworks of symphonic and chamber music only the distillations of human emotions—impersonal joy, sadness, exultation—are heard. The *specific* as adumbrated by words set to music and sung, the expressions of petty man—"I love, I hate, I envy, I yearn"—are left out.

Over the years I have noticed that lovers of chamber music (perhaps the most abstract of musical forms) are most likely to reject the singing voice. Only when the voice is used instrumentally, as in some of the Bach cantatas or when the voice itself has the pure, abstracted quality of a boy soprano or countertenor will they abide and even cherish it.

Then there are the more specific prejudices that certain types of voices engender. A sensitive woman and excellent writer who likes *only* the male voice explains her distaste for its female counterpart: "I'm not prepared to take in all those women's animal passions." Some people shy from the "vapid," "foolish" sounds made by a coloratura soprano. Others are dismayed by the reticent tones of the average English oratorio tenor—"the sort of noise one would expect a giraffe to make were it so to forget itself as to yawn during the obsequies of a president of the Royal Zoological Society," as Sir Thomas Beecham once put it.

Our reactions then, to the singing voice are as subjective as to people themselves. We have "types": we prefer blondes to brunettes; we don't like men with hair on their chests. As in the crowd, there are misogynists who live with total indifference towards their fellow beings. So we love or loathe the singing voice, each and every one of which is a characterization. Like the human face and personality it is all but impossible to mistake one for another. This has recently been proved scientifically: prints, like those of the tips of the fingers, can now be taken of the voice. Each one differs; each has a unique, characteristic pattern as varied as man himself. As one of the characters says in Willa Cather's *The Song of the Lark:* "The voice simply is the mind and is the heart."

CONTENTS

Introduction: Vocal Spells   XI

Part One: THE HEARSAY VOICES   1

Part Two: THE OPERATIC VOICES OF TODAY   27
Coloratura Soprano Roles, 45, Soubrette
Soprano, 45-46, Lyric Soprano, 46, *Spinto*
and Lighter Dramatic Soprano, 47-48,
Dramatic Soprano, 49. Lyric Mezzo-Soprano, 60-61, Dramatic Mezzo-Soprano,
61. Contralto, 62. Lyric Tenor, 78-79,
Spinto or Dramatic Tenor, 79-80, Heldentenor, 80. Baritone, 89-90. Bass 90-92.

Part Three: THE NON-OPERATIC VOICES   109

Part Four: MAGIC: THE ILLUSORY SCIENCE.
HOW IS IT DONE?   139

Part Five: THE AGES OF VOICE   177

Appendix   295

Glossary   299

Reference Notes   301

Bibliography and Recommended Reading   307

Index   317

ILLUSTRATIONS

Coloratura by Gerald Hoffnung   33
The Wagnerian Soprano by Gluyas Williams   53
"The King"—Caruso Self-Portrait   70
Bonci and Chaliapin by Caruso   80
Basso by Gerald Hoffnung   85
Rossini by Caruso   126
Verdi by Caruso   129
The Mixed Chorus by Gluyas Williams   137
Tetrazzini by Caruso   203
"Madama Butterfly" by Caruso   241
At the Rehearsal by Caruso   257
Don José by Caruso   260
"Signorina acknowledges applause" by Gerald Hoffnung   265
Jean de Reszke by Caruso   285

Following page 76:

The Concert Singer by Thomas Eakins
Manuel Garcia
Maria Malibran-Garcia
Malibran's Debut
Madame Viardot-Garcia

Emma Eames
Geraldine Farrar
Giovanni Rubini
Lina Cavalieri
Conchita Supervia
Maria Callas
Mary Garden

Following page 204:

Felia Litvinne
Albert Alvarez
Edouard de Reszke
Therese Tietjens
Enrico Caruso
Luigi Lablache
Clara Butt
Gioacchino Rossini
Reynaldo Hahn
Jean-Baptiste Faure
The Singer and the Listener by Edgar Degas

PART ONE

THE HEARSAY VOICES

A proper survey of a subject should begin with its history, but in the case of the singing voice an authentic history really cannot be written. Our information as to how singers sounded before the invention of the phonograph is entirely dependent on hearsay— the highly subjective observations and reactions of people who set them down in writing. Since science now tells us that no two ears hear a singing voice precisely the same way, these commentaries on singers of the past that are so often quoted must be regarded with increased skepticism. Some idea of the range and flexibility of the voices of legendary singers is provided by the music they performed. But previous to the twelfth century only the scantiest fragments survive; before the Age of Pericles, virtually nothing. Once more then, we are forced into the realm of speculation, a place, however, in which any true lover of singing is delighted to find himself.

*　　*　　*　　*

First Songs.　　How and when man first evolved his remarkable ability to speak and to sing is of course not known. The usual stereotype of the caveman is an ape-like creature who makes only grunting sounds. Darwin believed that the voice evolved from man's need to attract a mate, thus eliminating the task, so often depicted, of having to go out and drag one back to the cave. Darwin's theory is made more believable because of the direct

connection that exists between man's voice and his sexual development. Other anthropologists, however, decry the idea that man first
lifted his voice in imitation of the mating calls of animals and
birds, pointing out that of the very earliest songs known to us,
the themes are not erotic, but relate to religion, battle or domestic
matters.

Some scholars believe that when man first discovered he possessed the power to make a variety of sounds differing in pitch and
duration, the result was neither speech nor song, but a combination
of the two—a kind of intoning. When this marriage broke up is
of course again not known. "It is indeed tempting to surmise,"
writes C. M. Bowra in his *Primitive Song* "that in the late Paleolithic Age, c. 30,000-15,000 B.C., when men delighted in painting
and carving and modeling, they delighted also in the melodious
arrangement of words and that the hunters of mammoth, bison
and rhinoceros who recorded their hopes or their achievements so
splendidly on the walls of caves celebrated them in song. But just
as we know nothing of their speech . . . so we know nothing of
any specialized purposes to which it may have been put. Certainty
of any kind is out of the question . . ."

If we have no knowledge of how our primitive ancestors actually
sang there are at least some indications of the subject matter of
their songs. This hasn't varied, with the exception of perhaps a
greater preponderance of love songs, from what we feel the need
to sing about today. There were religious songs—the church hymns
of twenty millenniums ago; there were songs that described heroic
deeds of war, just as only a few years back the country's favorite
hit was "The Battle of New Orleans." There were songs describing the evil and tragedy in fighting, atavistic counterparts of the
"protest" songs heard all over the world in our time. There were
songs of animal life and nature:

> Glittering stars of the white night,
> Moon shining on high,

Piercing the forest with your pale beams,
Stars, friends of white ghosts,
Moon, their protectress.

A feeling towards the moon in this song handed down among the Gabon pygmy tribe quickly brings to mind Norma's apostrophe to the moon, "Casta Diva," or the thousand and one popular songs of which the moon is the subject. And then there were songs of death and resurrection such as this invocation to an ancestor:

My departed one, my departed one, my God!
Where art thou wandering?

If none of the music of these songs is known to us, though presumably it was as primitive and limited as the people who sang them, scholars nonetheless believe that they were very often sung accompanied by some kind of rhythmic body action—the waving of an arm, the stamping of a foot. This sounds totally contemporary when one thinks of the average popular songstress performing on television who snaps her fingers or twitches the cord on the microphone that she holds a few inches from her mouth; or today's pop groups wracked, it seems, by rhythmic spasms as they give their all to their numbers. Many of the songs of earliest man were antiphonal, that is, a question and answer pattern between two groups, the answer returned in a kind of refrain. This too seems entirely familiar when we remember the arrangements of many pop groups today with one singer delivering the line of a song and the others immediately echoing it.

The feminist writer, Sophie Drinker, suggests that among the singers of ancient times women were superior to men, who couldn't sing as readily while out chasing and killing the day's rations. A woman's more routinized domestic duties allowed for a greater cultivation of the art and Mrs. Drinker believes that the peculiarly rapt expression often seen on the faces of women choristers even today is simply a continuance of how females many thousands of years ago looked as they went about their daily domestic routines singing. The birth of a baby in many tribes was also an important occasion for which women would sing in order to ward off evil spirits and ease the labor of the mother. Once delivered, women have of course sung to their babies from time immemorial. (The syllables "lu lu" seem to have had a peculiar fascination for primordial women for purposes of singing: hence the word "lullaby," also "alleluia," and "ululate" which means "to wail.")

Other anthropologists agree with Mrs. Drinker that our female ancestors may have sung better and certainly more frequently than the males. If then modern man has evolved by making new and increased demands on his intelligence and physical equipment, this would explain why over the aeons, women, in asking more of their voices, now generally have a range of at least three more notes (and sometimes up to an octave) than the finest male singers.

Anthropologists also tell us that with the exception of a few tribes in which women were forbidden to sing, the female maintained a complete equality with the male. Allowing a thousand years out for the time when the Christian Church restrained the singing of women on the grounds that it was lascivious, the female has continued to maintain her rare equality with the other sex. Singing is at least one field in which a woman can and does compete successfully with the male, enjoying the fullest possible recognition of her status.

At first the songs of our ancient antecedents seem to have been mainly communal. But as the singing voice began to develop it was natural that certain individuals among the group should be discovered to have superior voices and musical talent. Solo singing on a very limited scale therefore slowly developed and the soloist in a tribe by skillful use of his voice—sometimes by mere mimicry of animal noises—was often expected to drive away evil spirits. These solo singers were powerful and held in awe, but also feared and even disliked. In the minds of a superstitious, primitive people the magical effect of the singing voice seemed to be linked in some way with the terrifying spirits themselves. Something of this superstitious awe, I think, carries over in our worshipful attitude towards singers today. They are creatures not as we, but in touch with supernatural forces that evoke incomprehensible responses to the vocal art which seem almost frightening.

*　　*　　*　　*

Voices of Antiquity. Let us now move on to comparatively recent times, that is to say the seventh century B.C. Then for the first time we have a visual documentation of an attempt at a vocal "method" among the Mesopotamians, as shown in a bas-relief in the British Museum. Together with a group playing various instruments, we see a choir of six women and nine children. One of the women has her hand on her larynx and is squeezing it so as to produce the thin, whiny high notes favored in the East to this day.

By this time the epics of Homer, his *Odyssey* and *Iliad,* had come into being. Though the hexameters of these poems are believed to have been sung, no one is certain what kind of singing was involved. Evidence points to an extremely limited type of vocalization, with an occasional chord plucked from the lyre or *kithara* to mark a change of mood. We know of course that the Greeks of Homer's time and in the later years of the Golden Age revered music, so much so that as Paul Henry Lang points out in his monumental *Music in Western Civilization:* "an educated and distinguished man was called a musical man (ἀνὴρ μουσικός), whereas an inferior and uncouth person was simply 'unmusical' or a man without music (ἀνὴρ ἄμουσος) . . . They [the Greeks]," he goes on to say, "had two souls in their breasts, one striving for clarity, temperance and moderation (σωφροσύνη), the other driving them towards the fantastic and orgiastic, the cult of Dionysus. For this very reason they preached the idea of σωφροσύνη with great fervor."

It seems probable that in ancient Greece the singing voice and its art—the attractions of which it has to be admitted come down fully on the side of Dionysus—never approached the range and power of the other performing arts of acting and dancing. Singing there certainly must have been—both religious and secular. Plato disapproved of the latter, the professional singers who could be hired to entertain during dinner parties, but then Plato, like most of the high-minded Greeks, conceived of music as a moral force, controlled, subservient to the word, the idea. Of the various modes or primitive scales that had come into being Plato held disapproving views. The Ionic and the Lydian he considered "effeminate and gossiping harmonies," and in general saw no need for "a great many strings, nor a variety of harmony in our songs and melodies." Music was conceived of by men such as Plato in intellectual terms, and regarded as a placator of passions not a stimulant to them as an unrestrained voice lifted in song can so easily be. Music was meant to ennoble the character and perfect the soul. In such a moral climate the art of singing was not likely to develop and at least one authority has concluded that Greek vocal music "was not music in our sense of the term at all, but a special way of reciting poetry, determined by nuances of expression which had been steadily and continuously refined by the most artistic people on earth but throughout their history more akin to the method of speaking than of the singing voice."

A people who evolved the beautiful myths of Orpheus, the first great solo singer, cannot however be considered entirely anti-vocal. Greek legends do not describe the range nor quality of the voice of Orpheus, but no book whose subject is the singing voice would be complete without mention of its magical beauty: ". . . there was every kind of bird brought under the spell of the singing, and all beasts of the mountains and whatever feeds in the recesses of the sea, and a horse stood entranced, held in control, not by a bridle, but by the music . . . You could see . . . the rivers flowing from their sources toward the singing and a wave of the sea raising itself aloft for love of the song . . ."

Orpheus, son of Apollo and grandson of Zeus, also knew the secrets of magic and astrology, thus confirming the association of the supernatural with singing. In what must have been one of the most thrilling song contests of all times, Orpheus protected the Argonauts from the deadly dangerous singing of the Sirens by the greater enchantment of his own vocal art. With the vanity characteristic to vocalists, the Sirens could not bear being outsung by a rival and threw themselves into the sea and became rocks.

As for Orpheus, after singing his way down through Hades to Eurydice, only to lose her again by looking back on the way up, his subsequent fate was one that has threatened many a famous singer —that of being torn to pieces by a mob. (Two squealing girls once grabbed on to each end of Frank Sinatra's bow tie and almost strangled him to death.) In the case of Orpheus these were not hysterical teen-agers attempting to rip off a piece of his robe as a memento, but the Maenads, a group of wild Bacchic women furious at his rejection of them out of faithfulness to the memory of his wife, Eurydice.

*   *   *   *

With the rise of the Roman Empire history definitely instructs that the ascendancy of music and singing as an art is linked with the moral spirit of the people—a fact that the newly founded Christian Church began to recognize about the same time. The Romans took much from the earlier Greek civilization but not its moral spirit of control and restraint. Quite the opposite: the Roman ideal came to be pleasure, surrender to the senses. In this spiritual atmosphere, Greek music speedily changed, quickened, gained rhythm, became more animalistic and sexy. Oriental music full of elaboration was brought to Rome from the campaigns in Egypt.

By the third century A.D. music seems to have become an integral part of Roman life. Rather the way music follows us about today in elevators and restaurants and airport lounges, a wealthy Roman would have his slaves make music for him at home while he dressed or ate, or when he made journeys by land and sea. At banquets it was customary for the warlike Romans to sing songs accompanied by flutes in praise of famous heroes. They also attended concerts of massed vocal choirs or instruments at which, according to Cicero, "the audience would give vent to its disapproval if the singer or player made mistakes"—a custom that sounds suspiciously similar to the behavior of Italian audiences today.

With such a national enthusiasm for music, virtuosi naturally emerged, among them great singers together with the usual jealousies, rivalries and claques that swirl about great vocal stars. One of the renowned singers of his day was Tigellius who sang and composed at the court of Augustus. As capricious and temperamental as the most explosive prima donna, he was quite capable of refusing to sing even when commanded by the emperor, if the mood was not upon him; equally he might perform throughout an entire banquet whether bidden or not. A number of the emperors themselves, most notably Hadrian, were amateur singers of talent, though some condemned the practice of music as unmanly. All Roman society was shocked by the Emperor Nero, not because he was obsessed by music but for appearing as a professional singer and actually competing in contests, in which, not oddly, there was little suspense as to who would be the winner. Suetonius tells us that Nero had a "thin, husky voice" and in an effort to improve it would lie with a metal weight on his chest to strengthen his breathing. This vain, decadent emperor also kept close watch over his diet in case certain foods injured his voice, and refused to command his soldiers in person lest he strain his vocal cords—all practices that might be prescribed in the vocal studio of today. Nero made his first public appearance in Rome in 59 A.D., sang in the contests at Naples in 64 and reappeared at the Theatre of Pompey in Rome the following year. Towards the end of 66 he made a professional tour of Greece singing and accompanying himself on the *kithara*, as he had been instructed by his Greek master, Terpnus. Nero's performances usually consisted of personal interpretations of a tragic role or theme, such as Orestes killing his mother, or Oedipus blinded. His success in these roles cannot be doubted given the fact that he possessed a claque numbering five thousand which had been carefully instructed in the three ways of making applause gratifying to the Emperor's ears: *bombi,* a sound like the buzzing of bees; *imbrices,* resembling the noise of rain or hail falling on a roof; and *testae,* the crashing of pots together. Suetonius found one of Nero's performances "interminable." This, an early instance of the rich and powerful buying public appearances as a singer, is certainly not the last.

No account exists of the range and general quality of the voice of a celebrated singer such as Tigellius, nor do we know what vocal feats, if any, he may have performed. Contemporary reports do tell us that a number of singing teachers existed, that singers practiced scales and were expected to lead the healthy temperate life necessary to the maintenance of their art. "Quintilian relates how they protected their throats by holding handkerchiefs before their mouths when speaking," writes Dr. Lang, "and how they avoided the sun, fog and wind. On the other hand Martial reports that some of the singers overexerted themselves to such a degree that they suffered ruptured blood vessels. This was due, no doubt," he adds, "to the large proportions of the theaters and rooms, which demanded loud singing."

To what extent vocal art at this period might have developed is entirely a matter of conjecture, for by about the third century A.D. a force had come into the world that was to have the greatest possible effect on the singer and his song. This, of course, was the Christian Church.

The Devil's Songs. That singing was godly there could be no doubt. The disciples themselves sang after the Last Supper before going up onto the Mount of Olives. And did not Paul exhort the Ephesians to "be filled with the Spirit, speaking to yourselves in psalms and hymns and spiritual songs, singing and making melody in your heart to the Lord"? Earlier religions had employed chanting and song in the performance of their rites; it was natural for the founding fathers of the Church to adopt the same practice. Chants, mainly Jewish, using one or at the most two notes to a syllable and having melodic sequences but no rhythm or measures were intoned by the congregations of the first Christian churches. As Christianity spread, Greek and Byzantine influences were brought to bear on the music of the service and it became enriched. Certain men of the early Church recognized that music could be a powerful stimulus to belief and a means of attracting converts. They composed new psalms and hymns and encouraged enthusiastic singing among their flocks. By the third century it had become customary to hear at a service the men of the congregation singing out a verse of the psalm, the women and children replying with another, and both joining together in the refrain—a pattern of song already thousands of years old.

Though singing was capable of raising religious exaltation, the Church fathers soon became aware that it also brought out other emotions and impulses of a kind distinctly in contradiction to the teachings of Christianity. Within an orthodoxy of obedience and self-denial, the free, exhilarating expression of singing sat most uncomfortably. Above all, the Church preached the sinfulness of sex and the desirability of celibacy. But the warm, sensuous tones of the singing voice, particularly of a woman, evoked all too powerfully the earthiness of man's nature. "So often as I call to mind the tears I shed at the hearing of the church songs . . . whenas I am moved not with the singing but the thing sung," wrote St. Augustine. "And yet so often it befalls me to be moved with the voice rather than the ditty, I confess myself to have grievously offended, at which time I wish rather not to have heard the music." In 318 A.D. the Church fathers moved against the disturbing power of the singing voice by forbidding the voluptuous song of women to be heard in church. By 367 neither men nor women of the congregation were permitted to lift their singing voices in praise of God, only specially trained members of the clergy.

These men were called canons—"singing men"—and at their ordination, as W. J. Henderson writes in his interesting *Early History of Singing,* they were charged as follows: "See that thou believe in thy heart what thou singest with thy mouth, and approve in thy works what thou believest in thy heart." Specially instructed in vocal technique and musicianship, able to embellish their solos with *appoggiaturas, portamenti* and ornaments of various kinds, these canons soon developed into the singing stars of their time. The world does not change and we learn from Henderson that "they speedily acquired the self glory which has clung to singers ever since . . . and began to swell with vanity." This was expressed in terms of personal adornment, particularly by the length of their hair, the luxuriance of which these Beatle-like canons doubtless believed added to the effect of their singing as they stood before their congregations.

Again we have no actual description of how these men sounded nor what the range and power of their voices were like. We do know something about their training at the Schola Cantorum, which is usually thought to have been founded by Gregory when he became Pope in 590, but which was probably started at a somewhat earlier date. The course, for example, lasted nine years, much of this time evidently consumed in memorizing the chants. What we know of this music suggests that the voices of these canons may have possessed some of the power and flexibility which have long been associated with the best Italian singing, or "bel canto" as it has come to be called. Technical problems such as breathing, the placing of the voice, learning to sing a controlled legato line must have all been studied at the Schola Cantorum and presumably mastered. An ability to sing florid passages was also a necessity, for coloratura-like phrases were common in the liturgies of the Eastern Church, and later, in that of Spain, the latter's being derived from the much turned, highly ornamented music of the Moors.

For the next seven or eight hundred years the Church held the curious position of building and maintaining a technical and aesthetic standard of singing by presenting to the public, so to speak, fine professional vocalists, while at the same time trying to prevent the public from singing themselves. All secular music, love songs, work songs, the folk songs that are as natural to people as breathing itself were denounced as sinful and lascivious. Particularly suspect was the woman's singing voice. In the fifth century Bishop Hippolytus declared an edict: "A woman who attracts people with her beautiful but deluding sweetness of voice (which is full of seduction and sin) must give up her trade and wait forty days if she is to receive communion." Another bishop, a hundred years later, complains with horror, "How many peasants and how many women know by heart and recite out loud the Devil's songs, erotic and obscene." The only female singing condoned was that of nuns, and their tones were trained to sound sexless and devoid of human expression. It is odd to realize that the present designation of women's voices, "alto" and "soprano," have in fact masculine endings and refer to boys' voices, "higher" and "highest" above the normal range of men's voices. No words existed to describe the type and range of sound that women made while singing.

Forbidding men and women so natural a means of expression as lifting their voices in song proved, of course, as unrealistic as trying to prohibit the birds their notes. Secular singing, though much suppressed, continued to give vent to man's feeling about his life and the life of others. Singing also became associated with magic and incantations. "If we have a headache," remarks St. Augustine, "we run to the singer of incantations; I see this occur every day." Since Church music was all that people were exposed to, often parts of the liturgy were simply borrowed and given different words. By the eleventh century when men were beginning to feel the first stirring of their own individual worth, secular singing, far from being blotted out, had increased, and it was

then that the first solo singers of note came into being. These
were the troubadours.

Singers of Grace.   For centuries the Church had suppressed the
singing voices of women, had condemned their sound as lewd and
a device for sexual ensnarement. Now curiously—and then again
perhaps not so curiously—when the solo secular voice was raised
again in Western Europe it gave extravagant praise to women. Of
the various kinds of wandering musicians and singers during the
eleventh century the first was the *jongleur,* the tough, bawdy,
traveling entertainer of his day, a one-man vaudeville show with
his songs, dances, funny stories and tricks. Like all such troupers
of any age he was a sound and experienced musician. At the opposite end of the social scale were the troubadours of noble, sometimes royal birth who appeared in the twelfth and thirteenth
centuries. Perhaps the most celebrated among these was Richard
Coeur de Lion, skilled in the art of composing and singing verses
in praise of chivalric love, as was his friend, Blondel de Nesle.
Legend has it that when Richard was imprisoned secretly in a
castle high on a hill overlooking the Danube, his friend found his
way to this rocky retreat and climbing up under one of the windows of the castle began to sing a lay which he and the monarch
are thought to have composed together. To Blondel's joy and delight he heard the familiar voice of Richard take up the song
along with him. Thus the singing voice proved its power to effect
the rescue of one of Europe's most important rulers.

Passing the tedious months in prison, Richard is also said to
have composed and sung in the customary Provençal these sad,
yet rather threatening lines:

> No prisoner can tell his honest thought,
> Unless he speaks as one who suffers wrong;
> But for his custom he may make a song . . .
> My friends are many, but their gifts are nought.

Shame will be theirs, if, for my ransom here
I lie another year.

Brothers to the Gallic troubadours were the German minne-singers who with Teutonic thoroughness constructed an elaborate set of rules and regulations on the composing of songs—those strictures which Wagner mocks so thoroughly in *Die Meister-singer*.

But what kind of voices did they possess, these the first solo secular singers to emerge in comparatively recent times? From all that can be adduced their sounds seem to have been very limited. Most of the troubadours' music that has survived reveals that the singer was required to have a compass of no more than an octave; frequently the range of a song is a sixth. Here again emphasis was on the word and there was no ideal of either vocal beauty or display for display's sake. Professor Donald Jay Grout, a noted musi-cologist, believes that the quality of tone of the troubadours—light, thin, clear and without vibrato—was quite different from that of singing voices we are used to today.

Meanwhile inside the churches vocalists were still seizing the opportunity to indulge themselves in various types of vocal dis-play, suggesting that their voices may have had considerable range and flexibility. "These people break up their melodies with hock-ets, debase them with discants, and load them with moteti and tripla in the vulgar style," thundered Pope John XXII in 1324 and ordered the singers to desist or undergo penalties. The Church, however, was not the place at this time where the voice could really get its wings and soar. Sacred music until the seven-teenth century was highly polyphonic, a musical style which does not aid in the evolution of the singing voice nor in the highly in-dividual art of solo singing.

To bring out all the brilliance, power and expressiveness in-herent in the workings of the human lungs and larynx, a new kind of musical form was needed. Not until the start of the seventeenth century did it finally emerge and the first age of bel canto was born.

The Counterfeit Voices. The development of the singing voice as we know it today very much parallels the development of man as we know him today. With the coming of the Renaissance and the so-called Age of Humanism, men really began to emerge as individuals. Until then they had mainly been as members of a unit, as were their voices, since vocal music was almost entirely polyphonic. When individual man began to assert his uniqueness, the singing voice responded with its special claim to uniqueness too.

In 1600 Jacopo Peri, himself a singer, wrote what is generally conceded to be the first opera, *Euridice,* and there commenced in Italy a golden age of singing, which some look back upon and rue will never come again. Peri took his example from the Greeks, as did many artists of that period, and composed a declamatory kind of music in which the sense of the word was all-important. The greatest master of this kind of vocal writing was Claudio Monteverdi. His full-length opera, *L'Incoronazione di Poppea,* which has been produced and recorded in recent times, is a work that seems strangely modern to us today, telling a story of very real, passionate people wonderfully characterized by the music. No display of the voice of any kind is introduced; if there are repeated notes or embellishments it is purely for emphasis. The voice is the complete servant of the word and never has it been used in a more human way.

But as a taste for the baroque gathered this almost austere vocal music gave way to display, ostentation and artificiality; to lines that were long, serpentine and highly ornamented. The singing voice, as it was uniquely capable of doing, led the way in creating this style of music, mainly through the performances of the celebrated *castrati,* who initiated what is generally thought of as the first golden age of bel canto.

"Viva il coltello"—"Hooray for the knife"—audiences sometimes shouted after a particularly remarkable performance by one of these tall, full-chested male singers who produced the sound of a woman's voice. For the development of this curious vocal taste the Church, ever a force over the destinies of the singing voice, must take the perhaps not so unwitting blame. Having banished the sexually arousing sound of the female voice from services it now had to rely on the capabilities of boys to cope with the higher ranges that rightfully belong to women. When by the end of the fifteenth century a number of polyphonists began to emerge— particularly in the Netherlands—who composed highly complex and glorious music that required voices of power and stamina, it soon became evident that the voices of boys were inadequate. At best, boys had never been totally satisfactory; after years of careful musical training and practice their voices, maddeningly, might break overnight, and all their valuable instruction and experience be instantly lost. Unless . . .

Tampering artificially with the sex of a male and his ability to procreate was definitely interfering with one of the basic works of God, and the Church promised excommunication to anyone participating in such a crime against nature. Nevertheless the Church also took the attitude that if a husky male well-trained musically and in vocal production, from whom emanated a voice with a female range, appeared on the doorstep, so to speak, this was the will of God. Accordingly the singer would be promptly accepted into the choir to gain honor, wealth and, above all, security in this most insecure of times. As a result, all over Italy, mainly among desperate peasant families, boys displaying any kind of singing voice and musical talent were put to the knife. Most of them never made careers and were left to finish their lives as eunuchs— the targets of mockery and derision.

Shame, indignation, revulsion have generally been the reactions of people towards the unsexing of a man by surgery for the sake of retaining his boy's range and quality of tone. "Can British matrons

take their daughters to hear the portentous yells of this disen-
franchised of nature, and will they explain the cause to the youthful and untutored mind?" demanded the London *Times* when
one of the last celebrated *castrati*, Giovanni Velluti, appeared in
the English capital in 1825. Here, however, is a modern view on
the castrating of boys to preserve their singing voices which I
came across in a letter to *Stereo Review*, November 1966, from a
lady in California:

"I do not believe the practice of producing *castrati* for their
special musical purpose 'ghastly' or 'shameful' when the operation
is performed on the initiative of the individual, as was often the
case, nor do I regard the *castrati* themselves as being 'mutilated'
. . . I have many friends, some of them quite prominent in musical
circles, who agree with me that if there is to be a serious and
widespread revival of Baroque and *bel canto* opera, there must
necessarily be a return of the *castrati* to sing the roles they alone
can handle with dramatic and vocal legitimacy. . . . I definitely do
not advocate force, but if a young singer should possess a fine
voice which he wishes to preserve, I can sympathize with no reason for discouraging him. Children in general are far more reasonable, intelligent beings than most adults want to believe, and a
gifted child is a thorough pragmatist to whom nothing is more
important than his talent."

From appearances in church the next obvious step for the
castrati was to invade the more glamorous and exciting theaters
and opera houses where they were at greater liberty to indulge
themselves in what they were most adept at—embellishments
and interpolations of highly elaborate cadenzas into their music.
Certainly from a vocal point of view the knife created a unique
physical situation. During puberty a man's vocal cords or folds
lengthen to an average of seven-twelfths of an inch and also
thicken; so do a woman's, only less so. For this reason a woman's
voice is more flexible. The vocal folds of a boy are proportionately
smaller and thinner still, and these by one stroke of the knife

were placed in a male body with male strength, stamina and above all lung power. An examination of the music in which *castrati* excelled usually shows that they were able to execute tremendously long, elaborate phrases in one breath.

The vocal feats of the castrati are legendary and with all such tales perhaps subject to some disbelief. Johann Quantz, the flautist, who heard many of the great singers of this first golden age of bel canto, tells us that Farinelli had a range the same as today's lyric or dramatic sopranos—that is, slightly more than two octaves rang- ing from A, below middle C to the high C″ or even D″. Yet when one examines excerpts of the music that he is supposed to have sung, replete with an infinite number of trills, runs and other complicated embellishments, it appears that he lacked comfort and ease above the G′ below high C″, nor does the music go lower than the D just above middle C—a range in fact of eleven notes. Difficult as these fast-moving, scale-like figures, runs, jumps and rapidly repeated notes are to execute, I do not think they would hold any terrors for Joan Sutherland, though she might require a greater number of breaths to sing the same amount of music.

Contemporary accounts of the *castrati* also sometimes proudly point out that the intonation of such and such a singer was good and that he always sang in tune. This mention of the ability (or lack of it) to sing on pitch also frequently occurs in descriptions of the great vocalists of the pre-recording days in the nineteenth century, suggesting that audiences in both eras seemed to have been far more tolerant of out-of-tune singing than we are today.

Would we have admired the vocal art of these strapping, often gawky men who appeared in female parts, lavishly gowned and adorned with jewels? Certainly sexual inconsistency does not worry audiences in opera houses of today when a well-busted woman puts on the breeches of amorous youths like Octavian and Cherubino. But would we have reacted with the same adoring adulation that English and Italian audiences gave to these artificially created vocal anomalies? (The practical French, incidentally, never had a taste for the singing of the *castrati*.) Naturally it is almost impossible to judge. Certainly we would have been impressed by their remarkable vocal technique just as we are amazed and delighted by the coloratura abilities of a Sutherland or Berganza today. On the other hand I wonder how we would react to the actual quality of the voice of a *castrato*. Contemporary accounts often speak of its sweetness and the pathetic quality that it possessed, but into more than one description creeps the word "shrill." Certainly these voices lacked (literally) any sexual quality and were without the warm, pulsating vibrato that we expect to hear in today's voices. On the other hand such is the diversity of vocal tastes that the lady from California whose letter I have quoted and others besides would undoubtedly welcome the return of this counterfeit voice.

The Bel Canto Mystique. By now the reader will have noticed several references to the term "bel canto" or "bel canto singing." What is meant by bel canto and do we have bel canto singers today?

As with so much concerning the singing voice, utter confusion reigns over the meaning of the term which in English is literally "beautiful singing." Some people regard bel canto as a technique of wonderful singing, the secrets of which are lost forever. If this is so, at what period in history did it exist? Already by 1723, when highly developed solo singing had been known for about a century, the *castrato*, Pier Francesco Tosi, is wailing over a *decline* in vocal standards. "The fault is in the Singers," he complains in his *Observations on the Florid Song,* the first of countless volumes that have poured forth ever since purporting to teach the reader a singing technique. "They praise the Pathetick, sing the Allegro," he continues. "They know the first to be most Excellent, but they lay it aside, knowing it to be the most difficult." From this we may infer that the singers at this period—which some declare to be the golden age of singing—lacked the ability to sing a long, sustained line, the flowing legato that those who claim to understand what bel canto is would say was its essence. Well then, perhaps true bel canto singing came later . . .

"In Italy music is decadent, there are no more schools, nor great singers . . . I do not know to what may be attributed the real cause, since the ancient systems have fallen into disuse, and the good customs of ancient schools no longer regulate our Profession." It is now fifty years later, the time of another supposedly golden age of song. The writer is the celebrated singing teacher Giambattista Mancini. While offering some faint recognition to the great vocalists of his era—the celebrated *castrato,* Pacchierotti, for example, or the extraordinary soprano Lucrezia Agujari, with her range up to C''' above high C'', whom Mozart heard—he bewails the demise of true bel canto singing and the methods that produced it . . .

On to the next golden age, the one in which singers such as Maria Malibran, Giuditta Pasta, Giulia Grisi, Henrietta Sontag, Giovanni-Battista Rubini and Luigi Lablache starred, and which many people take to have been the truly great age of bel canto. "Today one hardly ever hears a really beautiful and technically correct trill; very rarely a perfect mordent; very rarely a rounded coloratura, a genuine unaffected soul-moving portamento, a complete equalization of the registers, a steady intonation through all the varying nuances of crescendo and diminuendo. Most of our singers, as soon as they attempt the noble art of portamento, go out of tune; and the public, accustomed to faulty execution, overlooks the defects of the singer, if only he is a skilled actor and knows the routine of the stage."

This was published in 1834 at the very height of a supposedly great era of bel canto singing, and the writer is none other than Richard Wagner, who, though he is supposed to have destroyed bel canto as it was once known, appears to be familiar with its concepts . . .

Let us move on still later in our search for the true period of great singing. "Singing is becoming as much a lost art as the manufacture of Mandarin China or the varnish used by the old masters." Here the writer is the immensely knowledgeable singing teacher, Manuel Garcia II, lamenting "the disappearance of the race of great singers, who, besides originating that art, carried it to the highest point of excellence." The year is 1894 when the celebrated nonagenarian pedagogue could have heard Adelina Patti, Nellie Melba, Lillian Nordica, Emma Eames and the two de Reszkes, to choose a random selection from the luminaries of that reputedly golden age.

"It is plain to every careful observer that the race of beautiful singers is diminishing with every year, and that in its place there is growing up a generation of harsh, unrefined, tuneless shouters." By now we've reached 1938 and the eminent music critic, W. J. Henderson, an expert on voices, who wrote those words, could have heard in New York that year Kirsten Flagstad, Lauritz Melchior, Kerstin Thorborg, Helen Traubel, Lawrence Tibbett, Lily Pons, Bidu Sayão and, making his debut, Jussi Bjoerling.

Every earlier age, so it seems, was the golden one when bel canto reigned supreme. It resembles old men sighing for the bright days of their youth when everything seemed fresh and beautiful and wonderful. But was it? Did an age of singing ever exist more glorious than at any other time in history? As one observer shrewdly sums it up:

"From the beginning [vocal reformers] have insisted that the art of bel canto is lost . . . Three of the greatest teachers of the old Italian school all lamented the decadence of the art of singing. Others before and since have done the same thing . . . From this we draw some interesting conclusions: first, that the real art of singing was lost immediately after it was found. Second, the only time it was perfect was when it began. Third, that ever since it began we have been searching for it without success."

Nonetheless the quest for bel canto as a method of singing continues. Many people believe that the old Italian singers, including the celebrated *castrati,* practiced some secret vocal technique, perhaps a way of holding the tongue or taking breath, which is now lost, and if it could but be recaptured true bel canto singing would be restored to the world. Hopes high, they turn to an early work on singing technique but are rebuffed by its generalities: "Learn to breathe so that you can sing through the phrases." "Do not sing too loudly." "Do not sing too softly." If there were specific technicalities in the so-called "Italian" method, Tosi was not prepared to divulge them. Nevertheless to some bel canto will continue to mean a method of singing, lost forever, a kind of fantasy vocalism the like of which they have never heard.

Others conceive of bel canto as a tremendous agility of voice. A male or female to be a true bel canto vocalist must possess the ability to trill, to sing runs quickly, execute turns, big jumps and so forth—in other words bel canto means to them all the *batterie de la voix* that the human larynx possesses. The only trouble with this concept of bel canto is that all voices do not possess innate flexibility. To quote from what some regard as one of the great manuals on bel canto, Mancini's *Practical Reflections on Figured Singing* (1774): "The agility of the voice cannot be perfect if it is not natural; and if it is not perfect, instead of bringing pleasure and delight to the listener, it will bring annoyance and boredom.

"Then," goes on the author, "he who does not have it from nature should never lose time vainly in trying to acquire it . . . thus the prudent master, finding the scholar to lack a natural disposition for singing agility, should cease to conduct him by this route, but lead him to another, since in this profession the ways are many, the styles are varied, as are the dispositions by which one may arrive at the desired honor of being a good and admired virtuoso."

For still others, bel canto is simply a concept: round, beautiful tones melting one into the next, forming a line to the singing that is an essence of the art. Of the bel canto voice, one observer has conceived the tones as having a "rock-like steadiness" which are "shot through with an astonishing vibrance, or to use the Italian term, *vibrazione* . . . This extreme intensity of tone, this emotional-tone, is the main character of the bel canto singer."

To return to our original question, do we have bel canto singers today? If we accept the last definition of the bel canto voice as having astonishing vibrance and rock-like steadiness of tone, then such artists as Leontyne Price, Birgit Nilsson, Sherrill Milnes and Nicolai Ghiaurov triumphantly affirm that we certainly do have bel canto singers. Though it may shock purists I would go so far as to say that vocalists such as Ella Fitzgerald and Dinah Shore with their creamy, supple voices and round tones are also exponents of bel canto singing.

If, however, we take the bel canto voice to mean one possessing great flexibility then we can also look to such singers as Joan Sutherland, Monserrat Caballé, Beverly Sills and Marilyn Horne, all of whom are capable of performing remarkable feats of florid singing. In the last twenty years there has been a revival in taste of what some regard as the "bel canto" music of Rossini and Donizetti. The artist who unquestionably reawakened this interest was Maria Callas with her ability to move a large voice combined with a dramatic sense mounting to near genius. Though identified with this so-called revival of bel canto, Callas never gave her listeners unalloyed pleasure from the actual beauty of her voice. Indeed some have found the break in its registers and pronounced wobble at the top of the range positively painful. Callas' ability to breathe drama and life into what had hitherto seemed old-fashioned, trivial music written only to display the voice was her particular gift to her vocal era. Many would be appalled to hear Callas described as a singer in the bel canto tradition, on account of her vocal faults. And yet if Giuditta Pasta with her uncertain intonation and Maria Malibran with her stretched voice are remembered as great bel canto singers of an earlier age, then unquestionably Maria Callas must be considered one in her own time.

PART TWO

⌒

THE OPERATIC VOICES

OF TODAY

I have read somewhere that our modern voices are supposed to sound the same as those heard around 1700 (with the exception, of course, of the *castrato* voices) but this seems to me to be unlikely. Man constantly evolves. We know, for example, from clothing that has survived, as well as the scale of early eighteenth-century beds and chairs that today's human beings are of much larger average size. It is reasonable to suppose then that many of today's singing voices are much larger and more powerful than any that might have been heard two hundred years ago. One wonders what the *castrati* with their celebrated lung power would have thought of our Wagnerian singers and their ability to make themselves heard over an immense orchestra of more than a hundred players. It is difficult to believe that such huge voices existed two centuries ago. They evolved, as have all singing voices, when there was a demand for them.

Today, too, we have another comparatively "new" kind of voice in the husky, almost masculine sounding tones produced by most female pop singers. Before about 1925 this kind of singing was scarcely ever heard except among folk singers in Spain who have always had a taste for that particular vocal quality. We also ought to consider the modern ranges. Today a high C″ is around three quarters of a tone higher than the C″ of a hundred years ago. String players have forced up the pitch to draw a more brilliant sound from their instruments. This trend shows no sign of abating. Thus the famous F″ above high C″ that Mozart wrote for his sister-in-law, the first Queen of the Night in *Die Zauberflöte,* really only required her to hit a note that we would consider between E″ flat and E″ natural.

When it comes actually to cataloguing today's voices it is essential that we enter the opera house. Only there can be heard in the greatest variety the capabilities of man's singing voice. However beautiful the voices of concert singers may be, or especially those of pop singers, they are no more than diminished versions of the operatic voices. By examining what type of voice sings what roles in the standard operatic repertory we ought to be able to cover the amazing variety of today's singers.

Unfortunately there is a great deal of overlapping among the various kinds of voices and before making a catalogue of them (however imprecise) we should perhaps bear in mind that every voice is a broad characterization. A high, light, woman's voice, for example, suggests girlishness, innocence and fragility. With an increase in the size of the female voice, it assumes greater pathos, while the largest take on dramatic force and qualities either tragic or heroic. The same is more or less true with the various high male voices. In both sexes the lower ranges have a darker quality sometimes associated with sexiness, but more often with evil. Frequently a parental or authoritarian connection is made with these lower tones.

Each operatic composer, therefore, writes for the particular kind of voice that will best suit the character whom he is bringing to musical life. How carefully Giuseppe Verdi considered this aspect of his art we know from a letter to his librettist when Eugenia Tadolini had been suggested to take the part of Lady Macbeth. "Madame Tadolini sings to perfection and I should prefer Lady Macbeth not to sing. Madame Tadolini has a splendid voice, clear, pure and powerful; and I should like in Lady Macbeth a hard, hoarse, gloomy voice." Rossini as a creator of operatic character has been done an injustice by the high coloratura sopranos who

steal the role of Rosina in *Il Barbiere di Siviglia* from the darker
voiced coloratura mezzo-soprano for whom it was written. These
high, light, twittering voices have the effect of turning Rosina into
an arch, kittenish creature. When the role is sung by the lower
voice as the composer intended, warmth and womanliness come
into the character.

While the range and tessitura of an operatic role largely determine what kind of voice will sing it, the personal tastes of the
manager of an opera company may influence its casting, also singers
themselves anxious to extend their repertories and appear in new
roles. Let us now try to break down the different kinds of singing
voices into their varied categories.

Highest of all.   Generally the soprano voices are loosely classified as coloratura, lyric and dramatic. In addition we hear of the
lyric-coloratura, also the *spinto*. And what is the soprano *leggiero?*

Of the coloraturas there are several kinds. Highest of all is the
soprano *acuto sfogato* with a range

Soprano Acuto Sfogato

Voices with these dizzying top registers are extremely rare, but it
is interesting to note that at least two occurred during the lifetime of Mozart. One belonged to his sister-in-law Josephine Hofer,
born Weber, for whom he wrote the high-lying arias of the Queen
of the Night. The other, Lucrezia Agujari (whom the Italians
graciously nicknamed *La Bastardella*), Mozart heard sing at Parma

when he was fourteen years old. We know that she sang the following phrases because he copied them out in a letter to his sister:

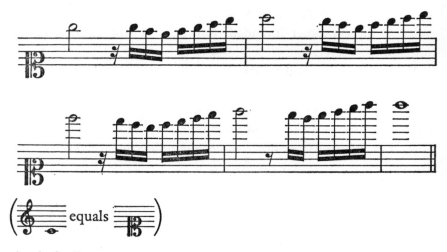

Agujari's Range

The quality of tone of the acutely high coloratura soprano is almost always thin and childlike in the upper register. Indeed, by some physical accident, this singer seems to have retained the range of her childhood pre-pubescent voice (often little girls can make a sort of squeak up to the C''' above high C'') coupling it with fuller but still very light tones in the middle of the range. The lowest notes in these voices are usually unsubstantial and almost lacking in tone, a fact which introduces an almost implacable rule that applies to all singing voices: one extreme has always to be sacrificed for the other. Voices most brilliant at the top almost invariably lack the same power and fullness at the bottom. Examples among today's great singers are Leontyne Price, whose tones are weakest in the lowest part of her range, glorious and soaring at the top, and Joan Sutherland, whose bottom notes are also thin. If a full, round lower register is developed as Renata Tebaldi has done lately, it seems to drag down the extreme top

Coloratura by Gerald Hoffnung.

notes so that they are sung flat or have to be screamed. Birgit Nilsson has both brilliant top and bottom notes; the weakest part of her voice lies in the middle. This price—power for flexibility, brilliance for subtlety, high notes for low, whatever it may be— is almost inevitably paid in the process of singing, leading to the observation: "There has never been a perfect voice."

Small and girlish is the voice of the soprano *acuto sfogato,* and so often is its possessor. (This explains why the ragings of the tempestuous Queen of the Night which must be sung by this type of coloratura rarely come over effectively in the opera house.) Some notable high coloratura sopranos of recent times have included Frieda Hempel, Selma Kurz, Maria Ivogün, Lily Pons, Mado Robin, Erna Berger and Rita Streich. There have been one or two sopranos with freak ranges extending to the C''' above high C''' among them Erna Sack and Yma Sumac whose extreme top notes suggest the quality of a peanut vendor's whistle. The effect of these extremely high tones must be accounted more freakish than artistic. Nonetheless the records of both sopranos continue to be available, showing that there is always a demand for a stunt, be it on a vocal or a real trapeze.

These highest of all sopranos have the roles of the Queen of the Night and Zerbinetta (in Strauss's *Ariadne auf Naxos*) pretty much to themselves. They also specialize in singing the glassy, not quite human Queen of Shemakha in Rimsky-Korsakov's *Le Coq D'Or* and the mechanical doll Olympia in *Les Contes d'Hoffmann* for whom their bright, slightly meaningless tones are perfectly suited.

Soubrettes.   A second type of light high woman's voice, having some kinship with the soprano *acuto sfogato* because it often has a similar girlish, delicate quality, is sometimes called the soubrette soprano. This voice is as small, light and flexible as the high coloratura but simply lacks her extraordinary top range. (It will, in consequence, have more fullness in the middle and lower part of the compass.) The soubrette soprano sings roles such as Susanna in *Le Nozze*, Zerlina in *Don Giovanni*, Despina in *Così fan Tutte* and Sophie in *Der Rosenkavalier*, and not surprisingly the very high coloraturas—Roberta Peters is one—looking for new opportunities will climb down from their heights to sing these juicy, non-coloratura roles.

Possibly because this bright, pretty voice often emanates from young ladies with bright, pretty faces and figures to match, the composers of light operas, operettas and musicals have demanded it of their heroines. As far back as the eighteenth century when John Gay put together *The Beggar's Opera,* he cast Polly Peachum as a soubrette soprano. The heroines of the Gilbert and Sullivan operettas such as Patience, Phyllis in *Iolanthe*, Yum-Yum in *The Mikado* (with her charming "The Moon and I") all call for this type of voice sometimes with a slight coloratura technique as in the staccato passages of Mabel's "Poor Wandering One" in *The Pirates of Penzance*. Offenbach's naughty heroines are light soubrette sopranos as are Victor Herbert's virtuous ones. Lehar, Friml and Romberg all wrote some of their most attractive melodies for this most attractive, if small kind of voice. So did Jerome Kern for his heroine, Magnolia, in what might be described as the first significant American musical, *Showboat,* which he composed a year or so after the new technique of amplifying and recording the voice electrically had been introduced.

This invention of course has had a staggering effect on singing and the singing voice. As far as the soubrette or operetta kind of soprano was concerned it enabled pretty singers to make a career in the theater with a voice of small carrying power. The introduction of the sound movie allowed a number of smiling soubrette sopranos to sing their way into the hearts of millions of people. Jeanette MacDonald, the girlish Deanna Durbin, whose pretty soprano matured when she was in her early teens (as this kind of voice often does), Jane Powell, equally girlish in looks and positively infantile and tiny in sound, were but a few of the stars that people crowded into the movie houses to see and hear. Irene Dunne, though only secondarily a singer, could often be expected to break into a song with her attractive soubrette soprano voice during a quieter moment of one of the madcap comedies in which she frequently played. It is true that in this era various opera stars such as the sopranos Lily Pons and Grace Moore, and the mezzo-sopranos Gladys Swarthout and Risë Stevens also appeared in movies, but they of course never actually needed the amplification that, say, Jane Powell or Kathryn Grayson required. About this time, singing in a low, chesty, insinuating voice Mary Martin came to fame with her famous "My Heart Belongs to Daddy." Not content to be typed by her "cute" style of singing she studied diligently to turn herself into a soubrette or operetta soprano, with a style of singing that is always more stiff and formal than a "show biz" way with a song. How well she succeeded can be judged in a disastrous movie, *The Great Victor Herbert,* which comes back occasionally in the lateness of the TV night. Needless to say Mary Martin returned to a casual, unpretentious singing style that was one of her greatest charms.

On the American radio too, light sopranos such as Jessica Dragonette, Vivian Della Chiesa and Margaret Speaks had their innings
and even sang fairly heavy operatic selections secure in the fact
that their voices were riding a boosting system of electronic impulses. One who had the volume to fill the largest of opera houses
was strangely enough created by radio. In the 1940's CBS put on
an interesting program called "Invitation to Music" which, lacking a sponsor, could be heard late in the evening after the "prime
time" hours. On it appeared a young soprano with an extraordinarily beautiful voice who had the opportunity to sing all kinds
of music—arias, lieder, French songs and folk songs to the delight
and wonder of, I suppose, a limited radio audience. This was
Eileen Farrell, the short, chubby wife of a policeman in Staten
Island, not committed to the exigencies of a concert and opera
career until her children were raised. No one, hearing her only
over the radio, could be absolutely certain of the size of her voice
because of the power of the microphone to deceive, so that when
she finally appeared in person, unamplified, in a stunning recital
at Carnegie Hall the audience was left gasping.

The vogue for light operetta sopranos carried into the "golden
age" of musicals during the late forties and fifties. The heroines
of *Carousel, Most Happy Fella* and *Kiss Me Kate* all call for this
appealing, feminine sounding voice, and though today the electronic clangs and bangs of the pop singers and their groups would
appear to be drowning it out in popularity let us not forget the
mighty drawing power of pert, winsome, slightly prissy Julie
Andrews—and her pert, winsome, slightly prissy sounding soubrette soprano voice.

A Selection of Sopranos.   Most of the great coloraturas of past
and present such as Patti, Melba, Tetrazzini, Galli-Curci and
Sutherland are most properly classified by the Italian term, *leggiero*. Their range does not comfortably exceed E″ flat or E″
natural and looks like this:

Soprano Leggiero
(usual coloratura soprano range)

None except Sutherland attempted the Queen of the Night and when she did she found it necessary to transpose the second aria down. Nor was her singing of the part considered a success.

In the main, the soprano *leggiero* usually has the same light, sparkling, fluty quality of her acutely high-ranging sister, combined with an agile coloratura technique. Hers then are most of the great coloratura parts such as Lucia di Lammermoor, Rosina, and Gilda in *Rigoletto*. Some with a more emotionally compelling character to their voices and who call themselves lyric-coloraturas, also sing Mimi in *La Bohème* or Micaela in *Carmen,* roles which have no coloratura passages at all. They will also be heard as Marguerite in *Faust* and the Massenet Manon, parts which offer them only a small amount of vocal display. Equally, these roles can be sung by the slightly larger-voiced lyric soprano, who usually has a limited (if any at all) coloratura technique and cultivates the following range:

Lyric Soprano

The lyric soprano has a generous and appealing repertory from which to choose. She may sing Puccini's much put-upon Madama Butterfly or Liu in *Turandot*. She can get stabbed as Nedda in

Pagliacci or strangled as Desdemona. If she prefers a more cheerful evening's work she can always move in on the soubrette soprano territory and sing the charming roles of Susanna and Zerlina. Classic examples of the lyric soprano at the Metropolitan Opera House have been Dorothy Kirsten and Licia Albanese. Their repertory has included Mimi, Manon Lescaut, Violetta in *La Traviata,* Micaela and Marguerite. Both these singers, however, eventually went in the other direction and pushed on to the part of Tosca, a role usually undertaken by the next-size larger soprano, the *spinto,* or even the largest, the dramatic.

"*Spinto*" is the Italian for "pushed, urged on" which exactly defines this type of voice—a lyric soprano "urged on." The *spinto* has the same range as the lyric, but her low notes must have more power and emphasis to do justice to such roles as the Leonoras in *Trovatore* and *Forza del Destino,* Tosca, Aida and the Countess in *Le Nozze.* At the same time the possessor of this voice must be able to shade it down to a fine pianissimo, right up to the high C" called for in Aida's Nile Scene aria, and to move it in passages where flexibility is demanded, as in the fast-moving sections of Leonora's arias in *Trovatore.* The voice of Leontyne Price is a perfect example of a *spinto* and Verdi might almost have had her in mind when he wrote the operas of his middle years, *Forza, Don Carlo, Un Ballo in Maschera* and *Aida,* as well as the soprano part of the *Requiem.* It would probably be correct to describe Renata Tebaldi as a *spinto* also, though with great versatility she will essay an essentially lyric part such as Mimi as well as taking on the heavy roles of Maddalena in *Andrea Chénier* and La Gioconda. In passing, it is interesting to note that Joan Sutherland originally possessed a voice capable of being trained as a *spinto,* but instead lightened it to gain the wonderful agility it now possesses—another example of the inevitable bargain that has to be struck in the vocal process. Nevertheless Miss Sutherland has an unusually large voice for the soprano *leggiero* roles that she most often sings.

With the *spinto* we reach the first kind of soprano heavy enough to perform a Wagnerian heroine—Eva in *Die Meistersinger* (the lightest); Elsa in *Lohengrin;* Elizabeth in *Tannhäuser;* Senta in *Der Fliegende Holländer* and Sieglinde in *Die Walküre.* This is a repertory that Gwyneth Jones has been exploring along with Italian parts. The rest of the Wagnerian soprano roles, Isolde, the Ring's three Brünnhildes and Kundry in *Parsifal* require the services of the heaviest of high women's voices, the dramatic soprano.

One of the less manic and more intelligent authorities on the subject of the voice, Blanche Marchesi writes, "The dramatic soprano is the rarest voice produced by nature . ... It is like a new-born Newfoundland dog, clumsy, heavy, shapeless . . . The heavier and bigger the voice the more carefully must it be trained."

The dramatic soprano has about the same range as the *spinto.*

Dramatic Soprano

This voice must be able to soar over great Verdian ensembles or the heavy Wagnerian orchestra as well as to sustain literally hours of singing in one evening. The three Brünnhildes, Isolde, Elektra, Leonore in *Fidelio,* Donna Anna in *Don Giovanni* and Norma are all usually sung by a dramatic soprano, though the last three are also undertaken by singers with slightly lighter and smaller voices. In our own time Zinka Milanov was described as a dramatic soprano but rarely assumed Wagnerian roles; Rosa Ponselle never did (though there is a ravishing early recording of her singing Elsa's "Traum" in Italian). Both, on the other hand, sang Norma, which Lilli Lehmann, the extraordinary dramatic soprano at the turn of this century who sang practically everything, declared to be much more demanding and exhausting than the *Götterdämmerung* Brünnhilde.

The whole classifying of voices is made still more troublesome by the fact that singers change and that as they grow older their voices become bigger, darker and less flexible. Eleanor Steber, for example, began her career at the Metropolitan singing a light, lyric part such as Sophie, and ended up portraying the Marschallin, and Elsa and Donna Anna as well. Tebaldi has ranged from Mimi through the *spinto* Tosca and two Verdi Leonoras (*Trovatore* and *Forza*), to the dramatic La Gioconda. In days of yore these progressions from light parts to heavy were more extreme. The hard working American, Lillian Nordica, made her way from Gilda to Isolde, while the most amazing of all, Lilli Lehmann, sang everything from the Queen of the Night to the three Brünnhildes. Age appears to be an important factor in the maturing of the dramatic soprano voice. Flagstad, for example, working her way through the lighter parts—Mimi, Nedda and eventually Aida—never sang a Wagnerian role until she approached thirty-five. She did not possess a coloratura technique like Lilli Lehmann but her voice, while lacking flexibility was definitely larger and more opulent.

In our own day we have had the extraordinarily versatile Birgit Nilsson who switches from the *spinto* parts of Aida and Amelia in *Ballo in Maschera* to Elektra, Isolde and the three Brünnhildes. Nilsson has never sung Norma because it requires too much of a coloratura technique; nevertheless, I was astonished to read in a *New Yorker* profile of her, that she can sing the second act Queen of the Night aria with its repeated F‴'s above high C″ but only *after* her voice has been warmed up for several hours. When the conductor, Karl Böhm, impugned her claim, she bade him come to her dressing room after conducting a performance of *Götterdämmerung* in which she was the Brünnhilde. Böhm complied and Nilsson knocked off the aria just as she had said she could.

Throughout this discussion the reader may have noticed that I have scarcely mentioned one of the most celebrated of all operatic roles—Violetta in *La Traviata*. What kind of soprano sings this rich, starring part? So wonderfully complex and complete is the musical characterization that almost every kind of soprano voice suits it. Violetta's gaiety, her shallowness, her frailness can all be well expressed by the tones of the soprano *leggiero* and so such artists as Patti, Tetrazzini, Galli-Curci, Lily Pons and Joan Sutherland have taken the part. Violetta is still a young woman, warm, feminine and lovely so that lyric sopranos such as Bori, Sayão, Albanese and Freni have also sung the role. Violetta is also a woman with a certain grandness of character, noble in her sacrifice of Alfredo and her struggle against affliction, so that the larger-voiced *spinto* sopranos such as Claudia Muzio, Rosa Ponselle and Renata Tebaldi proved equally effective in the part.

All sopranos, of course, long to sing Violetta and since only the very heavy dramatic voices are unsuited to it, most great singers have attempted the role over the years. Some, not already mentioned, include Christine Nilsson, Sembrich, Nordica, Melba, Geraldine Farrar, Mary Garden and Maria Callas. The tremendously self-disciplined Lilli Lehmann sang in all 170 different roles in 119 operas. Towards the end of her career when she was close to sixty, she gave an interview to the music critic W. J. Henderson, at her home just outside of Berlin. Among the questions raised was whether Frau Lehmann would retire as usual to the Tyrol for the summer. Not before she first sang three engagements at Ischl, was the reply. And what part would she be singing, inquired Henderson.

"A beautiful and yet somewhat roguish smile broke across her noble face," he writes, "as she said in a half whisper: 'Violetta.' "

The Mystical High C". Before climbing down from the altitudes of the soprano voice let us linger a little longer to consider that famous note around which whirls such excitement and glamor

—the high C". In giving the *spinto* and dramatic soprano ranges I have indicated what notes *ideally* these kind of voices should possess. Many of us recall the effortless high C" of Flagstad in her prime, and today we have the amazing Birgit Nilsson who approaches this note from the top and sometimes sings it a tiny bit sharp. But for every Nilsson and Flagstad there are dozens of *spinto* and dramatic sopranos for whom the high C" is just out of reach or else is achieved by what must in all honesty be called a scream. Is it any wonder? To utter a high C" absolutely on pitch the tiny edges of a soprano's vocal cords must flutter over a thousand vibrations per second.

Usually high C" comes easily enough to a lyric soprano. The natural extent of some beautiful *spinto* and dramatic soprano voices, however, seems often to be only to a high A' or B' flat; after that extreme difficulty is encountered in reaching the B' natural and top C". This appears to be another example of the inexorable rule of sacrifice in vocalization: since these larger-voiced sopranos have very full middle and lower registers they must pay the price for it with their high tones.

"When you wish to discuss great singers," soprano Geraldine Farrar is supposed to have said, "there are two you must put aside. One is Caruso, the other is Rosa Ponselle." Yet the wonderful Ponselle with her "seamless" scale and fascinating quality of tone never seems to have had secure top notes. She transposed the "Casta Diva" in *Norma* down a whole tone and after she cracked on a high C" in *Aida* one evening never sang the role again. Helen Traubel during a radio broadcast of *Tannhäuser* broke on the high note in Elizabeth's joyous greeting to the Hall of Song. Cruel and inhuman it would seem for a great artist to be remembered for one blot on an otherwise sensitive and beautiful performance, but it is often the case.

In more recent times Madame Tebaldi with her increasingly powerful middle and lower registers now must scream her top C" if she makes it on pitch, and Victoria de los Angeles who always possessed unusually luscious middle and lower sections to her voice has come more or less to do the same. Time and age of course have something to do with the destruction of a singer's high C" but in their younger days neither of these artists ever had an easy top. Their B' naturals and high C"s always sounded a little bit forced and shrill.

Is it possible for a soprano with a fine *spinto* or dramatic voice but lacking a proper top C" to make a career? Let us examine a random sampling of roles. All the heavier Mozart parts, with the exception of Constanze in *Die Entführung,* are available to her— that is, Donna Anna, Donna Elvira, the Countess and Fiordiligi. Though Richard Strauss often wrote cruelly for the singing voice, she can also do the Marschallin. Wagner has a reputation for having made impossible demands on the voice, but in fact it is possible to sing almost all his heroines without a high C". Elsa, for example, goes no higher than a hysterical high B' natural when the nobles rush in to kill Lohengrin. In fact Ortrud's music, peppered with A' sharps, would appear to have a higher tessitura than Elsa's though Ortrud is not required to sing beyond A' sharp or B' flat. In *Walküre* Brünnhilde only touches high C" in her opening shout, but must sustain a high B' natural at the conclusion of it— a cruel test for a singer on making her entrance. Thereafter she has no more of these extreme top tones to perform. Nor does Sieglinde, ever. The *Siegfried* Brünnhilde however, full of B' flats and naturals, also has two high C"s (the second optional) and for this reason must be accounted the most arduous of the three Brünnhildes even though it is the shortest.

It is when we examine the Italian repertory that still more difficulties arise for our high C"-less soprano. Some of the fascinating heroines of Verdi's middle and late operas she can manage, Leonora in *Forza,* in which she must sustain a B' natural, but nothing higher. Verdi, however, gives the high B' flat a tremendous workout as he does also in *Trovatore.* Here, there are high C"s and even D" flats in the runs and cadenzas of the other Leonora's

music, but these can be either lightly touched—far easier than
sustaining the note—or the D″ flat in the cadenza of the last act
aria changed to B′ flat.

What if a soprano lacking a high C″ wishes to sing the role of
the hapless Aida? Lurking in the second part of her aria "O Patria
Mia" is a top C″ within the following slow phrase:

From "O Patria Mia"

There is no escaping it. It cannot be transposed nor glossed over.
Mercilessly it demands that the soprano reveal the state of her
high C″ to the audience, a revelation which unfortunately may
not be altogether pleasing. Sometimes we are treated to a scream.
At others it will be a musical note of a sort but sagging below the
pitch. When Leontyne Price sings this passage she soars up to the
C″ with total assurance, diminishes the note as Verdi demands,
and glides back down the phrase in one breath, triumphantly as-
serting that the art of great singing has not been lost.

SOPRANOS

True Coloratura Roles

Amina (*Sonnambula*)

Gilda (*Rigoletto*)   Toscanini chose Zinka Milanov, a dramatic soprano, to sing Gilda's fourth act music, but it is usually done by a girlish, innocent-sounding voice.

Lakmé

Lucia di Lammermoor

Olympia
  (*Contes d'Hoffmann*)

Oscar (*Ballo in Maschera*)

Philine (*Mignon*)

Queen of Shemakha
  (*Coq d'Or*)

Queen of the Night   A part that usually can only be sung by
  (*Zauberflöte*)   the high soprano *acuto sfogato*.

Rosina (*Il Barbiere*)   Originally written for the coloratura mezzo but grabbed by the coloratura soprano who sings the music whenever possible an octave higher.

Zerbinetta (*Ariadne*)

SOPRANOS

Some Soubrette Soprano Roles

Adele (*Fledermaus*)

Adina
  (*L'Elisir d'Amore*)

Blonde
  (*Entführung*)

Despina (*Così fan Tutte*)

Gretel
  (*Hänsel und Gretel*)

Lauretta (*Gianni Schicchi*)   Florence Easton created the part at the
                                 Metropolitan the same season she sang
                                 Isolde.

Manon
Marcellina (*Fidelio*)
Musetta (*Bohème*)
Nanetta (*Falstaff*)
Norina
  (*Don Pasquale*)
Sophie
  (*Rosenkavalier*)
Susanna (*Le Nozze*)
Zerlina (*Don Giovanni*)   Recently at the Metropolitan the mezzo-
                                 soprano, Rosalind Elias, was cast in this
                                 role, but it is not customary.

SOPRANOS

Some Lyric Roles

Antonia
  (*Contes d'Hoffmann*)
Cio-Cio-San   A heavy lyric part which might also be
  (*Madama Butterfly*)   classified as light *spinto.*
Desdemona (*Otello*)   See note on Cio-Cio-San.
Euridice
  (*Orfeo ed Euridice*)
Juliette (*Roméo et Juliette*)
Louise
Manon Lescaut
Marguerite (*Faust*)
Micaela (*Carmen*)
Mimi (*Bohème*)
Nedda (*Pagliacci*)
Pamina (*Zauberflöte*)
Rosalinda (*Fledermaus*)
Violetta (*Traviata*)   See discussion in text.

SOPRANOS

Some Spinto and Lighter Dramatic Roles

Aida	
Amelia	
(*Ballo in Maschera*)	
Ariadne	
(*Ariadne auf Naxos*)	
Chrysostemis	
(*Elektra*)	
Constanze	
(*Entführung*)	A role requiring a *spinto*-sized voice having the technique of a soprano *leggiero*. Difficult to cast.
Countess (*Le Nozze*)	The versatile Marguerite Matzenauer, a mezzo-soprano was cast—or perhaps miscast—in the 1917 revival at the Metropolitan.
Donna Anna	Requires considerable agility.
(*Don Giovanni*)	
Donna Elvira	Slightly lighter voice than Donna Anna,
(*Don Giovanni*)	but also demands some agility.
Elisabetta (*Don Carlo*)	
Elizabeth (*Tannhäuser*)	Also sung by heavy dramatic sopranos such as Flagstad or Nilsson.
Elsa (*Lohengrin*)	As Elizabeth.
Fiordiligi	
(*Così fan Tutte*)	
Gioconda	A heavy part, taxing to the light *spinto* voice.
Giulietta	
(*Contes d'Hoffmann*)	
Gutrune	
(*Götterdämmerung*)	
Lady Macbeth	Sometimes sung by mezzo-sopranos, with their darker, more evil sounding tone quality.

Leonora
  (*Forza del Destino*)
Leonora (*Trovatore*)
Marie (*Wozzeck*)
Marschallin
  (*Rosenkavalier*)   The first Marschallin at the Metropolitan was Frieda Hempel, who the same season sang the Queen of the Night. Another was the heavy dramatic soprano, Helen Traubel.

Mistress Ford (*Falstaff*)
Norma   A tremendously taxing role, requiring great stamina, extreme flexibility and a voice of noble proportions. Joan Sutherland is the sixth singer ever to attempt the part at the Metropolitan; eight have tried it since the present Covent Garden Theater opened in 1858.

Salome   Also sung by heavy dramatic sopranos like Nilsson who however lightens her voice to make it sound more girlish.

Santuzza
  (*Cavalleria Rusticana*)   An in-between part, heavy, difficult to cast and sometimes given to a mezzo-soprano.

Senta
  (*Fliegende Holländer*)
Sieglinde (*Walküre*)   Also sung by heavy dramatic sopranos.
Tatiana (*Eugen Onegin*)
Tosca
Turandot   The versatile Birgit Nilsson, a heavy dramatic soprano, sings this role. It requires a brilliant top to the voice.

SOPRANOS

The Heaviest Dramatic Roles

3 Brünnhildes (*Walküre, Siegfried, Götterdämmerung*)	Melba, a soprano *leggiero,* sang one disastrous *Siegfried* Brünnhilde. The mezzosopranos Marguerite Matzenauer and Karin Branzell sang the *Walküre* Brünnhilde at the Metropolitan.
Elektra	
Isolde	Matzenauer sang this role at the Metropolitan too. Irene Dalis, another mezzo, recently sang it in San Francisco.
Kundry (*Parsifal*)	Has been sung by mezzo-sopranos.
Leonore (*Fidelio*)	Lotte Lehmann sang this part with great effect but never attempted the Brünnhildes or Isolde.

THE LOWER WOMEN'S VOICES

Some people use the word "alto" to describe all women's voices that are not sopranos, but the term is a loose one, to say the least, if one considers that there are at least four categories of lower women's voices (which, needless to say, overlap) and indeed a fifth if we include that large band of lady pop singers who belt out their songs entirely in what is known as the chest register. Let us begin with the most unusual of these five.

The Rare Mezzo. Equivalent to the soprano *leggiero* is the coloratura mezzo-soprano, an agile honey-sounding voice for which Rossini wrote a number of the heroines of his operas. Having a range

Coloratura Mezzo

this type of voice had fallen out of fashion until the recent revival of interest in the ebullient works of the Italian composer. Its possessor must have all the agility and coloratura virtuosity of her sister sopranos, but perform in a range lower down the scale. Since the mezzo-soprano's vocal folds are apt to be thicker and longer, an ability to sing with great swiftness and precision becomes that much more difficult. Therefore the voice is rare.

Two current coloratura mezzo-sopranos who give the lie to the oft-repeated declaration that bel canto singing is dead are the Spaniard Teresa Berganza and the American Marilyn Horne. The former is a lyric coloratura mezzo while the latter possesses an astonishingly big voice which does not, however, prevent her from singing all kinds of runs, turns and trills with consummate skill. The size of Miss Horne's voice has enabled her on occasion to even sing—incredible though it may seem—the Immolation Scene from *Götterdämmerung,* though she has perhaps not been well advised to do so. The size of her voice combined with its extraordinary flexibility enables her to shine particularly in the role of Adalgisa in *Norma* and the man's part of Arsace in *Semiramide.*

Lyric and Lighter. With the same range as their coloratura counterparts, lyric mezzo-sopranos are heard in such roles as the comic Dorabella in *Così,* the poignant Mignon in Thomas' opera and as Charlotte in *Werther.* They also frequently turn up as amorous youths, Cherubino in *Le Nozze,* Octavian in *Rosenkavalier,* cynical youths such as Nicklausse in *Contes d' Hoffmann* or just plain boys like Hänsel in *Hänsel und Gretel.* Sopranos however, sometimes steal Cherubino and Hänsel from the mezzos, particularly in Germany. It has happened in New York as well: Geraldine Farrar sang Cherubino at the Metropolitan as does today another charming soprano, Teresa Stratas. *Spinto* sopranos such as Maria Jeritza or more recently Gwyneth Jones are more likely to make off with Octavian.

Another part that the lyric mezzo-soprano claims on the basis of tradition but has a dreadful time holding on to is Carmen. Georges Bizet originally offered the title role of his opera to a beautiful Frenchwoman with a light soprano voice named Marie Roze. Fortunately she recognized that she was not suited to "the very scabrous side of this character," as she put it, and turned down the offer. Bizet's next choice was a mezzo-soprano, Célestine Galli-Marié, and she became the first Carmen. Thus we are not really enlightened as to what kind of voice the composer intended for his wonderful operatic creation.

Carmen is like Violetta, a varied role full of every kind of opportunity in which to shine. Not only do the various kinds of mezzos battle among themselves to sing it, but the sopranos have also moved in to wrest the role—with variable results however—from their darker voiced sisters. The kittenish Adelina Patti, for example, sang Carmen and it was pronounced one of her few failures. The majestic Lilli Lehmann sang Carmen and it was pronounced one of *her* few failures. The much admired singing actress, Olive Fremstad, though popular in the part in Germany, gathered little enthusiasm for her Carmen in the United States. The beautiful sopranos Geraldine Farrar and Maria Jeritza did not wholly please with their interpretations of the role, and even the fabulous Rosa Ponselle was scathingly reviewed when she sang the gypsy; however though some of these criticisms were later retracted. This would seem to prove that Carmen was perhaps intended for the darker, more voluptuous sounding mezzo-soprano voice—though it is true that both Fremstad and Ponselle had darker voices than is usual for sopranos.

On the other hand, the most celebrated Carmen of all time was indeed a soprano, Emma Calvé, who had however richly colored middle and lower registers to her voice. Another highly successful soprano Carmen was Mary Garden, a remarkable singing actress. In three of the current recordings of Carmen the role is sung by sopranos, Maria Callas, Victoria de los Angeles and Leontyne

Price—none of whom, oddly enough, have ever portrayed the role on the stage.

Of the many mezzo-sopranos who have had their innings with Carmen one of the most notable was the Spanish Maria Gay. People who went to the Metropolitan in the thirties will remember the colorful interpretation of Bruna Castagna while those lucky enough to attend Covent Garden at about the same period will recall that of Conchita Supervia, who also possessed a remarkable coloratura technique.

Going Up!   The range of the dramatic mezzo-soprano is almost exactly that of the dramatic soprano:

Dramatic Mezzo-Soprano

What then is the difference between the two? The answer lies predominantly in the quality of the voice, the mezzo's being darker and more lush, with an emphasized lower end of the range. These attributes conjure up an atmosphere of seductiveness, perhaps used for an evil end; or even a feeling of dark, out-and-out villainy. Pity the poor dramatic mezzo-soprano, who loves but is unloved (Amneris, Eboli), who is wickedly voluptuous (Dalila, Venus), witchlike and obsessed (Azucena, Ulrica) or just plain bad news (Ortrud). Sometimes she has right on her side (Fricka) but the public considers her a scold. And sometimes she is totally ignored by operatic composers, as for instance, Puccini, who never wrote for the big mezzo voice. Since the dramatic mezzo-soprano approximates the range of the *Spinto* and dramatic sopranos, no won-

The Wagnerian Soprano by Gluyas Williams.

der she often dreams of escaping into more elevated realms where she is good, noble even, and where above all she gets her man— if only in heaven.

Sometimes in training the singing voice an inexperienced or incompetent teacher can make a serious mistake. Hearing the full, dark lower notes of a young, exceptionally musical girl born in Sweden but who grew up in Minnesota, the first vocal pedagogue of Olive Fremstad trained her as a contralto. He in doing thus so emphasized the bottom and middle tones of her voice perhaps up to F'. With the immutable law in singing of sacrifice, this meant that any higher notes the handsome young woman with a splendid dramatic talent might have possessed were slighted and therefore left weak.

Let us follow Fremstad's most unusual career. Fortunately she was able to come to Europe where she sang for Lilli Lehmann, who at once advised her to train as a mezzo-soprano or even true soprano, and gave her scales and exercises that removed the stress from the low, dragging down notes of the voice. This produced a brighter quality and strengthened the upper tones of its long range. After two years of study Fremstad made her debut as a mezzo-soprano in Germany in 1895 and for the next eight years sang the entire mezzo repertory, lyric and dramatic, all over Europe and at Covent Garden.

Fremstad, one of the most dedicated of singing artists, however, was never satisfied. When she made her debut at the Metropolitan in 1903, it was in the soprano role of Sieglinde, a part, however, which in range and tessitura lies comparatively low. That same season she also sang Venus, Brangäne and Fricka, all parts usually considered the property of the mezzo. The next year she added the marginal role of Kundry to her repertory, and the one after that found her interpreting the *Siegfried* Brünnhilde, a role that can only be sung by a true soprano. In 1907 she became New York's first Salome in a single gripping performance before the opera was forced off the boards on the charge of prurience. Finally on New Year's Day, 1908, she sang her first Isolde with Gustav Mahler as conductor. Quite literally she had turned into a soprano before the very ears of the public. The critics were amazed:

"Mme. Fremstad's voice is of indescribable beauty in this music, in its richness and power, its infinite modulation in all the shades and extremes of dramatic significance. It never sounded finer in quality and never seemed more perfectly under her control. And her singing was a revelation, in the fact that the music was in very few places higher than she could easily encompass with her voice. The voice seems, in truth, to have reached a higher altitude and to move in it without strain and without effort."

Thereafter, during a career that seems all too short for an artist whose singing "in her highest moments . . . took on the quality of genius," Fremstad also sang the other Brünnhildes, Tosca and Elsa.

This gradual transition effected in numerous and continuing performances before the public was a most unusual feat. In subsequent years at the Metropolitan audiences occasionally heard mezzo-sopranos such as Marguerite Matzenauer and Karin Branzell in the soprano role of the *Walküre* Brünnhilde with Matzenauer singing Isolde and the Countess in *Le Nozze* as well. These ladies, however, did not *remain* up. One who did with fine artistic if not totally successful vocal results was Rose Bampton, who made her debut at the Metropolitan on her twenty-third birthday in November 1932 singing the mezzo part of Laura in *La Gioconda*. For four seasons she sang a limited number of mezzo roles while working to transform herself into a soprano. This transition took place at the end of the 1937-38 season as Donna Anna. Thereafter, she slowly added Aida, Elizabeth, Sieglinde, Elsa and Kundry to her repertory. One of the biggest moments of her career was when Toscanini chose her to sing Leonore in *Fidelio* in the first of his celebrated series of broadcast operas. An intelligent, sensitive singer, Bampton's transition to a soprano never entirely worked. Neither properly a mezzo nor a soprano but something in between, she was the victim of one of those malicious tricks that nature sometimes plays on singers.

In 1943 in a performance when Bampton undertook her first Sieglinde at the Metropolitan, the ninth Valkyrie, Schwertleite, was a young American mezzo-soprano, Margaret Harshaw. By 1947 she had thoroughly established herself in the big mezzo parts such as Amneris, Azucena and Ulrica. Four years later she was engaged by Covent Garden as a soprano to sing the three Brünnhildes in the *Ring,* appearances she was unfortunately prevented from making. The following year she appeared in Wagnerian roles in New York and returned to London in 1953 for her first *Walküre* and *Siegfried* Brünnhilde. Thereafter she dropped all her mezzo roles, usually a necessity in the process of going up, lest they drag the voice down. Like Bampton, Harshaw was an intelligent, admirable artist with a powerful, silvery voice that proved effective for a number of years in the Wagnerian soprano repertory. And yet again she never sounded effortless, never could make her voice soar with the ease and brilliance of the true dramatic soprano. Would it have been better not to have made the transition? At the time Harshaw turned soprano there was a dearth of Brünnhildes and Kundrys: certainly the dimensions of her career were much extended by making it.

The temptation for a mezzo-soprano to go up when the juicy and sympathetic soprano roles hang so temptingly near is therefore sometimes very great. Just a slight stretch (so it seems) and they are plucked. Actually, stretching the compass of a voice and singing in a tessitura that is not comfortable, while possible, is also very dangerous. The two marvelously talented Garcia sisters, Maria Malibran and Pauline Viardot, appear to have been mezzos who added top notes to their voices to sing such parts as the soprano role of Norma. Whether Malibran's voice would have endured very long the treatment to which she subjected it is difficult to say as she died so young. Viardot, who at the age of thirty was described by Gounod as "already nearing her end, and singing out of tune all the time," summed it up in advice she gave to a young singer: "Don't do as I did. I wanted to sing everything and I spoilt my voice." In our own time the fine mezzo-soprano Christa Ludwig began to sing and record a number of soprano roles and seemed to be tending towards a take-over of the entire repertory. The strain, however, on her resplendent voice soon began to show in her performances and though announced to sing the *Siegfried* Brünnhilde under von Karajan, she stepped down in a return to her old mezzo ways.

Nonetheless there have been a number of women singers who began as mezzo-sopranos and made highly successful transitions to the soprano roles. Outstanding examples are Edyth Walker, Gertrude Kappel, Dusolina Giannini, Anny Konetzni and currently,

Marta Fuchs, and Gwyneth Jones. Also the attractive English lyric soprano Jennifer Vyvyan was first a mezzo. Improbably, the coloratura Erna Sack, with her extraordinary peanut whistle register, began her career in Berlin in 1928 as a contralto.

Much rarer are the cases of sopranos who have moved down to darker levels of the mezzo. In our own time we have had one outstanding example—the inimitable Regina Resnik. She made her Metropolitan debut on twenty-four hours' notice with an hour and a quarter rehearsal as Leonora in *Trovatore* in December, 1944, and thereafter sang many *spinto* soprano parts such as Aida, Tosca, both Donna Anna and Donna Elvira, Sieglinde and Butterfly. Her voice was full and luscious in the middle and lower parts of the range, but her top tones were often shrill and unreliable. After ten years Resnik began to make fewer and fewer performances at the Metropolitan and in the 1954-55 season dropped out altogether, only to appear the following year singing mezzo roles exclusively. Her voice by then had assumed a darker quality with more heavily emphatic low tones. Thus the career of this fine artist renewed itself. Interestingly, almost twenty-five years after her debut as a soprano her voice has taken on the quality of the lowest of all women's voices—the contralto.

"Une Voix Obscène." The distinction between the mezzo-soprano and the contralto is often ill defined. The range of the two is more or less the same,

Contralto

and people frequently use the terms interchangeably. A true contralto has an even darker, sometimes lugubrious sounding voice. But while the mezzo, like the sister soprano above her, strives to show off her high notes, the contralto heads in the other direction and pulls out as *her* trump card her low notes. For this reason contraltos singing recitals are often fond of choosing a song like Schubert's "Der Tod und das Mädchen" with its optional ending of D, below middle C. Marian Anderson used to bring out this note with a kind of awesome profundity. Interestingly, this great contralto tells in her autobiography that as a young girl in her teens she sang the "Inflammatus" from Rossini's *Stabat Mater*, undaunted by its repeated high C″'s, which shows that she possessed a phenomenal range of almost three octaves. Having these top notes, she was occasionally advised to transform herself into a soprano. Aware of the richness and sonority of her lower range she wisely resisted the temptation and never sang in public, anyway, music that carried her much above a high A′. Thus, while her middle notes had a brighter mezzo-soprano quality, the low part of her voice had the haunting dark tones we think of as belonging to a true contralto. Many contraltos with their much emphasized low notes and rather inflexible voices (Marian Anderson, however, possessed a beautiful trill) do not sing above F′.

True contralto roles are infrequent in opera as the voice, particularly in America, is rare. Erda, full of forebodings as she rises from the bowels of the earth, is best performed by a singer with an authoritative lower register. (The *Siegfried* Erda must sing one high A′ flat, but otherwise the part lies very low indeed.) I also unhesitatingly prefer the role of Gluck's Orfeo to be sung by a contralto. There is some precedent for this since the part was originally performed by a *castrato* contralto, though Gluck later altered it for tenor when the opera was given in Paris (the French never having had a taste for an artificially created female voice emanating from a large male frame). Berlioz revived and arranged Gluck's *Orfeo* for the extraordinary Pauline Viardot in November, 1859, who evidently had a voice best described as a mezzo-soprano with very well emphasized low tones. It is this version that we are most accustomed to hearing today with a woman singing the male title part. The part lies low and requires a voice of great nobility and dignity; it must at the same time be tenderly poignant, a quality which is sometimes lacking in the forceful bottom of contraltos, most particularly in what one observer has amusingly described as "the dark hooting tone of the traditional English contralto."

Because of a love for oratorio as well as for the Gilbert and Sullivan operas that call for gloom-ridden contraltos to limn such parts as Katisha in *The Mikado* or Lady Jane in *Patience,* England has produced more than its share of this unusual type of woman's voice. A famous contralto of days gone by who possessed stentorian low tones was Clara Butt. "C'est une voix obscène," remarked the composer, Reynaldo Hahn, himself a singer, when he heard her. Dame Clara's voice, at least heard in records, almost completely lacked a vibrato, giving the effect of the singing of a huge mannish choirboy.

Another peerless English contralto of more recent times was Lancashire-born Kathleen Ferrier, who embarked on a professional career at the extraordinarily late age of twenty-nine during the height of the war. She had taken two years of singing lessons when in 1943 she came to the well-known singer and teacher, Roy Henderson. At that time, he writes, "the quality of the voice was rich, but rather too dark and it possessed but one colour." (This, incidentally, is a classic analysis of what irks and displeases certain people about the contralto voice: darkness and monotony.) "The range was only moderate," continues Mr. Henderson of Ferrier's voice. "The high E' tended to sharpen in pitch and lost much of the quality of the lower notes, while F' was about the upper limit and was only supported by an extra push of breath. The interpretative side of singing hardly existed."

Ten years later Kathleen Ferrier was dead of cancer. It is difficult to believe that in this time she added two whole tones to the top of her range, that she lightened and brightened her voice and molded it into the wonderfully expressive instrument that it became; that she also mastered languages omitted in her original rather rudimentary education (she left school when she was fourteen) and that she learned a large repertory of lieder, oratorio arias and other works for voice which she sang under the great conductors of her time. One of these, Bruno Walter, so admired the beauty of her voice and art that he often accompanied her in recitals. Kathleen Ferrier's last two heart-breaking appearances were in the role of Orfeo at Covent Garden. After the second performance, having smilingly received a crowd of backstage visitors and cheerily waved the last one away, when asked by her sister Winifred if there was anything she wanted, Ferrier replied, "Get me a stretcher, love." On it she left the opera house—forever.

Kathleen Ferrier seems to me to have had the perfect voice for Orfeo. It entirely lacked any harsh or astringent quality throughout its compass, having instead a strange kind of radiance which made her singing almost unbearingly moving to hear. As with Mozart, it seems as if she had some foreknowledge of the shortness of her destiny, so much did she accomplish in so little time.

THE LOWER WOMEN'S VOICES

Lyric Mezzo-Soprano Roles

Carmen	See discussion in the text.
Cenerentola	A luscious part for the coloratura mezzo.
Charlotte (*Werther*)	
Cherubino (*Le Nozze*)	Sometimes sung by a lyric soprano.
Dorabella (*Così*)	Also sung by a dramatic mezzo.
Hänsel	Sometimes sung by a lyric soprano.
Laura (*Gioconda*)	Also taken by a dramatic mezzo.
La Cieca (*Gioconda*)	Same as Laura.
Lola	
(*Cavalleria Rusticana*)	

Maddalena (*Rigoletto*)

Mignon   Farrar and Bori, lyric sopranos, sang
                                this part; so did Christine Nilsson, a so-
                                prano *leggiero*.

Mistress Page (*Falstaff*)
Nicklausse
  (*Contes d'Hoffmann*)
Octavian
  (*Rosenkavalier*)   Sung by lyric and even *spinto* sopranos.
Preziosilla (*Forza*)
Rosina (*Il Barbiere*)   Usually taken away from the coloratura
                                mezzo by the soprano *leggiero*.

Siebel (*Faust*)
Suzuki
  (*Madama Butterfly*)

THE LOWER WOMEN'S VOICES

Dramatic Mezzo-Soprano Roles

Adalgisa (*Norma*)   Ideally, a dramatic mezzo sings this, but
                                lyrics also do it.

Amneris (*Aida*)
Azucena (*Trovatore*)
Brangäne (*Tristan*)
Dalila
Eboli (*Don Carlo*)
Fricka (*Rheingold* and
  Walküre)
Klytemnestra (*Elektra*)
Magdalene (*Meistersinger*)   Can be sung by a lyric mezzo as well.
Marina (*Boris Godounov*)
Ortrud (*Lohengrin*)
Ulrica
  (*Ballo in Maschera*)
Venus (*Tannhäuser*)

THE LOWER WOMEN'S VOICES

Contraltos

Note: These roles can be sung by mezzos, but they should have very strong, deep low notes.

    Dame Quickly (*Falstaff*)
    Erda (*Rheingold* and *Siegfried*)
    Orfeo
    Orlofsky (*Fledermaus*)

Also various middle-aged ladies in Gilbert and Sullivan operettas such as:

    Katisha (*Mikado*)
    Lady Jane (*Patience*)
    Little Buttercup (*Pinafore*)

* * * *

THE HIGH MEN'S VOICES

"There are men; there are women and then there are tenors," is the familiar saying * about these singers whose voices are scarce and tremendously in demand in the opera house. One might carry it a step further and say that there are men, women, tenors and countertenors since the male who can produce this odd, not exactly feminine but rather sexless sound is of incredible rarity. There exists a not uncommon fallacy in the public mind that a countertenor is the modern version of the *castrato,* his voice, if not artificially created, at least resulting from a lack of sexual maturation. Writing rather sourly of countertenors, Ralph Morse Brown declares that they have delicate skin, little or no facial hair and never a beard, a statement belied by the appearance of the most famous countertenor of his generation, Alfred Deller. In addition, Mr. Brown counsels the prospective teacher of a countertenor to prepare himself to deal with a person "ultra clever,

---

* Another, made by Hans von Bülow: "A tenor is a disease."

highly nervous, refined and charming, peculiarly nice and correct in interpretation, and hypersensitive," or else one "stupid, phlegmatic, unreliable and a hopeless bungler"—a catalogue which would appear to cover almost all the attributes of human character.

Though the countertenor may incline to white flesh and hairlessness, he is generally no less sexually mature than his female counterpart, the contralto, who can sometimes have a sturdy, virile appearance (the famous contralto, Clara Butt, was six feet tall) and possess hair on her face and body where it does not ordinarily appear in most women. The countertenor and the contralto then, share the twilight world that society seems to be tending towards today where pronounced male or female sexual qualities merge. As young men and women today dress alike and even share the same clothes, so the countertenor and the contralto sing almost exactly the same range

Countertenor

Like the contralto, who by muscular adjustments within the larynx can sing the low, manly sounds of *her* extra register, the countertenor by actions within his larynx, produces in *his* extra register the high, slightly hooty tones that are correctly described as falsetto. (In earlier times the high head tones of an ordinary tenor came to be called "falsetto" but these are not produced in the same way and the term applied to them is inaccurate and misleading. But this will be discussed more fully in a later section.)

A high, feminine sound, his falsetto voice, emanating from a

man, usually makes us laugh. Puccini asks Marcello to use it when
he's pretending to be the girlish dancing partner of Schaunard in
the last act of *Bohème*. Verdi calls for the portly Sir John Falstaff
to sing a few falsetto notes when he describes with irresistibly
comic effect how Mistress Ford has fallen in love with him. The
male falsetto can also sound macabre and mad to our ears, greatly
adding to the impact of an opera such as *Wozzeck*.

While the ordinary tenor or baritone voice (but infrequently the
low bass) can make brief excursions into this extra male register,
the countertenor uses it almost the entire time. And because he
has enforced and strengthened his falsetto register to such an extent, the lower, what we might call "ordinary" light tenor or baritone part of his voice becomes weak and inaudible, just as the
female pop singer using only her chest register enervates the ordinary, more feminine quality of her voice.

In an interesting passage in the biography of Alfred Deller, *A
Singularity of Voice,* the celebrated countertenor discusses the
existence of another kind of "high tenor who can either dispense
with falsetto entirely, or use it for the top fourth or fifth of the
compass, without perceptible break. Some people say this is a true
countertenor; others that it isn't a countertenor at all, but merely
a high, light tenor. Certainly, some singers one hears who are
billed as countertenors seem to be tenors with an exceptionally
high range." This type of countertenor, however, lacks the astonishing ease and effortlessness that Deller, who sings mainly in his
falsetto register, possesses.

Though the world has come to accept—welcome even—a lady
who belts out her songs with the raucous quality of a buzz saw,
reactions to the sounds of a countertenor tend to be more am-
bivalent. Michael Tippett, who has composed for Deller, is quoted
as saying in the same *A Singularity of Voice:* "It was the voice for
which Bach wrote many of the alto solos in the Church cantatas;
and Purcell, who himself sang countertenor, gave to it some of
his best airs and ensembles. To my ear it has a peculiarly musical

sound because almost no emotional irrelevancies distract us from the absolutely pure musical quality of the production. *It is like no other sound in music* * and few other sounds are so intrinsically musical." Along with a delight in the sound of a choirboy's voice, a particular fondness for the countertenor seems to exist among the English. In addition to Tippett, Benjamin Britten has also composed for the countertenor, including the part of Oberon in his opera, *A Midsummer Night's Dream.* Can it be a national feeling for reticence, for understatement that responds to the lack of what Tippett calls distracting "emotional irrelevancies" in this type of voice? On the other hand I have heard this reaction from an otherwise unaggressive and mild-mannered Englishman, a most knowledgeable lover of music and singing. "Down with the countertenor!" he cried, turning slightly red in the face as his eyebrows worked up and down. "He always sounds unnatural, constrained and affected, as well as ugly." A taste for the countertenor voice, however, has spread to other countries, particularly Germany and America where now that there is a demand for them countertenors are emerging in greater quality.

In keeping with the modern crossing of the sexes, male pop singers breathing moistly and warmly on the shiny metal domes of their hand mikes, frequently sing their numbers in the soft, veiled tones of their falsetto registers. And recently we have had the phenomenal success of middle-aged Tiny Tim, who thinks nothing of bounding into his falsetto register to the immense satisfaction of his fans.

Tenore Leggiero. On an average the length of the ordinary tenor's vocal chords is around seven-twelfths of an inch † and slightly thicker than those in the throat of the female. As a result, men are far less adept at performing florid music. Handel calls

---

* Italics R. Rushmore.
† Caruso's were said to be one inch long, the nonsensical information that tends to arise about legendary figures.

upon the heavy bass voice to move with agility through such arias
as "O Ruddier than the Cherry" from *Acis and Galatea* or "Why
do the Nations" from *Messiah*, but the result is all too often a
heavily aspirated and muddily articulated series of runs and skips,
not at all what the composer would have wished for. The male
voice most capable of a coloratura technique is the small, often
rather pale-sounding tenor known as the *tenore leggiero* or sometimes *tenore bianco*. His range is the same as the heavier but less
flexible lyric tenor

Tenore Leggiero

though this gentle, suave-sounding tenor, as Alfred Deller has
noted, can sometimes extend his compass by shading his high tones
off into falsetto, turning himself into a kind of countertenor. Because the *tenore leggiero* favors the middle and upper part of his
range and also emphasizes lightness and agility, he usually lacks
body in the lower part.

Notable examples of the *tenore leggiero* have included Alessandro Bonci, and Tito Schipa and more recently, Cesare Valletti
and Luigi Alva. They have all shone in the light roles of Almaviva
in *Il Barbiere*, Nemorino in *L'Elisir d'Amore* and Don Ottavio in
Don Giovanni. Fenton in Verdi's *Falstaff* is also most attractive
when sung by a tenor with a gentle, almost petal-like softness to
his voice. These singers, however, in their search for more repertory often take on slightly heavier parts such as Rodolfo in *Bohème*,
Alfredo in *Traviata*, or Massenet's Des Grieux. The *tenore leggiero*
who sings the last named part usually fares beautifully with the

evocative "Le Rêve," Des Grieux's aria in the second act that should be sung almost entirely in a finely spun *mezza voce*. But the same tenor then has difficulty in mustering the size of voice needed for the dramatic third act aria, "Ah, fuyez douce image."

Interestingly, at the outset of his career Tito Schipa sang in addition to the light tenor repertory some of the heavier tenor roles such as Cavaradossi and Turiddu, but soon gave them up. The glowing, youthful sheen of his voice continued to last throughout a career that endured over forty-five years. We must not forget, too, the so-called "Irish tenor" with its light, pale quality which should properly be classified as *tenore leggiero*. The most obvious famous example is John McCormack's sweetly flexible voice with its faultless trill.

America is a country that has not produced many light tenors of fame, yet the first American Negro to make a distinguished international career was not, as might be supposed, a man with a big rolling voice and expansive art to match, but Roland Hayes, who possessed a small tenor voice of extreme refinement. Against all kinds of odds and prejudices Hayes set out on a singing career in 1911, opposed by his mother, who though ambitious for her son, thought that if he became a singer it must be as a night club entertainer. A famous story is told that when Roland Hayes was commanded to perform at Buckingham Palace in 1920, he jubilantly wired his mother the news. "Remember who you are," she promptly cabled back. Like Schipa, Hayes made no attempt to enlarge his light, finely controlled voice, with the result that his career lasted thirty-five years.

The Lyric and the Dramatic Tenor. When it comes to the bigger-voiced tenors the distinction between lyric and dramatic is very indistinct indeed. Much *va-et-vient* goes on, the lyric tenors pushing into heavier dramatic roles such as Radames in *Aida* or Andrea Chénier, the dramatic tenors stepping back to sing lighter, more graceful parts like Rodolfo or Alfredo. All these tenors have about the same range as their lighter voiced confrères

Lyric and Dramatic Tenor

but considerably less agility, and in a part such as Tamino can experience difficulty with the passage in Act One, Scene Three, when he must sing embellishments—as a coloratura loves to do— of the melody he has played on his Magic Flute.

A perfect example of a true lyric tenor was Jussi Bjoerling, one of the phenomenons of modern vocal times. Bjoerling received his first singing lessons at the age of five and with his father, Carl David, and brothers Olle and Guerta sang throughout his child-hood in a group known as the Bjoerling Male Quartet. He first came to the United States, not as is generally supposed, in 1937 when he made his debut with the Chicago Opera Company, but many years earlier with the quartet as a lad of thirteen. The Bjoerling family were all tenors and recordings of one of Jussi's brothers show a striking similarity of quality to that of the more famous tenor, lacking only his brilliance of tone.*

Because the careers of singers are constantly overshadowed by effects of aging, their birthdates as given to the public are open to constant suspicion. Bjoerling is usually supposed to have sung his first important operatic role—Don Ottavio—at the amazingly youthful age of nineteen. Actually he was four years older, so that by the time of his debut he had already eighteen years ex-perience of performing. To this fact we can attribute his superb

* Jussi Bjoerling's son, Rolf, is also a tenor with a timbre much like his father's.

musicianship, phrasing and diction—qualities not always found in tenors of whatever sized voice.

Jussi Bjoerling unlike many lyric tenors never tried to move on to the bigger, more dramatic tenor parts. True, he recorded such heavy roles as Canio in *Pagliacci* and Calaf in *Turandot* but he avoided them in the opera house. The heaviest parts he undertook at the Metropolitan were the name part in *Don Carlo* and Manrico in *Trovatore,* the latter reluctantly. As a result Bjoerling's crystalline sheen of voice lasted until his untimely death from heart disease at the age of fifty-three. How little his voice varied over the years, except to darken a bit, can be heard by comparing his records made in the thirties to the last, a concert in August 1960, less than a month before his death.

One who has almost kept pace with Bjoerling is Richard Tucker who in the Metropolitan revival of *Luisa Miller* in 1968 sang the opening performance with a freshness of vocal quality that put time back to his debut in the winter of 1945—and Tucker's repertory, unlike Bjoerling's, has included many of the heavier dramatic roles such as Don José in *Carmen* and Turiddu in *Cavalleria Rusticana.*

The King. And what of the greatest tenor of them all? His face with its comic, wide-set eyes and broad gash of a mouth rising above a ludicrously dumpy figure, Enrico Caruso by means of a richly dark voice, almost muscular in feeling, and a way of using it with total conviction, exerted a spell over those who heard him greater than any singer in modern vocal history. This was partly due to the introduction of phonograph records that paralleled his career, and also to the fact that Caruso happened to record extremely well. For many, he became the ideal singer through whom they could hear operatic music that had been denied them or rationed out on far-spaced occasions. But Caruso meant even more than that. He reached people all over the world, even those who were otherwise indifferent to singing. To many he was not just a

"The King," a Self-portrait by Caruso.

singer—but a spirit. In his vocal art could be heard an accent of humanity to which the public gave its unfaltering response. Even if one had never listened to a Caruso record it is possible to understand his unique quality from his letters that Dorothy Caruso published in 1946 in her deeply moving memoir, *Enrico Caruso.* These, full of comic misspellings and grammatical errors, give the measure of the man's character and of his heart. As Mrs. Caruso points out in a little introduction to her book: "At times they are curiously Biblical."

Caruso was no exception to the rule that boy altos are more likely to become tenors (as boy sopranos become baritones and basses). At the age of twenty-two he made his first important appearance at Caserta as Turiddu, a fairly heavy tenor role that he probably should not have undertaken, for during the beginning

of his career he was given to breaking on his high notes. Caruso
was a true lyric tenor and in his early years at Covent Garden
and the Metropolitan he sang mainly the lyric roles. During this
time there lay on his voice when he sang *mezza voce* that peculiarly
haunting peach fuzz quality (I cannot describe it better) which is
unique to the Italian tenor. (The voice of the young Gigli and
to some extent the young di Stefano also had this gentle, vulnerable sound not to speak of Kerruccio Tagliavini.)

Unfortunately, if the Italian lyric tenor pushes on to more
strenuous dramatic parts this bloom goes from the voice, which
was the case with Caruso, who by the end of his career had sung
thirty-six different roles at the Metropolitan, many of them very
taxing to an intrinsically lyric voice. This, as Irving Kolodin
writes, "cost him the command of his early lyric eloquence. No
voice could withstand unaltered the amount and kind of usage
to which Caruso's was subjected. Only his extraordinary physique
and robust constitution limited what could have been deteriora-
tion to merely a change of timbre." This change took the form
of a thicker, darker, certainly more dramatic quality, but with
some of the sweetness gone. By performing the heavy tenor roles
such as Samson or Eleazar in *La Juive,* Caruso actually strained
his voice to the extent that he developed dreaded wartlike nodules
on his vocal cords which had to be removed surgically.

In his fascinating pictorial biography of Caruso, Francis Robinson declares that the great tenor could easily have sung the
lighter Wagnerian tenor parts such as Lohengrin and Tannhäuser
—certainly Walther in *Die Meistersinger.* Being a completely ori-
ented Italian, with English, as we know from his letters, totally
his own, he shied away from the difficulties of singing in German.
Mr. Robinson, however, publishes a picture of the program of
Caruso's only Wagnerian performance—*Lohengrin* in Italian at
Buenos Aires in 1901 with Toscanini as conductor.

Ever since what might be described as the mystique of Caruso,
tenors have been hailed (possibly by their own press agents) as a

second Caruso. Mrs. Caruso is supposed to have declared that
Jussi Bjoerling's voice came nearest to that of her remarkable husband whom she outlived for so many years. The comparison does
not seem entirely apt, but does illustrate the difference between
a pure lyric tenor which Bjoerling remained and the kind of tenor
who pushes his voice into more dramatic parts. Bjoerling always
kept his pristine, slightly uninvolved quality; Caruso came to
sound more like a baritone. In other respects, however, there were
certain similarities between the two: both, as tenors so often are,
were short and plump with Caruso the stouter and more massive.
Both, despite the sincerity of their acting when they played romantic figures, demanded a certain suspension of disbelief from
their audiences. (When Jussi Bjoerling sang his first, impassioned
Des Grieux in Puccini's *Manon Lescaut*—one of his finest parts—
at the Metropolitan, a friend of mine commented that he looked
strangely like Lotte Lehmann dressed up in breeches. And of course
some of the photographs of Caruso in costume are absurdly comic.)
Of their temperaments, though Caruso appeared outwardly calm
when he sang, he was not: "Of course I am nervous," he is quoted
as saying. "Each time I feel there is someone wanting to destroy
me, and I must fight like a bull to hold my own." Bjoerling, on
the other hand, never even went through the routines of trying his
voice that Caruso practiced on the day of a performance. Once
when asked why not, Bjoerling replied, "If I'm well it's not necessary. If I'm not what good does it do?" Both tenors were conscientious artists, but Caruso, with far less musical background and
training than the Swedish singer, had to work harder to develop
his musicianship. B. H. Haggin, one of America's sharpest music
critics, has this comparison to make of the singing of the two
tenors on records:

"In his recorded performance of 'O Paradiso' Caruso arriving
at a high B flat holds and expands it from *pp* to an overwhelming
ff, then breaks off to take breath before completing the phrase;
whereas Bjoerling in his recorded performance, connects the ex-

panded B flat with the next note as part of the continuous and beautifully shaped phrase: in the Caruso performance, then, one hears an exceptionally beautiful voice and a mastery in its manipulation; in the Bjoerling not only these but the art in musical phrasing that Caruso did not have."

Beniamino Gigli was sometimes considered a second Caruso, but his lovely lyric voice which he pushed on into more dramatic parts never possessed the thrilling richness and drive of his predecessor. In our own time, for sheer versatility and the size of his repertory Richard Tucker comes nearest to the record established by Caruso, though he still has some way to go to achieve the 607 performances that Caruso gave at the Metropolitan.

Caruso was of course the great best-selling recording artist of his time and made the fortune of what was then called the Victor Talking Machine Company. Jussi Bjoerling made over three hundred records, many of which sold extremely well. But at this writing the operatic tenor who has chalked up the biggest sales for RCA Victor is the incredible phenomenon—Mario Lanza.

A Second King.   I don't think it's an exaggeration to say that because of the mass public attending the movies and buying records, Mario Lanza was the most popular operatic singer who ever lived—despite the fact that he sang in only two actual performances of opera, *Madama Butterfly* in New Orleans. "A great voice," was the reaction of Serge Koussevitsky when the twenty-one year old, boyishly handsome tenor auditioned for him in 1942. At that time Lanza had a year and a half of voice lessons behind him. The conductor invited the young tenor to Tanglewood, which Lanza had never heard of, for a summer of study in company with Leonard Bernstein. Intense musical training that Lanza so badly needed—most of his knowledge of singing had been derived from constantly playing the records of Caruso—was unfortunately interrupted by the draft. In the Army, at that time weighing 287 pounds, he eventually made it into an Army Air Force

Show. After his discharge he embarked on a career of small town concerts and a few radio shows, but his voice, though naturally beautiful, was incorrectly produced. The young tenor's greatest break came when a wealthy real estate operator and failed singer heard him, and combining his knowledge of singing with a shrewd business sense, decided to invest in Lanza's career. He stopped Lanza from singing in public, sent him to one of the best singing teachers in New York and supported the singer and his wife through more than a year of extensive training, during which Lanza for the first time learned how to read music. In 1947 the tenor sang a Hollywood Bowl concert and the next day was signed to an MGM contract.

Piggish, lazy and with a conceit about his singing that probably disguised his enormous musical insecurity, Lanza believed that he would one day reach La Scala and the Metropolitan. Certainly he had the voice for it. Warm, Italianate, its sound was glorious. It also had the requisite size, though Lanza tended to force. Many, however, doubted that he possessed the necessary musicianship as well as self-discipline to sing in the great opera houses of the world. His singing career as movie star and recording artist was nonetheless fantastic. Lanza was the only operatic artist ever to sell over one million copies of a record, "Be My Love," in a single year and he is still RCA Victor's best-selling "classical" singer.

The Heavier Tenor. Though I have said that Caruso could undoubtedly have sung very beautifully some of the lighter Wagnerian roles, a tenor who begins singing the Italian and French lyric roles, as Caruso did, is more than likely to remain with them. (True, late in his career Martinelli sang Tristan in Chicago, but this was exceptional for an essentially Italian tenor.) Yet today we do have such dramatic tenors as Jon Vickers or Jess Thomas who switch back and forth from the lighter German parts to French and Italian roles. Thus Vickers sings Don José, Radames,

Peter Grimes, Siegmund and the exacting role of Florestan in *Fidelio.* Thomas can do most of this repertory too, also Calaf in *Turandot,* Lohengrin, and heavier Wagnerian parts such as Sieg-fried and Tristan. Neither of these singers, however, shades his voice down for an evening as Alfredo or the Duke in *Rigoletto,* as does Richard Tucker, who also sings Don José and Radames—but no German parts. Thus confusion and ambiguity will be seen to infect the nomenclature, "lyric tenor," "dramatic tenor," or *"ten-ore robusto"* as the latter is sometimes called.

So far, we have mainly discussed the Italian and French rep-ertory. Before looking into the intricacies of who sings what in the various German operas, it would be appropriate to say a word about the German tenor himself. In certain cases, like the Italian tenor with his peach fuzz quality, the German tenor will have a peculiar national sound difficult to describe but unmistakable. It is partly innate but also compounded by the scooping, slurring way (mostly in operetta) in which the voice is employed. Richard Tauber, possessor of a glorious but unmistakably Teutonic voice, was capable of singing Mozart or lieder with impeccable style, but could also ladle out a generous helping of rich Viennese chocolate and whipped cream when he rendered such favorites as "Dein ist mein ganzes Herz" for which he was so famous. This national voice and style of singing has been apostrophized in verse by M. W. Branch in a poem called "Schmalztenor."

> O hark! 'tis the note of the Schmalztenor!
> It swells in his bosom and hangs in the air.
> Like lavender-scent in a spinster's drawer
> It oozes and percolates everywhere.
> So tenderly glutinous,
> Soothing the brute in us,
> Wholly unmutinous
> Schmalztenor.
>
> Enchanting, his smile for the third encore
> (Cherubic complexion and glossy curls),

His nasal nostalgia, so sweetly sore,
   Vibrates on the sternums of swooning girls.
      Emerging and merging,
      Suggestively urging,
      Receding and surging—
         The Schmalztenor.

The Absolute Last of the Schmalztenor
   Is heard in Vienna in lilac-time.
He's steaming and quivering more and more
   And dowagers whisper, "He's past his prime!"
      Young maidens have drowned for him:
      Pass the hat round for him:
      Open the ground for him—
         Schmalztenor.

The tenors (not necessarily German, however) who can sing the heavy German repertory consisting of Tristan, Parsifal, Siegmund, the two Siegfrieds, Florestan and Herod in *Salome* are rare indeed. In the past twenty years there have really only been two, the late Set Svanholm and more recently, Wolfgang Windgassen. Neither of them should be strictly classified as heroic or *heldentenors,* any more than the celebrated Jean de Reszke.

As is well known de Reszke began his career as a baritone singing such parts as Figaro in *Il Barbiere* and *Don Giovanni* as early as 1874. Bernard Shaw, then a London music critic, much admired de Reszke in the latter part. After appearing for three years in this guise the baritone retired from the stage and re-trained his voice, a time which, incidentally, while not appearing before the public he once described as the best years of his life. After his reappearance ten years later he sang what might be called the *spinto* tenor roles in the Italian-French repertory: Faust, Roméo, Radames, Don José, and then cautiously embarked on Wagnerian parts such as Walther von Stolzing and Lohengrin, but first singing them in Italian. His beautiful interpretations at a time when

The Concert Singer by Thomas Eakins

Is physical beauty necessary to a singing career? Let the reader decide from the following selection of some of the world's most celebrated singing artists.

Most celebrated of all the singing families were the Garcias. What they may have lacked in sheer beauty of voice, they made up in intelligence, musicianship, or sheer intensity.

Manuel Garcia, age 100, detail from portrait by John Singer Sargent

Museum of Art, Rhode Island School of Design

Maria Malibran-Garcia

Victoria and Albert Museum

Detail of Malibran's Debut,
1825 Self-Caricature

Victoria and Albert Museum

Victoria and Albert Museum

Madame Viardot Garcia

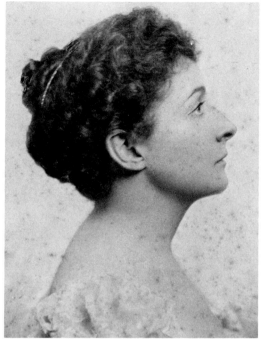

Emma Eames

Some Beauties...

Collection of author

Geraldine Farrar

Liff-Stuart Collection

Giovanni Rubini

Collection of author

Collection of author

Lina Cavalieri

Conchita Supervia

Liff-Stuart Collection

Maria Callas

Mary Garden

there was increasing excitement over Wagner, led him to push on through most of the Wagnerian repertory but now singing the parts in their original language. Some say this was fatal to his career and that he overtaxed his voice, causing his early retirement. (He was fifty-two.) Certainly de Reszke cancelled many performances towards the end of his career, particularly *Siegfried,* an especially arduous role. Some say that he wasn't a tenor at all, but a baritone with high notes. But then an awful lot is said in the world of singing that is sheer nonsense.

[De Reszke was not the only tenor to sing Wagnerian roles who began as a baritone. Others have included Rudolf Berger, Ramon Vinay, Set Svanholm (who sang as a baritone for six years before going up) and the inimitable Lauritz Melchior. Outstanding tenors who sing the Italian repertory such as Carlo Bergonzi and Bruno Prevedi also began as baritones.]

For reasons best known to herself, spiteful nature usually chooses to inflict on the man with a tenor voice—he who must portray a whole series of dashing, youthful heroes—lack of height and a tendency to corpulence. Indeed, one tenor, the Roumanian-born Joseph Schmidt, possessor of a rich, soaring voice, never could make an operatic career because of being so extremely short. Even in the opera house where credibility is not the commonplace of an evening, he would have looked too ludicrous. In our own day we have such strapping and handsome six-footers as Franco Corelli and Nicolai Gedda who sing the Italian-French repertory, but they are really quite unusual. When we come, however, to that most exceptional of all tenor voices—the *heldentenor*—there can be no exception to the rule of his physique. He will be *enormous.* Not only tall, like Jean de Reszke who was six feet (though not a true *heldentenor*), but also having a chest of massive proportions, greater than photographs of de Reszke show him to have possessed.

During the twentieth century there have so far been but two tenors of international fame who properly fit into this category of the gigantic and vocally indefatigable tenor. They are Leo

Slezak and Lauritz Melchior. Others, like James McCracken, meet the physical requirements but lack the untiring vocal ability of a true heroic tenor; while there have been a number of Wagnerian tenors, Max Lorenz, Ludwig Suthaus, Svanholm and Windgassen already mentioned, able to get through their parts, but not having the reserve or ease which the colossal size and girth of a Melchior might have accorded them.

Melchior, as has been said, began his career as a baritone, but one night while singing the Count in *Trovatore* with an observant American mezzo called Madame Charles Cahier, he added an unwritten high C' to his part. Amazed, she urged him to re-train his voice. A year later he had gone up and stayed there for twenty-five years, an incredible eye-shattering figure in the bearskin of Siegfried, a moving, but hopelessly robust and healthy-looking Tristan on his deathbed. During his career he sang opposite Frida Leider, Kirsten Flagstad, Marjorie Lawrence and Helen Traubel, sopranos with voices of prodigious size and opulence. During that time there was only one Melchior. No other tenor could be compared with him.

TENORS

Some Lyric Roles

Beppe (*Pagliacci*)	The first six roles are most appropriately sung by a *tenore leggiero*.
Count Almaviva (*Barbiere*)	
Don Ottavio (*Don Giovanni*)	
Ernesto (*Don Pasquale*)	
Fenton (*Falstaff*)	
Nemorino (*L'Elisir*)	
Alfred (*Fledermaus*)	Most of these parts can be sung by heavier, *spinto*-type tenors.
Alfredo (*Travtata*)	
Cavaradossi (*Tosca*)	

Des Grieux (Both *Manons*)
Duke (*Rigoletto*)
Faust
Ferrando (*Così*)
Pelléas   Sometimes sung by a high, light baritone.
Pinkerton (*Butterfly*)
Rodolfo (*Bohème*)
Tamino
  (*Zauberflöte*)

TENORS

Spinto *or Dramatic Tenor Roles*

Andrea Chénier
Calaf (*Turandot*)
Canio (*Pagliacci*)
Dimitri (*Boris*)
Don Alvaro (*Forza*)
Don Carlo
Don José (*Carmen*)
Enzo (*Gioconda*)
Erik
  (*Fliegende Holländer*)
Florestan (*Fidelio*)
Herod (*Salome*)
Hoffmann
Julien (*Louise*)
Lenski (*Eugen Onegin*)
Lohengrin   Also sung by the heroic tenor.
Manrico (*Trovatore*)
Otello   An Italian *heldentenor* role.
Radames (*Aida*)
Riccardo or Gustav
  (*Ballo*)
Samson

Tannhäuser   Also sung by the heroic tenor.
Turiddu
  (*Cavalleria*)
Walther
  (*Meistersinger*)

TENORS

The Heavy German Heldentenor *Roles*

> All these parts have been sung by tenors with less than heroic voices.

Parsifal
Siegfried
Siegfried
  (*Götterdämmerung*)
Siegmund (*Walküre*)
Tristan

Tenors are usually short, basses tall.
Bonci and Chaliapin by Caruso.

THE LOWER MEN'S VOICES

Villain, Father or Friend. Next in order to the tenors as we descend the depths of the male voice are the baritones, usually designated lyric and dramatic, but again with a certain amount of spilling over between the two categories. What I choose to call the "Verdi" baritone, who sings Rigoletto or di Luna in *Trovatore* (but also Valentin in *Faust* and Gérard in *Andrea Chénier*) requires a range of

Baritone

with particular power and brilliance towards the top. The baritone who sings Tonio in *Pagliacci* must have a ringing high A flat for the Prologue, though it isn't in the score. The baritone who sings Iago must be able to touch lightly a high A natural in the first act Brindisi and that *is* in the score.

This husky, virile-sounding voice with its much emphasized middle and top (to the detriment of the power of the low notes, naturally) is a comparatively modern invention having evolved from the time of Rossini. Mozart, writing for his baritones, gives them a lower, less demanding tessitura and scarcely ever asks them to hit even a top F. This is why the higher bass singers, or bass-baritones as they frequently call themselves, have sneaked out from their usual run of characterizations—monarchs and ponderous paternal figures of other kinds—to grab the dashing role of Don Giovanni and the delightful one of Mozart's Figaro. Ezio Pinza, a high bass, was the first to initiate this practice at the Metropolitan. (The previous Don was Scotti, who sang all the Verdi baritone roles.) Since Pinza's time the baritones have continued to lose out to a series of attractive basses and bass-baritones such as Cesare Siepi, George London and most recently, Nicolai Ghiaurov, all having voices bright and light enough to suit the dash and verve of these characters.*

As far as leading operatic roles go the possessor of a light lyric baritone is rather restricted in the opera house. Mozart is his most generous benefactor with Papageno in *Die Zauberflöte*, Masetto in *Don Giovanni* and Guglielmo in *Così*. He has a nice love duet as Silvio in *Pagliacci* and he is onstage through most of *Bohème*, though the role of Marcello offers him few places really to shine. This voice can manage the rewarding part of the elder Germont in *Traviata* but few of the other fat Verdi roles. The part of Pelléas lies low in the tenor range and sometimes lyric baritones undertake it. Lacking the usual robustness of the big baritone voices, they can do justice to the grace and subtlety of this music. Above all, lyric baritones such as Charles Panzéro, Gérard Souzay and Hermann Prey make good recitalists.

As with all voices the lyric baritone can grow in size, strength and robustness. Inexperienced in opera, Robert Merrill made his debut at the Metropolitan as the elder Germont while he was still in his late twenties. Soon afterwards he was offered the heavy and demanding part of Rigoletto but had the good sense to turn it down until he and his voice were more mature. Gradually he took on some of the other exacting dramatic baritone parts, di Luna in *Trovatore*, Iago in *Otello*, and, twenty years after his debut, Scarpia in *Tosca*, always retaining the freshness of his voice.

Some men are innately equipped with big "Verdi" baritone voices but at the outset these can be thick and unwieldy. The young Leonard Warren had some trouble refining his gloriously

---

* Covent Garden, however, has reverted to baritone Dons such as Kostas Paskalis and Georges Bacquier.

large, sometimes wobbly voice and this is now true of the young Yorkshire baritone, Peter Glossop. The palm for the widest, richest, most thrilling "Verdi" baritone of all generally goes to Titta Ruffo. There is a remarkable similarity of virile tone quality between Ruffo's voice and Caruso's, and since Ruffo was one of the few baritone draws in vocal history (for some reason, however superb they may be, baritones don't seem to affect the box office like sopranos and tenors), this may account for the fact that while Caruso sang at the Metropolitan Ruffo did not, only appearing there after the great tenor's death. The two Italians made one record together, the duet *"Si per ciel,"* from *Otello,* and it is hair-raising.

So far I have discussed the kind of baritone who sings the high-lying Italian-French repertory. There are other artists, however, legitimately termed baritones, who usually remain entirely with German works. Big-voiced, sometimes dark-voiced, these singers devote themselves to the Wagnerian baritone parts, Wotan in the first three operas of the *Ring,* Telramund in *Lohengrin,* Kurvenal in *Tristan* and so forth. They will also portray the villainous Pizarro in *Fidelio* and the sanctimonious Jokanaan in *Salome,* and in the Italian repertory Scarpia in *Tosca* and Amonasro in *Aida.* These roles are also taken by vocalists who call themselves bass-baritones with a range

Bass-Baritone

and a darker tone quality than the true baritone.

A distinguished bass-baritone of recent time has been George

London who sang such bass roles as Boris Godounov and Méphistophélès, bass-baritone parts like Wotan and Eugen Onegin, and
the "Verdi" baritone role of Amonasro in *Aida*. "Verdi" baritones are usually assigned the part of Escamillo in *Carmen*, which
London also sang, but this is a difficult role for either type of baritone to manage. Much of the bull-fighter's music lies too low for
a high baritone to project it successfully, and yet it has high notes
discomfiting to the lower bass-baritone kind of voice.

Another fine singing actor, the Welshman Sir Geraint Evans,
moves around among the bass, bass-baritone and baritone roles
in a way that mocks any attempt to explain what kind of voice
sings what and why. Calling himself a baritone, Evans sings Falstaff, Wozzeck and Pizarro, all considered true baritone parts. He
sings Mozart's Figaro, a baritone or bass-baritone role, and then
in *Don Giovanni* switches not to the name part but Leporello,
which is almost always sung by a bass.

Baritones are usually manly, sturdy-looking fellows, often tall,
causing them to loom over the hero of the opera which the baritone, poor fellow, almost never is. Villainy is frequently his evening's work: Scarpia, Iago, Telramund, Barnaba in *Gioconda* are
all unbelievably depraved. Sometimes the baritone is a father—the
elder Germont, Rigoletto, Amonasro—though his relationships
with his various children never turn out to be very satisfactory due
to their mismanaged love affairs. Sometimes he is just a friend like
Rodrigo in *Don Carlo*, Wolfram in *Tannhäuser* or Renato in
Ballo. All too often he is in love with a lady who doesn't love him
and suffers devastating rejections. Gioconda and Leonora in *Trovatore* both prefer to sink dead at the feet of the baritone than
into his arms, while Tosca carries the rejection even further by
causing *him* to drop dead at *her* feet. Even when he gets to play
such a dashing symbol of sex as Don Giovanni his wooing is always interrupted, and while it is true that as Escamillo the baritone may have won Carmen between the acts, it is only a short

time before he finds her, like so many of his sought-after con-
quests, again dead at his feet.

Lowest of All. When sopranos sail up to a high C″ their
vocal cords or folds are fluttering at well over a thousand vibrations
per second. When the very rare *basso profundo* sings a D, two
octaves less one note below middle C his cords are pulsating at
around seventy-six vibrations per second. Like a low pedal point

Basso by Gerald Hoffnung.

held on the organ the effect is awesome and slightly forbidding. As
a result the bass voice is often used to portray gods, monarchs and
paternal figures with an occasional devil (Gounod's or Boïto's) or
dragon (Fafner) thrown in to vary the diet.

The higher type of bass, the *basso cantante,* who sometimes
calls himself bass-baritone, does not usually have the incredible
low buzzing notes of the *basso profundo,* but on the other hand

can reach an F at the top of his range which his much darker voiced confrères cannot:

Basso Cantante

The terms "lyric" and "dramatic" do not apply to the deepest male voices. These singers, big of stature, almost invariably have voices of a sonorousness and size that carry easily across the stretches of the largest opera houses. On the other hand, like tenors and baritones, they tend to divide up between those who sing the Italian-French repertory and those specializing in German operas. If none of them quite achieved the spectacular appeal of that former six day bicycle rider, Ezio Pinza, New York has been fortunate in having during the past twenty years a series of fine *cantante* basses including Jerome Hines, Cesare Siepi, Giorgio Tozzi and most recently, Nicolai Ghiaurov with his sumptuous voice. A favorite in London during this period has been Boris Christoff, rougher of voice but a great singing actor. On the whole, all these singers have remained within the Italian-French repertory, dividing up such star parts as Méphistophélès in *Faust,* Don Giovanni, Mozart's Figaro, Sarastro in *Zauberflöte* and of course the outstanding Russian role of Boris Godounov. They also have sung less important but vivid characters such as Don Basilio in *Il Barbiere,* Padre Guardiano in *Forza* who has much beautiful music and Colline in *Bohème* with his touching apostrophe to his overcoat. If an opera house rich in first-class basses can afford to cast one of them in the relatively small part of Monterone (*Rigoletto*) or the Commendatore (*Don Giovanni*) these operas are bound to have a greater impact in performance. Those implacable men of religion, Ramfis, the High Priest in *Aida* and the Grand Inquisitor in *Don Carlo*—far more powerful than the ruling monarchs of their respective countries—offer fine opportunities to the bass who is an excellent singing actor. Of the singers listed above, it should be pointed out that Jerome Hines made a not totally successful foray into the German repertory singing the *Walküre* Wotan in which the high-lying parts proved trying to his voice, while Giorgio Tozzi has demonstrated his versatility by singing both Daland in *Fliegende Holländer* and Hans Sachs at the Metropolitan. Another versatile bass is David Ward who switches from Wotan and the Dutchman to either King Philip or the Grand Inquisitor in *Don Carlo*.

The bass who ordinarily sings German roles usually has a darker, rougher quality to his voice and a more declamatory way of singing. Some higher German basses, notably in recent years Hans Hotter, opt for such parts as Wotan and Hans Sachs. Others with a slightly deeper range and sometimes darker quality will stay with King Marke, the Landgrave Hermann in *Tannhäuser* and garrulous Gurnemanz in *Parsifal*. They may also perform the winning role of Pogner in *Meistersinger* and the stellar one of Baron Ochs in *Rosenkavalier*. Finally there is a truly black type of bass sometimes afflicted with a wobble who hails almost exclusively from Germany or Austria and sings mainly the Wagner villains, Fafner, Fasolt, Hunding and Hagen.

Gloom is not entirely pervasive among the basses for there is another type of deep-voiced singer who has a surprising number of delightful roles in which to shine. I refer to the *basso buffo*. Within living memory we have had the wonderfully comic Salvatore Baccaloni and more recently, Fernando Corena, who have made a specialty of singing low-voiced humorous roles in grand opera. Of these, Don Pasquale, Dr. Dulcamara in *L'Elisir* and Falstaff (if he can manage the high-lying notes of the last named part as Corena has) are star roles for the *basso buffo*. Then there are rewarding secondary parts such as Leporello or the precursor of Falstaff, the fussy, scolding Fra Melitone in *Forza*. There are also the two Dr. Bartolos in *Il Barbiere* and *Le Nozze* and any number of what one might call vignette characterizations: the drunken Varlaam in *Boris;* Benoit, the landlord, and Alcindoro, Musetta's elderly admirer in *Bohème* (usually taken by the same *basso buffo*); and the Sacristan in *Tosca*. Like comedy actors who long to play Hamlet, undoubtedly a *basso buffo* would love to portray Méphistophélès or Don Giovanni. But something about his size, expression and general ambience of character dooms him to comedy in which, nonetheless, he can make a fine and busy career in the opera house.

The *basso profundo* is an exceedingly rare voice. In Russia one even deeper called the *contrabasso* used to emerge with a range down to the $B_{,,,}$, two octaves and one note below middle C. These could be heard mainly in the impressive Russian liturgy since such a voice is too woolly and slow-moving to serve in the opera house. With the reduction of the church and religion as practiced in the Soviet Union during the past fifty years these rare and extraordinary voices are said to be dying out, showing again how a singing voice will evolve to serve a particular need and, equally, disappear when there is no longer a demand for it. There is little need for the thick, unsupple voice of the *basso profundo* in the opera house, any more than for the stolid, unpliant contralto. However the low notes of Sarastro's two majestic arias in *Die Zauberflöte* are well served by a *basso profundo,* and he can also add a proper dragonlike growl to the role of Fafner. On the whole the dark unwieldiness of his voice leaves the *basso profundo* with little opportunity for a variety of characterizations.

Outside the opera house Ezio Pinza proved that a bass could be a sexy and magnetic figure (but then so he was in it) even in middle age, when he played opposite Mary Martin in *South Pacific*. The pop singer with a bass voice seems to be something of a rarity in the history of popular music. One who never sang in an opera house—not because he couldn't have, he wasn't asked—and gave concerts of a mixture of classical and folk music, was the extraordinary Paul Robeson, the sound of whose burry, deep voice was spine-chilling. One of the most admired singers of his time, Robeson had a limited range and never aspired to be a great vocal artist. He was a presence with a majestic voice to enforce it. What Paul Robeson stood for we are only just beginning to realize today.

BARITONES

Belcore (*L'Elisir*)	The first eight roles are more lyric than the rest.
Germont (*Traviata*)	
Golaud (*Pelléas*)	
Guglielmo (*Così*)	
Marcello (*Bohème*)	
Masetto (*Don Giovanni*)	
Papageno (*Zauberflöte*)	
Silvio (*Pagliacci*)	
Alberich (*Rheingold* and *Götterdämmerung*)	
Alfio (*Cavalleria*)	
Amfortas (*Parsifal*)	
Amonasro (*Aida*)	
Barnaba (*Gioconda*)	
Beckmesser (*Meistersinger*)	He has to sustain a difficult high A for three measures.
Count Almaviva (*Le Nozze*)	
Count di Luna (*Trovatore*)	
Dappertutto (*Contes d'Hoffmann*)	Tibbett, a baritone, sang this and the other three low-voiced villains. So did Pinza and George London.
Don Alfonso (*Così*)	
Don Giovanni	
Enrico Ashton (*Lucia*)	

Escamillo (*Carmen*)	Pinza, a *basso cantante*, and George London both sang this role.
Falstaff	
Figaro (*Il Barbiere* and *Le Nozze*)	
Flying Dutchman	
Ford (*Falstaff*)	
Gérard (*Andrea Chénier*)	
Gianni Schicchi	Can be sung by a bass as well.
Gunther (*Götterdämmerung*)	
Hans Sachs (*Meistersinger*)	
High Priest (*Samson*)	Sometimes sung by a bass.
Iago (*Otello*)	
Jokanaan (*Salome*)	
Lescaut (Both *Manons*)	
Eugen Onegin	
Orest (*Elektra*)	
Ping (*Turandot*)	
Pizarro (*Fidelio*)	
Rangoni (*Boris Godounov*)	
Renato (*Ballo*)	
Rigoletto	
Sharpless (*Butterfly*)	
Simon Boccanegra	
Telramund (*Lohengrin*)	
Tonio (*Pagliacci*)	
Valentin (*Faust*)	
Wolfram (*Tannhäuser*)	
Wotan (*Rheingold, Walküre, Siegfried*)	
Wozzeck	

THE BASSES

Alvise (*Gioconda*)	The first eight roles are the biggest for the *basso cantante* in the Italian and French repertory. He also has the Mozart Figaro and Don Giovanni.

Avito (*L'Amore dei Tre
 Re*)
Boris Godounov
Don Basilio
 (*Il Barbiere*)
Méphistophélès (*Faust*)
Padre Guardiano (*Forza*)
Philip (*Don Carlo*)
Ramfis (*Aida*)
Arkel (*Pelléas*)

This section lists smaller *basso cantante*
roles in which there are opportunities for
effective characterizations.

Colline (*Bohème*)
Commendatore
 (*Don Giovanni*)
Dr. Miracle
 (*Contes d'Hoffmann*)
Elder Des Grieux
 (*Manon*)
Father (*Louise*)
Ferrando (*Trovatore*)
Grand Inquisitor
 (*Don Carlo*)

Sometimes sung by a German bass with
his harsher, more declamatory way of
singing.

King (*Aida*)
Pimen (*Boris Godounov*)
Sam (*Ballo*)
Sparafucile (*Rigoletto*)
Timur (*Turandot*)
Tom (*Ballo*)

THE BASSES

Some Basso Buffo *Roles*

Alcindoro (*Bohème*)
Benoit (*Bohème*)

Dr. Bartolo (*Il Barbiere*
  and *Le Nozze*)
Dr. Dulcamara (*L'Elisir*)
Don Pasquale
Fra Melitone (*Forza*)
Leporello (*Don Giovanni*)
Sacristan (*Tosca*)
Varlaam (*Boris
  Godounov*)

Roles Usually Sung by German-Oriented Basses

Baron Ochs
  (*Rosenkavalier*)
Daland (*Fliegende
  Holländer*)
Fafner (*Rheingold,
  Siegfried*)
Fasolt (*Rheingold*)
Gurnemanz (*Parsifal*)
Hagen
  (*Götterdämmerung*)
Hunding (*Walküre*)
King Henry (*Lohengrin*)
King Marke (*Tristan*)
Kothner (*Meistersinger*)   Who must negotiate very florid music re-
                               plete with trills in Act One.

Langrave Hermann
  (*Tannhäuser*)
Osmin (*Entführung*)
Pogner (*Meistersinger*)
Rocco (*Fidelio*)
Sarastro (*Zauberflöte*)

THE COMPRIMARIOS

There are opera singers with the various kinds of voices already
described who perform only minor roles. As maids, confidantes, at-
tendants, courtiers and messengers they are sometimes the vital

means by which a plot is forwarded. These so-called *"compri-mario"* singers are of two kinds: young artists with fine voices hoping to work their way into leading roles, and singers with un-exceptional voices but who are good actors and build a career out of singing these small, but essential parts. In recent years New York heard the sopranos Lucine Amara and Martina Arroyo grad-uate from tiny parts such as the offstage Celestial Voice in *Don Carlo* to leading lyric and *spinto* roles. Londoners can remember the occasion on which Joan Sutherland was Clothilde, maid to the Norma of Maria Callas.

Frequently, however, the singer who takes smaller roles may find himself stuck in them, possibly because there is too much com-petition from older leading singers with his type of voice, or perhaps because he lacks a final star quality, that mysterious com-bination of voice, personality and projection. Thus they may con-tinue for years acting as "covers" in case the leading singer falls ill, sometimes getting a break, but somehow never quite making it to the big time. In his story, *Once More from the Beginning*, Robert Merrill tells how after having won the Metropolitan Opera auditions and a contract to sing with the company, his heart sank when he was asked to study Marullo in *Rigoletto*, the Herald in *Lohengrin* and Schaunard in *La Bohème*. With a kind of courage born of desperation lest he be singing these *compri-mario* parts for a lifetime, he dared *not* to learn them. Such *chutzpa* paid off and Merrill made his debut as the elder Germont and has never sung anything but leading roles since. An earlier fine baritone, Lawrence Tibbett, made a most unobtrusive debut as Lovitzky, buried in the huge cast of *Boris Godounov*, and con-tinued to sing small parts (with an occasional Valentin thrown in) until assigned the role of Ford in *Falstaff*. The opera was es-pecially revived for Antonio Scotti, still the leading baritone of the Metropolitan in the 1920's. Ford's part is small but it does have the biggest aria in the whole score and Tibbett seized his opportunity. Thereafter, he never looked back until some nineteen years later he sang the part of Falstaff himself.

Some singers with fine voices have been offered contracts with the Metropolitan to sing small roles, but resist the tempting title "of the Metropolitan Opera Company" and turn their faces east to Europe. From there, having earned valuably needed experience that is so difficult to obtain in America and made a reputation, they return in triumph to New York. One of the early great and glamorous singers to establish this pattern was Geraldine Farrar, who turned down a contract with the Metropolitan and set out for Europe where she became a star of the Berlin Opera. Not many years ago the American tenor, James McCracken, was singing the few lines of the toymaker, Parpignol, in *La Bohème*. Fortunately for lovers of *Otello* and other Italian operas, McCracken threw down his basket of toys and headed across the Atlantic, whence he returned, his voice, his operatic experience and not least his physique vastly enlarged to sing the leading roles of the dramatic tenor repertory.

For the number of singers with lovely voices caught in the web of the *comprimario* parts, there are ones to match them with voices lacking in sensuousness. These artists, serious, conscientious, often fine actors, have made long careers by their musicianship and their ability to assume all kinds of bite-sized operatic characterizations. One of the most famous of these interesting artists was Angelo Bada, who first sang the few, but intensely significant lines of the Messenger in *Aida* on 16 November 1908, the evening also of the Metropolitan debut of Arturo Toscanini. Bada sang his last part, Arturo Bucklaw, rejected fiancé of Lucia di Lammermoor, in March 1938. For over thirty years he never sang a leading role, nor ever even appeared as soloist in the Sunday night concerts that used to be a feature at the Metropolitan for so many years. Yet his career, based on a pale rather bleaty kind of tenor, must be accounted a notable one. Another more recent *comprimario* was the Russian baritone George Cehanovsky. who made his Metropolitan debut in 1926, and sang seventy-eight different roles for the company until 1966—a total of forty years.

Though the roles he performs may be minor, the *comprimario* does not go totally unnoticed. In the comic scene for the deaf servant, Frantz, who dusts the Munich flat of Crespel in Act Three of *Contes d'Hoffmann,* a clever artist as was the *comprimario* tenor Alessio DePaolis can bring the house down. This same type of tenor can make a subtly evil characterization of the wily Prince Shuisky in *Boris* and the even more sinister Spoletta, Scarpia's henchman, in *Tosca.* The *comprimario* tenor may also be given the part of Beppe in *Pagliacci* which includes a graceful serenade, sung, unfortunately, offstage. (A story is told that Caruso once asked the secondary tenor singing Beppe if he might perform this little aria instead, which he did. There was applause but not of the lavish kind usually accorded any rendition by Caruso, proof to him that his fame and popularity were all illusion: the audience hadn't even recognized his voice.)

There are many other outstanding vignette characterizations for the skilled *comprimario* to create in the standard operatic repertory. The mezzo-soprano who sings the blind mother pleading before the tribunal in Act Three of *Andrea Chénier* has a superb opportunity to stir her audience and indeed so effective is the scene that sometimes a leading singer will gladly undertake the role though it is very brief. A mezzo with a gift for comedy can make much of the few lines of the Innkeeper in *Boris.* The soprano who sings the slight role of Lucia's maid participates in one of the most show-stopping numbers in all of opera—the Sextet in Act Two: so does the *comprimario* tenor who sings Lord Arturo Bucklaw.

Certain operas put tremendous pressure on the *comprimario* staff of an opera company, causing the general manager to call out all the reserves he possesses. These include *Boris Godounov* with its children, servants, boyars, peasants and sole simpleton, and *Die Meistersinger* which requires a bevy of male *comprimarios* to portray the stalwart citizens of Nuremberg. Perhaps the most demanding operatic work of all in this respect is *Louise,* Charpentier's lovely evocation of Paris at the turn of the century, in which there are no less than thirty-seven tiny little parts (six, however, heard offstage). There are a number of midinettes, a pair of philosophers, two rag-pickers (one old and one young, the latter sung by a woman), two policemen, a variety of vendors of different foods ranging from artichokes to watercress, a junkman, a street arab, a noctambulist and a character known as the "King of Fools." A certain amount of doubling can take place, but it provides a great evening for the *comprimarios*, and if their numbers run out the hard-pressed general manager can always move in fresh supplies from the chorus.

As with the *comprimarios*, it might be supposed that a position in the chorus would be a stepping-stone to stardom for the aspiring singer. If anything, it is even less so, firmly quenching the light (if there was one) of the potential star and establishing him as a chorister and no more. True, such fine leading artists as Leonard Warren and Jan Peerce sang in the Radio City Music Hall Glee Club as a means of getting on with their careers, but that was outside the opera house. Like *comprimarios*, opera choristers can make long, full careers with usually no more than an average voice. They work hard. Only a few operas such as *Salome*, *Walküre* and *Pelléas* give them a night off. They must memorize a large repertory and possess fine musicianship. (The extraordinary singing in the recent production of Schoenberg's extremely difficult *Moses and Aaron* at Covent Garden attests that the chorus of this company certainly does.) Even less than with *comprimario* singers does one hear of a chorister in a prominent opera company taking a leading role with a smaller one, nor, for that matter, moving into the field of concert singing. Though the singing voice remains the center of their lives they seem to become set in their ways and do not explore the musical by-paths along which their vocal art might take them.

NATIONAL VOICES

By this time the reader must have become aware in this cataloguing of voices that certain countries or regions seem to specialize in certain kinds of voices. We have the high soprano *acuto sfogato* from middle Europe, the English contralto, the Spanish coloratura mezzo, the baby-voiced Italian tenor, the Russian bass and so forth. Certain countries have a distinct national vocal quality as well. In addition they may produce singers of international reputation far out of proportion to their populations. I'm thinking particularly of Scandinavia. Why should three little nations with a combined population of about fifteen million have given the world scores of great singers from Jenny Lind through Christine Nilsson, Olive Fremstad, Kirsten Flagstad, Lauritz Melchior, Karin Branzell, Jussi Bjoerling and Birgit Nilsson, to name but a handful? And why should England with a population of over fifty million have produced so few vocal artists of international reputation over the years?

With this discussion we once again enter the realm of pure speculation and yet the conclusions to be drawn seem quite inescapable. Singers from a particular country are bound to be affected by its national taste and style in music, particularly folk songs. For example, the native music of Spain and southern Italy flows with Moorish-oriented runs and sinuous turns and embellishments of other kinds. Not surprisingly, a line of singers possessing remarkable agility has come from these regions, including the delightful coloratura mezzo Conchita Supervia, and later de los Angeles, Berganza and Caballé. The oratorio, beloved of the English for a century or more, usually requires a female singer with a commanding low voice. When there is a national demand for a type of voice to satisfy a particular musical taste that taste will be served, and so the English specialize in producing husky (sometimes manly sounding) contralto voices. The same has proved true in Russia where there exists a passion for the low bass voice that was once a requisite in religious services.

Next we should consider national tastes in the quality of singing voices. The German-speaking countries make an interesting contrast with those of southern Europe. Germany and Austria, besides specializing in "little girl" high coloraturas, produce a characteristic tone quality in their sopranos. These are trained towards the top of the range with little vibrato, so that sometimes a soprano like Schwarzkopf will make a sound like a mew on a high note. Above all, German and Austrian sopranos do not sing the gutsy low notes known as chest tones. The colorful, slightly aggressive vocal quality that many women singers are capable of producing is simply not taught.*

In Italy the soprano sound is entirely different, having a plentiful vibrato, and much fuller tones at the bottom which are frequently compensated by a shrillness and tendency to flat the higher notes. Among the heavier sopranos chest tones are a must. These tastes seem to match the respective national attitudes towards women. The Germans tend to keep their women subservient and dependent. The ideal is for her to be pure, girlish, with a seasoning of archness. The Italian woman, the responsible mother keeping the family together, is volatile, aggressive, full of temperament—all qualities which one hears in the Italian voice.

America, which prizes the strong, outdoor kind of male, frequently produces a kind of wholesome, clean-cut type of baritone appropriate to a not overly sensitive cowboy singing to his horse under Western skies. An American male who produced the vulnerable, almost feminine sound that proceeds from an Italian tenor singing *mezza voce* would be regarded with deep suspicion. Yet that quality matches the gentleness which often predominates in the Italian masculine character.

* "She did make an iron rule that the higher type of soprano, lyrical soubrette and coloratura, should on no occasion make use of chest notes even in a mixed form," writes Elizabeth Puritz in her *The Teaching of Elisabeth Schumann.* This is a characteristic attitude among all German-oriented teachers of singing.

Slavic voices can almost always be recognized by the shiver that afflicts them. I use the word "afflict" for this wiry, whirring vibrato certainly seems a fault to our ears. Yet the Russians, the Yugoslavs, the Bulgarians and the Czechs don't seem to mind. True, the characteristic Slavic voice singing various central and eastern European languages bothers Western ears less than in Italian or German music. This brings us to what is perhaps the most overwhelming factor of all in the shaping of national voices—language.

A Tug of War.

> No human singing can
> Express itself without
> Words that usurp the sounds
> That pour forth from the throat

In the art of fine singing an implacable war rages constantly between the word and the tone. In certain situations one is invariably sacrificed to the other. The soprano, for instance, must never sing a long "ē" sound above G' lest she ruin her voice. To the discomfiture of the Wagnerian soprano the great composer gave the names of Siegmund, Sieglinde and Siegfried to three of the leading characters in the Ring. If one listens closely to the end of the *Götterdämmerung* Immolation Scene, Brünnhilde will really be heard to invoke her beloved "Sahgfried." "It is for the singer to defend his voice against the pitfalls of words," warns that trenchant authority, Blanche Marchesi. "He must never sacrifice vocal beauty, and if anything be sacrificed let it be the words."

Pier Francesco Tosi, writing two hundred and fifty years earlier, disagrees with her: "If the words are not heard so as to be understood, there will be no great difference between a human voice and a hautboy." During the eighteenth century audiences were quite content to let the singer run along for a plethora of measures on one syllable giving no thought to the verbal content of his song; this was also true during the bel canto era of the early nineteenth century, in which Berlioz witheringly condemned the

great vocal artists of this period as "performers on the larynx."
(A descendant of that vocal age and one much criticized for her
watery enunciation is Joan Sutherland, who by sacrificing the
word—to be sure the word is often fairly inane anyway—produces
floods of beautiful tone with remarkable agility.) Certainly there
have been many singers with excellent diction and beautiful tone,
but usually much care and hard work has been expended to bring
about this somewhat grudging alliance. In the popular field no
such attempt is made: the word almost invariably has the upper
hand and the tone must adjust as best it can.

To return to the subject of national voices, two great European
countries have a rich treasure house of poetry which they love
and honor together with the language in which it is written. In
both France and England a kind of natural instinct exists to put
the word before the tone in singing, thereby causing muscles in
the throat to move to positions which produce a far less pleasing
quality of sound and may actually harm the singing voice. As
a result in France most professional singers have reedy, nasal-
sounding voices and are rarely heard outside the borders of their
country. England, where the word is also sacred, has continually
championed the cause of opera and lieder in her native tongue
since the time Handel first came to British shores—and has suffered a paucity of international singers almost to the present
day.* Now that Covent Garden has reverted to a policy of presenting opera in its original language, together with a general in-
ternationalization of the musical scene, artists such as Sir Geraint
Evans, Peter Glossop, the Stuart Burrows, Gwyneth Jones, Josephine Veasey and Janet Baker, have emerged on the world scene
with round, properly placed voices that will last.

Since the word conditions and affects the tone of a singing voice
the language that a human learns from infancy actually *places his*

* Note this attitude of a celebrated English singer and teacher at the turn of the
century: "Voice must grow out of language, and students must begin their student-
ship by singing THOUGHTS . . . No alteration of the character of the word is ad-
missible."—David Ffrangcon-Davies, *The Singing of the Future.*

voice. By this I mean that it accustoms him to feeling his tongue and above all his larynx, which can move up and down slightly in his throat, in a particular, familiar place. Because of his language this position becomes habit. Also because the language has been spoken over centuries by his forebears, it may have evolved a certain shape to the all-important resonator at the top of the throat, a cavity called the pharynx. In addition it may have sculpted in a certain way other cavities that lie behind the nose and the upper part of the face which are also resonators.

This being the case let us examine some of the languages—English, for example, the so-called Oxbridge accent. Generally considered genteel and desirable, words that are not mumbled are spoken very far forward on the teeth and lips, so that the "t's" and labials fall upon the ears of the listener like a little shower of pebbles. Nothing could be more disastrous for the creation of a natural singing voice, since this forward inflection draws the larynx up from the throat giving the average untrained English singing voice a white, breathy, all but toneless sound. Combine this with a terror of being rude—such as making loud noises—ingrained in the average Englishman who speaks with an Oxbridge accent and it is easy to understand why the English have produced so few natural voices. The Englishman who would become a singer must break two habits that are almost as natural to him as breathing: the way he produces his speaking voice and his mercilessly conditioned inhibitions. (The latter, of course, do not extend to the British as actors, who are superb and many in numbers, perhaps because they are dealing precisely with what comes naturally to the natives of this land of Shakespeare—the spoken word, not "rude noises.") Once out of London in the provinces, in Lancashire, say, whence emerged the great natural voice of Kathleen Ferrier, we hear an accent that places the voice further back in the throat. The same is true of the Irish brogue and though there have not been many great Irish international singers (one thinks of John McCormack and Margaret Sheridan, and today Heather

Harper and Maureen Lehane) the country abounds in lovely natural voices.

As to French it is probably the most difficult to sing of any language in which there exists an important vocal literature. This language, too, pulls up the larynx to a position not suited for producing a round, full tone, and in addition requires the vocalist, if he is to sing his words with an eloquent, idiomatic pronunciation, to produce some of his notes in his nose. The concept of correct singing *"dans la masque"* is well known, but *"la masque"* has nothing to do with *"le nez,"* though the two are frequently confused. The would-be French singer, therefore, has to overcome the evolution of his resonators and pharynx over generations of his French-speaking forebears together with the negative effect of the language on the positioning of his larynx. In addition there is the absolute Gallic insistence that the tone be sacrificed to the word. Finally he has to fight a certain lack of national enthusiasm for singing—certainly not the case in England. At the Opéra and the Opéra-Comique, the French continue to go through the motions of putting on works in the standard repertory as they always have, and occasionally someone comes along and tries to stir up the thin, barely simmering broth with a new production or some guest singers. But always everything seems to fall back into the old ways with indifferent performances sung to half-filled houses by voices which, if they start out fresh, quickly degenerate into the grated, nasal sound that typifies French singing. By putting the word first, as expressed in their own cherished language, it is not surprising that among these, the most rational people in the world, a love of great singing does not seem to bind the French.

Cross the border at Ventimiglia and everything is reversed. Everyone knows that to an Italian singing comes as easily as eating or making love. It is in his blood; he adores it—though doubtless there are thousands if not millions of exceptions to the stereotype of the singing, song-loving Italian. His language, of course, is beautifully conducive to singing, with its long vowels, often connecting two words in a manner which gives added line to a musical phrase such as Violetta's

"Dite alle giovine. . . ."

and its soft words pronounced well back in the throat. No inhibitions about rude noises in this country. The Italians thrive on noise. Nor is there any particular literary mystique here. The Italians love their language, too, though to be sure over the various sections of the country they pronounce it in a multiplicity of ways, but Dante, Petrarch and possibly Manzoni hold sway over the artistic imagination of only a few, as opposed to the way Shakespeare seems to dominate that of masses of English people.

Spain, as I have already mentioned, has supplied the world with a number of marvelous singers. Because of an idiosyncrasy of the language, Spanish vocalists can usually be detected by the aspirated way they attack certain notes in the middle and lower parts of their range. A sound like the tiniest of hiccups, it can be heard in the singing of both de los Angeles and Caballé.

Heading north again to the heavily populated Netherlands, this song-loving country has produced some, but not many, singers of international fame, probably because of the inflections of a harsh tongue. Further to the east, Germany and Austria have of course been most fecund, though not always so. "A German singer! I should as soon expect to get pleasure from the neighing of my horse!" the musical monarch, Frederick the Great, is supposed to have said. In an article entitled On Dramatic Song, Richard Wagner, an informed authority on the singing voice, set down his views on the inferiority of German singing around the time of his marriage to Minna Planer (1836). The German throat, he declared, was less adapted by nature to singing than that of the Italian; nor did the majority of German singers train sufficiently before appearing in public (a complaint made to this day about singers everywhere). Hence the early loss of voice by his idol, the dramatic Wilhelmine Schröder-Devrient, Wagner's first Senta and Venus.

Perhaps because of Wagner's demand from his singers for a more Italianate, flowing style of singing wedded to German art, a line of Austro-German giants began to emerge towards the end of the nineteenth century, including some of the first Bayreuth artists, Amalie Materna, Marianne Brandt and Albert Niemann; also the incomparable Lilli Lehmann and the equally extraordinary Ernestine Schumann-Heink. In more recent times there have been such superb singers as Maria Jeritza, Elisabeth Rethberg, Lotte Lehmann, the great Wagnerian soprano, Frida Leider, and the huge, black-voiced bass, Michael Bohnen. Recently Germany and Austria have supplied the international scene with sopranos such as Elizabeth Schwarzkopf, Hilda Gueden and Irmgard Seefried, the versatile mezzo, Christa Ludwig, baritones such as Dietrich Fischer-Dieskau and Hermann Prey, and the late much-lamented tenor, Fritz Wunderlich. German, a most expressive language, is full of harsh and guttural sounds. For this reason it produces a more declamatory kind of singer, particularly among the males. The language also puts into the voice, especially that of the tenor, a kind of taut brilliance that makes it recognizably German.

I have already mentioned the classic shiver almost inevitably heard in Russian and Slavic voices, again presumably due to language, though one occasionally hears it among Italians as in the case of the early Pinza. Certain great singers from middle Europe, however, eluded it and made international careers: from Poland, the de Reszke brothers and Marcella Sembrich; the great dramatic soprano, Emmy Destinn, from Czechoslovakia; Milka Ternina, a celebrated dramatic soprano of around 1900 from Yugoslavia, and her pupil Zinka Milanov. Hearing Milanov's luscious soprano with its beautifully floated pianissimi for the first time, it would have been difficult to pin down its nationality.* It was a truly international voice.

* Milka Stojanovic, a pupil of Milanov's, does not sound recognizably Slavic either.

Except for one or two basses, the Russians—again because of the quiver intrinsic to most of their voices—have sent few great singers out into the rest of the world. In days gone by there was the charming coloratura Lydia Lipkowska and the mountainous Nina Koshetz, whose artistry moved many in the recital hall. Today, as the world shrinks, we are beginning to hear Soviet artists such as the handsome, dark-haired soprano, Galina Vishnevskaya, whose slightly strident tone quality is offensive to some ears but not the artistry nor conviction of her singing.

À propos the pronounced vibrato in most Russian voices, Howard Taubman tells a story of days gone by in Moscow at the Imperial Opera during a performance of *Ruslan and Ludmilla* when the baritone entered on a horse to engage in a scene with an old sage sung by a tenor in this case no longer young. The baritone began the parley and the tenor was just about to reply when the horse took over with a loud neigh. "The sound," says Mr. Taubman, "with its high pitch and shake and breathiness, resembled that made by the tenor. That unhappy individual tried to go on with his part of the colloquy. The horse replied in a higher key. The tenor sang again. The horse went him one better." Ultimately, of course, the curtain had to be rung down.

Of this little European tour the only area that remains is Scandinavia, comprising three countries which have given us some of the most extraordinary voices the world has ever known—way out of proportion to their small populations. Why should this be?

It is not enough to say that the Scandinavians are an intensely musical people though; musicianship of the trained, not intuitive kind, is rife among them. A myth grew up that Flagstad came from ignorant peasant stock; both her parents were in fact professional musicians, which, if living in a musical atmosphere has anything to do with it, explains why she had perfect pitch. Birgit Nilsson can memorize a score spread out on her lap in an airplane. These are not the accomplishments of some of the great Italian singers, the famous coloratura, Luisa Tetrazzini, for instance, of whom it is said she could not read music and had to have every note drilled into her by a répétiteur.

The true reason for the amazing flow of great singing artists from Scandinavia, so it seems to me, is again a matter of language. In these countries the various tongues, somewhat interrelated, position the larynx exactly where it is best suited for singing. The "yup-yup" sound of Norwegian or Swedish and the mocking of it with such clichés as "Yonny Yonson" all instance this. Because of his language a Scandinavian has far less to accomplish in adjusting his larynx for singing than do the natives of most other countries.

The United States has given many remarkable singers to the world, producing at first mainly female artists, often of great physical beauty such as Emma Eames and Geraldine Farrar. With the exception of the baritone, David Bispham, who had to defy his Quaker family to go on the stage, American male singers arrived on the international scene somewhat later, probably due to the American mistrust of a male artist in general and his virility in particular. (Writing in *Opera News* the young tenor Jess Thomas says that as a boy in a typical midwestern small town, he had to sneak out to the garage to the Metropolitan Opera broadcasts lest he be caught in so sissy an act—and that's not very long ago.) Americans, of course, speak much further back in their throats than their English cousins and bear down on their "r's" in a way that the British have pleasure in mocking. But the curled accent of the mid-Westerner that seems to cling to the roof of his mouth like clotted peanut butter is far more conducive to the correct placing of a singing voice than the forward enunciation of the Englishman.

America is such an ethnic mixture that it is difficult to define a strictly American voice, though fine baritones such as Lawrence Tibbett, John Charles Thomas, and recently, Sherill Milnes would seem to be recognizably American. Chameleon-like, the American singer who trains abroad will sometimes take on the characteristics of singers of the country in which he has studied. A record by the American lyric tenor, Richard Crooks, who studied in Germany and sang at the Berlin Stadtsoper, of "Recondita armonia" from *Tosca* in German, would lead the most experienced analyst of national voices to think that this was a German tenor—by quality of timbre, style and inflection. Teresa Stich-Randall sang Nanetta in the Toscanini broadcast of *Falstaff* which was later issued on records. Contrast her voice then before she went abroad for training in the Austro-German methods with what it came to sound like subsequently. It now has a totally German quality with a pure, somewhat mewed top.

The one truly recognizable American voice, or used to be anyway, belongs to the Negro singer—though I have been accused of racism for saying so. Marian Anderson, Paul Robeson, Dorothy Maynor all had distinctly "colored" voices and I think today that if he did not know, a perceptive listener would instantly recognize the voice of Leontyne Price as belonging to a Negro. But this is beginning to change, presumably as the Negro becomes more assimilated into America. To my ears the sweeping voice of Grace Bumbry does not sound Negro nor the pert one of Reri Grist. One thing is certain, however, now that blacks have broken the barriers that used to keep them out of the opera house, we can expect as tremendous a contribution to the art of operatic singing as they have made already in the field of pop singing. Indeed, in her *Manual of Bel Canto*, Madame Ida Franca asserts that "frequently the range of the Negro singer—and especially the range of the Negro tenor—can be developed to outdo any white singer's range," and gives tables showing that the chest and head registers of Negro female singers are outsize compared to those of white ones. She also declares that a "tenorino" (countertenor) voice is peculiar to the Negro and goes on to say happily, "With appropriate training such a voice can, of course, be developed into a voice of no less power and charm than the voice of a castrated virtuoso."

Another somewhat ethnically crossed country is Australia, which has hatched out a number of noted singers,* mainly female as with the United States at an earlier time. Melba, Frances Alda (she was actually from New Zealand), Florence Austral, a Wagnerian soprano with a remarkable top to her voice, another fine Wagnerian soprano, Marjorie Lawrence, whose career was tragically reduced by polio, and in our own time the remarkable Joan Sutherland are some of the vocal products that Australia has put on the international market. † None of these singers, however, can be said to possess a characteristic Australian voice, but there is no doubt that the Australian accent, however grating to the ear, is more conducive to the breeding of fine singing voices than a purer English one.

As the world grows smaller and more international we can expect today's singing voices to emerge with fewer national characteristics. Nevertheless, as long as countries continue to preserve the precious heritage of their own individual languages, singing voices will continue to be shaped and conditioned by them.

---

* The native aborigines, supposedly because of the construction of their facial bones, usually have only rudimentary singing voices.

† Others of recent years have included Marie Collier, Ronald Dowd, Margreta Elkins, Elizabeth Fretwell, Joan Hammond, Albert Lance, Elsie Morison and John Shaw to name but a few.

PART THREE

THE NON-OPERATIC VOICES

Of the numerous kinds of voices heard outside the opera house all belong in some way, however limited, to one of the types of operatic voices already described. In opera, despite what anyone might say, the voice comes first. With non-operatic voices there is often far less emphasis on sheer vocal beauty. New factors now enter in, such as style, personality and, in the case of the concert singer, consummate musicianship.

The Recitalists. Many outstanding concert singers have possessed voices of true operatic calibre. In the case of such artists as Lotte Lehmann, Alexander Kipnis or Elizabeth Schwarzkopf they have been equally at home in the opera house and concert hall. Other artists with big, wide-ranging voices that would seem to be suitable for opera have eschewed it for reasons of personality and a lack of histrionic flair. At one point in her career it was suggested to Kathleen Ferrier that she sing Carmen. Certainly she had the voice to do so but not the dramatic temperament. Very wisely she refused. The great mezzo-soprano Elena Gerhardt began her career with a few operatic forays (she sang Charlotte in *Werther* and Mignon) but soon realized that she must dedicate her musical life to what it was most suited for—the art of lieder singing. Other recitalists have made outstanding careers with voices severely restricted in range and tonal beauty. No one ever praised the vocal sensuousness of the much admired French baritone, Pierre Bernac.

Povla Frijsh, the Danish soprano, held audiences in her sway but
not because of the loveliness of her voice. In the case of a concert
singer, Rossini's formula for a successful singing career—"voice,
voice, voice,"—does not apply. Here the necessary ingredients are
artistry, musicianship and only then, lower down on the ladder,
voice.

An opera singer has many supports in the distractions of scenery,
costumes and his own dramatic gestures, together with a large
orchestra led by a conductor giving musical cues and ready to cover
over any mistakes. Not so the concert singer. He stands exposed
and alone on a stage, bare except for a piano and an unobtrusive
accompanist. Through the colors of his voice he has to create a
different mood with each song—evoke a tiny little world in perhaps no more than three or four minutes' time. So effective must
his singing be that he holds an audience fascinated for a whole
evening. Small wonder that there have been fewer great concert
singers than their operatic counterparts.

Successful recitalists have possessed almost every type of singing
voice, but it is also true that of the various types some are better
suited than others to lieder (a term that has come to mean art
songs not only in German, but many other languages as well).
Erna Berger, the German soprano *acuto sfogato,* was an excellent
lieder singer. Exquisite in delicate songs like Mozart's "Das Veilchen" or the Strauss "Ständchen" she could not summon the
darker, more impassioned accents needed in the dramatic song
literature. Lyric and *spinto* sopranos such as those possessed by
Elisabeth Schumann, Lotte Lehmann, Elizabeth Schwarzkopf and
Victoria de los Angeles have served the cause of lieder singing to
inestimable advantage. Only with the very largest soprano voices
do reservations enter in. For instance Flagstad with her impeccable
musicianship and marvelous vocal line, gave fine recitals and yet
at times her voice seemed to overpower the songs that she sang.
There was too much of a muchness and the effect something which
every recitalist struggles to avoid—monotony.

The lower women's voices also can succeed in the concert hall, particularly in more dramatic selections such as Schubert's "Erl-könig" or "Der Tod und Das Mädchen." These songs were specialties of Ernestine Schumann-Heink and Sigrid Onegin, both of whom were equally at home on the operatic stage. Today we find the gifted Christa Ludwig switching easily between opera and lieder. In the case of the late Kathleen Ferrier, she showed less inclination to engage herself in operatic affairs.

Among the men a number of German tenors such as Julius Patzak, Karl Erb and Ernst Häfliger have proved to be outstanding lieder singers. Fritz Wunderlich was well on his way to establishing himself in this difficult branch of vocal art until his untimely death. One thinks too of the Dane, Aksel Schiøtz—less so of his Swedish compatriot, Jussi Bjoerling. Though the latter gave many recitals, again a certain monotony tended to creep into them— was it because of the unvarying beauty of his voice? Nor is the rich, sumptuous quality of the baritone voice as produced by, say, Leonard Warren or Peter Glossop an altogether desirable attribute in the concert hall. The most successful baritone recitalists have possessed leaner (Gérard Souzay), at times harsher (Dietrich Fischer-Dieskau), more malleable (Hermann Prey) voices that can give greater expressivity to the words with which they are so closely engaged.

From the lowest male voices one would expect a certain monotony of tone color in their need to transfer songs down to lower, darker keys. And yet the great Russian bass Alexander Kipnis brought chiaroscuro into his beautiful recitals by an ability to lighten and brighten his big, dark voice. And of course the incomparable Feodor Chaliapin also gave highly successful concerts, somewhat eccentric affairs to be sure, at which audiences were handed books containing a large collection of song texts and translations, but no announced program. Chaliapin, as if overtaken by a moment's inspiration, would then appear to decide spontaneously which one of the collection he would sing. It was noticed, however, that in fact the bass sang the same "inspired" program night after night, the way any concert singer does who puts together a fixed selection of songs for his tours.

In the challenge of holding the unwavering attention of an audience through a whole evening, singers, particularly those with operatic affinities, have been known to resort to gestures, extravagant facial expressions and even changes of costume which are entirely out of place in the subtle, intimate art of lieder singing. Ideally, nothing external must distract from the blending of word and tone. Before beginning his next song the singer thinks himself into the mood of it. The effect on the audience can be magical as he projects this mood across the footlights before having sung a single note. Far less flamboyant than his operatic counterpart, a lieder singer, nonetheless, remains a singing actor and a showman. He chooses songs that best display his voice and carefully puts together programs with effective contrasts of mood, tempi and rhythm—also of key signatures—in his selections. When one considers what a lieder singer undertakes, an hour and a half of delineating the varieties of human emotion, from love to rage, from ironic humor to naïvety, can there be any greater challenge to the singing voice and its master or mistress?

Church Voices. As we have already noted, a curious love-hate relationship exists between the Church and the singing voice. How easy and natural and thrilling for man to raise his singing voice in exaltation of the Lord, as anyone, for example, who has ever participated in a performance of Handel's "Hallelujah Chorus" well knows. Though the Church in its earliest days may have kept back the development of the singing voice, this very censorship might have given to singing an importance that it would never have possessed. Certainly the literature of vocal church music is fabulously rich, from the polyphonous masterpieces of the fourteenth and fifteenth centuries to the recent large sacred pieces of Britten and Penderecki.

Despite today's decline in religious interest, church voices are still much in demand thanks to the extensiveness and beauty of sacred music. The most perfect church voices have undoubtedly belonged to the angels, but we have no knowledge of their range and tone quality, only innumerable descriptions of their celestial beauty. Church voices as we know them today differ very little in range and volume from the various operatic voices already described. The pure, limpid tones of a lyric soprano are particularly suited to the ethereal atmosphere of much sacred music, and if the voice possesses flexibility as well, it will do justice to the florid runs of "Rejoice Greatly" in *Messiah* or the closing "Alleluia" of Mozart's *Exsultate Jubilate*. The bigger-voiced sopranos also fare well in church vocal literature ranging from a time long before Bach to the present century. Only the very largest type of dramatic soprano voice, the kind needed to sing Gioconda or Isolde, is not so welcome as a church voice, except when called upon to perform in the Italianate, quasi-operatic *Stabat Mater* of Rossini or Verdi's *Requiem*.

Mezzo-sopranos and contraltos, serene, sometimes sorrowing, are heard to advantage for example in the beautiful arias such as "All es Vollbracht" or "O Erbarme Dich" that Bach wrote for them. A nineteenth-century favorite is "O Rest in the Lord" from Mendelssohn's *St. Paul*, demanding a voice with accents of tranquillity and reverence.

Like his dramatic soprano counterpart, the heavy tenor voice with an emphasized vibrato does not sound appropriate in most church music except that of the synagogue, perhaps because a more dramatic note is struck in the Jewish liturgy. Not surprisingly, outstanding tenors like Jan Peerce and Richard Tucker have made an easy transition from the temple to the opera house. Worst off as a church voice is the baritone. Even Verdi, who very much fancied this type of voice, failed to write a baritone part in his *Requiem*. Indeed, when singing hymns in a church choir the baritone has to choose between taking the second tenor line or that of the first bass, neither of which lie comfortably for his voice.

One other, very definitely non-operatic yet church voice that should be mentioned here is the one belonging to the gospel singer. In the religious fervor of this kind of singing, bel canto goes out the window, and we are involved with a shouted kind of vocal production, rising at moments of exaltation high into the soprano register.

Finally there is the voice of the choirboy, who often at the insistence of his parents but to his shame and humiliation (particularly in America) is made to lift up his angelic voice in church and eke out the family income. The choirboy's voice usually has a compass:

Boy Soprano

The slightly rarer alto approximates the range of the ordinary contralto and uses, just as she does, a chest tone. Vibrato-free and innocent-sounding, the voice of the choirboy to many people's ears is the most perfect of all church voices.

Though emphasis is laid upon a serene, devotional quality in rendering church music, this does not mean that church singers are never expected to sound dramatic. One thinks of the many anguished passages in the *Passions* of Johann Sebastian Bach, particularly *St. John.* Handel calls for a bass with a highly developed sense of drama combined with a coloratura technique to sing the aria "Why do the Nations"—though alas! he is not always available. Many of the later oratorios and masses—Mendelssohn's *Elijah,* for example, or the arresting *Glagolitic Mass* of Janáček—

have also been highly dramatic. As for the Requiems of Giuseppe
Verdi and Benjamin Britten—they are pure theater.

Many an aspiring opera singer has gained experience and cash
by fulfilling often very lucrative church engagements, but on the
whole those artists who have appeared to greatest advantage in
sacred music have usually been less successful on the operatic stage.
This was said to be true of the noted nineteenth-century English
soprano, Clara Novello. Jenny Lind made her sensational success
as an opera singer, but retired from the boards at a comparatively
early age never having morally approved of the theater. Her piety
and religious faith illuminated the church music which she continued to sing. In more recent times this same spirit of reverence
was deeply apparent in Marian Anderson's renditions of religious
arias, or perhaps even more so in her singing of spirituals.

The Pop Singers of Today. Informality prevails in the world
of pop singing and this is true of descriptions of pop voices. We
do not hear of the coloratura mezzo, Sarah Vaughan, though she
certainly fits into this category when letting forth with a burst of
scat singing. Nor have I come across any references to the well-
known countertenor, Tiny Tim, though again the description is
technically apt. All pop voices have some connection with the
big operatic voices, however slight. Let us look at them from
that point of view.

The modern pop voices are almost entirely dependent on the
microphone. Before the invention of electrical amplification the
voices of the stars that our grandfathers admired—Lillian Russell,
Anna Held, George M. Cohan, Julia Sanderson—were much
nearer to opera or at least operetta voices. The microphone made
it possible for a singer to make a career with a wisp of a voice,
providing the personality was abundant and the way with a song
original and appealing. The introduction of the microphone coincided with a vogue for cute, "little girl" mannerisms in the
female. As a result the first women pop singers of our modern

amplified age, such as Ruth Etting or Helen Morgan, sang with small, almost helpless sounding soubrette soprano voices. Nowadays we no longer hear this girlish, innocent quality (except in folk singers) because of a change in taste combined with a peculiarity of women's voices.

The peculiarity I refer to is the fact that many women are capable of singing the notes from A, below middle C (and lower) up to C' (and even higher) in two different qualities of tone. One sounds warm, round and what we think of as feminine. The same notes can also emerge with the tough, gutsy, more masculine quality of what is known as the chest register. Opera and concert singers use this second bold-sounding tone with great effect, but sparingly and rarely, if ever, above E, knowing that if the chest register is carried higher it will drag down the rest of the voice and ruin it. Sometime in the 1920's, however, coinciding with a period when women gained greater freedom, a taste for females singing entirely in their masculine sounding chest registers came into being and has been with us ever since. Thus because they have the range (though usually more limited) and emphasized low notes, I think we have to regard the female pop singers of today as contraltos, even though their voices may sound thinner and more astringent than those of the true operatic and concert contralto. Actually a Billie Holiday or Ella Fitzgerald may have been endowed by nature with mezzo or even soprano voices, but because of today's taste in pop singing they force themselves to sing entirely in the contralto range.

One of the first of these brash, almost raucous-sounding vocalists was Sophie Tucker, who had a voice as ample and handsome as her presence. She called herself the "Red Hot Mama" but her voice, which sounds like that of a real contralto on records, calls more readily to mind the idea of a golden-hearted madame. One of the great blues singers, Ethel Waters, relied more on her gentler medium register at the outset of her career, and then as the taste for the husky "torch" voice took hold, began to bear down on her chest register in her later work. Ethel Merman couldn't have known ever what singing in her medium register was like: her tones are all brass. Billie Holiday, with an infinite melancholy permeating her tone, had a very limited range of F, below middle C to C' the same as Judy Garland—both voices entirely in the chest register. Sarah Vaughan has a most unusual range, from the true contralto note of E, below middle C, which she just touches in her record of "Lullaby of Birdland," to E'. The lower part of her voice bears more than a little resemblance to that of Leontyne Price; it also has considerable flexibility when Miss Vaughan goes into one of her ornamented "scat" passages. Most popular songs, however, require neither flexibility nor a range of more than ten or eleven notes. An exception is "You'll Never Walk Alone" which Frank Sinatra sings and which requires a range of just under two octaves. (In the original cast of the musical *Carousel*, it was sung by Christine Johnson, a former contralto of the Metropolitan Opera Company.)

Ella Fitzgerald possesses a honey-sweet voice which goes back and forth between these two different ways of singing the same note with great smoothness, and which she can move right along when she does one of her "scat" numbers. Deadly true in her intonation, Ella Fitzgerald can sing almost anything, and in the opinion of many is the finest all-around female pop singer since this type of singing began. (There will be, I realize, a million howls of indignation at such a sweeping statement: "What about Billie Holiday? Sarah Vaughan? Peggy Lee?" But then fans of singers are as vocal as the stars they worship and a hundred times more contentious than the most temperamental singing star.)

Intonation, in an age when the microphone is frequently held so close to the singer's mouth that one fears to hear an accidental crunch of teeth on metal, can be a perilous thing because the softer the singing the more difficult it is for a singer to keep on pitch. This is true of a hushed rendering such as Peggy Lee's "Love Letters," in which this usually reliable singer can be heard to stray occasionally from the desired note. This may explain too, why the Beatles, who crowd the mike with their murmured voices, are so often subject to vagaries of pitch.

When recording was first invented, singers addressed themselves to a large horn and backed away from it on high notes, lest the more intense frequencies of these tones blast the cutting stylus. With the invention of the electric microphone it was usually placed in a fixed position before or above the singer, or in the footlights, and it was up to the sound engineer to control the sound so as best to enhance the singer's voice. As the years have passed, the pop singer and his microphone have become more intimate, giving the listener the feeling that he and he alone is being sung to. The best pop singers today have well-practiced techniques in the use of the microphone, practically bedding down with it in intimate moments, waving it away at the climax of a song, but always utilizing this amazing invention that we now take for granted to emphasize the best or suppress the worst in their voices.

Over the years opera singers have occasionally invaded the pop field, usually with unsatisfying results. The effect of a large, somehow formal-sounding voice close up to the microphone is disquieting, like watching a dignified middle-aged woman trying to "get with" the latest youthful dance. Helen Traubel appeared both in the movies and in night clubs, and there was some novelty in hearing one of the great Wagnerian sopranos of her day belt out numbers in a hearty style, but little else. Eileen Farrell put out records which showed that she had a surprising grasp of a jazz style, and of late, the incredible Leontyne Price has done the same thing. Pop purists will cavil (they always do) but certainly one or two of her selections are very appealing.

Among the modern male pop singers the microphone made possible a new type of singing—gentle, casual, friendly rather than passionate. This was the style known as crooning introduced by the tenor Hubert Prior (Rudy) Vallee in 1928. Other little-voiced tenors immediately came along to imitate him, but none ever quite matched his success. Today we have such tenors with tiny voices as Johnny Mathis who in using a lot of breathy falsetto sometimes makes a sound not unlike that of the countertenor.

Light tenor voices of a more lyric kind held radio audiences in their sway during the thirties. These belonged to the Latins Tino Rossi, Tito Guizar and Nino Martini. (The voice of the last was sufficiently large for him to sing the light tenor roles of the operatic repertory.) Legitimate successors to these pop tenors, though with voices bigger and more virile in sound, have been Sergio Franchi and the late Mario Lanza.

Though a baritone may never get the girl in the opera house, once out of it what a time he has! He is the swaggering, devastating hero of a flock of musicals like *Oklahoma!*, *Kismet* or *Kiss Me Kate*. (Star of all three was Alfred Drake, a big-voiced baritone who earlier had entered but failed to win the Metropolitan Opera Auditions.) The non-operatic baritone can set hearts fluttering in nightclubs and over television, as does Robert Goulet, or in the movies, again as Robert Goulet, or as Nelson Eddy used to. After all, Nelson Eddy almost *always* got Jeanette MacDonald. (Eddy, incidentally, had a large voice and sang in opera before his movie career.) It was during this period of the 1930's when Nelson Eddy was such a star that another kind of pop baritone, smooth and suave and intimate also came into his own, replacing the Rudy Valleeish sound of the pop tenor voice that had been the taste until then.

Far and away the most famous of the early pop baritones was Bing Crosby. This was partly due to the many movies he made but also because of his unique voice, round, mellifluous, having a special quality of its own which is not always the case in the pop world where second-rate vocalists can and do sound alike. There have been successors to Crosby with round, smooth baritone voices and emulating his casual, rather uninvolved style. Some of these direct descendants include Dick Haymes, Perry

Como and Dean Martin, but none of them ever quite had the honey of The Groaner in their voices.

Though he had his precursors it was the extraordinary Frank Sinatra who introduced a whole new, personal, intensely emotional style of pop singing that turned him into one of the most phenomenal singing idols of all times. In his younger days during an engagement at the Paramount Theater in New York over eight hundred policemen with the aid of twenty radio cars and two emergency trucks had to be called out to control a queue of ten thousand teen-agers standing six abreast waiting to hear the skinny, fragile-looking singer. Another twenty thousand milled about in Times Square. During his various engagements at the Paramount the staff reported that the seats and carpets ran with the urine of hysterical fans—almost entirely female—unable to control themselves. At that time intellectuals on *The New Republic* and the London *Times* solemnly sought to analyze Sinatra's power over his audiences. Loretta Young, the apparently never ruffled movie actress of many years, seemed to know: "What is there about that boy," she is supposed to have said, "that makes you feel he is singing to you—and you alone?"

Sinatra sings the baritone range, but his voice is weak and poorly focused at the bottom. It also lacks the round, rich quality of many other pop baritones. He sings up to an F, the note where a tenor must make a certain change in his throat to reach his high notes, leading to the suspicion that possibly in his early days there was a whole set of untapped tenor top notes to his voice. The reader may be slightly startled when I say I hear a distinct similarity between the way of singing of Frank Sinatra and Kirsten Flagstad. Both, when they attack a note, often begin it without vibrato and then gradually let it come in. Both sing on the consonant "n" using the resulting resonance whenever possible to add a connecting line through their singing.

Now in his fifties, Sinatra has been before the public for about thirty years. As with most singers his voice has thickened and lost some of its boyish glow. In 1950, he even got into serious vocal difficulties, suffering a throat haemorrhage during an engagement at the Copacabana. This seems to have been due to nervous tension over his tempestuous romance with Ava Gardner and when that came to some kind of resolution, Sinatra's career continued unabated. Fine musicianship, exceptional phrasing, total involvement with his material which in turn he communicates to his listeners, in short, the attributes of a great singer, have made Sinatra's career what it is—together with shrewd showmanship and the pugnacious charm of his personality.

The Non-Voiced Singers. Paradoxical but true, some of our greatest non-operatic singers have had really scarcely any voice at all. Among concert singers not generously endowed vocally I have already mentioned Povla Frijsh and Pierre Bernac. In the case of Maggie Teyte she certainly began her career with a lovely vocal instrument but ended it with a sadly limited one. Nonetheless because of her art and charm she continued to delight audiences right up until her final appearances.

In the popular field, numbers of artists have also held audiences by their way of projecting a song, by their magnetism or personal beauty, but not by their singing voices. One of the all-time greats was Billie Holiday who had an extremely limited voice which she lacerated by the intensity of her cigarette and drug habits. Another example of a non-voiced singer is Mabel Mercer, who has held legions of fans in her thrall for years even though her voice is practically non-existent and her intonation not always precise. And what of another great singer with a voice not always in tune— Marlene Dietrich? Yet to hear one of her concerts is an absorbing even moving experience, as when she sings "Where Have All the Flowers Gone?".

In this category too belong the dancing singers, Fred Astaire and Gene Kelly. With no voice to speak of, but confident that if their song wouldn't win the girl they could resort to their wonderfully deft feet, they put over with charm and simplicity some of the loveliest melodies of Irving Berlin, Jerome Kern, George Gershwin, Leonard Bernstein and other great song writers.

As the voice diminishes with age the art grows. This is true of the concert singer or of entertainers such as Sophie Tucker or Maurice Chevalier, who in their seventies or eighties have talked more than sung their numbers. Even in his prime the versatile and charming Rex Harrison never seems to have possessed more than a feather of a voice, but that didn't stop him from making his way with infinite aplomb through one of the most successful musicals ever written, *My Fair Lady*—occasionally hitting some notes but rarely sustaining them.

The successful folk singers also belong in the category of non-voiced singers, usually having true, sometimes quite pretty voices (though this can scarcely be said of Bob Dylan) but small, thin in quality and limited in range. Here again the word is all important. The singer with a big, sumptuous voice would swamp this kind of vocal literature, as often happens when opera singers attempt popular songs. Style, very personal phrasing, clarity of diction and an intimate approach is what's wanted—not voice.

In addition to the non-voiced stars who have delighted a large public there is another kind, not usually thought of as singers at all and, with one or two exceptions, heard only by a limited few. I refer to the composer as singer.

Rossini once said, "He who wants to write well for singers must be a singer himself," and the history of music confirms that this is so. The first (and some say finest) era of bel canto was ushered in with the operas *Dafne* and *Euridice* by Jacopo Peri. Peri was also a singer as were a number of the sixteenth- and seventeenth-century Italian composers who came after him. Today, vocal students working to perfect the long, flowing line that is one of the secrets of beautiful singing, practice the *Arie Antiche,* songs and arias by composers who understood the voice because they themselves were singers.

An opera that survives from this same period is Henry Purcell's
Dido and Aeneas, and here again we learn that Purcell was an excellent singer, first as a countertenor, a type of voice for which he
wrote many compositions, and later, oddly enough, a bass. Purcell's
performance of his ode, "Hail, bright Cecilia" was praised by a
local music critic of the day for the "incredible graces" which he
bestowed on the aria " 'Tis Nature's Voice."

This bond of composer and his own singing voice as inspiration
continues into more recent times. Though Mozart sang duets with
his sister as a little boy, post-pubescence does not seem to have
left him with an impressive vocal organ. And yet his preoccupation
with the voice, his rare understanding of it which makes his vocal
compositions such a delight to perform, suggest that he had the
sensibility of a remarkable singer if not his physical equipment.
Quite the opposite is true of Beethoven, who wrote ungratefully,
almost aggressively for the singer. It is said that Beethoven himself could not sing in tune—though this may have been due to the
affliction that attacked his hearing so early in his life. Even then
Beethoven seems to have resorted to a kind of singing to assist
him in composing. A friend, Ferdinand Ries, relates how once
while out walking, Beethoven "had constantly hummed or almost
howled up and down the scale without singing definite notes.
When I asked him what it was, he replied that a theme for the
last allegro of the sonata (Opus 57) had come into his head."

Not surprisingly then, those who have written most sympathet-
ically for the voice and specialized in vocal music have been the
most proficient singers themselves. This is borne out by the case
of Rossini, who as the son of a soprano and the husband of another, thoroughly understood the technique of singing, besides having a fine high baritone voice of his own. In December 1823,
Rossini endured the torments of seasickness to cross the Channel
to England, where as a famed operatic composer, he was taken up
by the fashionable as well as the musical of the day. Though
ostensibly engaged as impresario at the King's Theatre for a

Gioacchino Rossini by Caruso.

"Rossini season" the composer, never at a loss for expediency, capitalized on his lionization by singing and playing one of his own buffo arias at the Brighton Pavilion before George IV. He also rendered (I'm certain smiling inwardly) Desdemona's Willow Song from his *Otello,* singing it in falsetto, which caused an uneasy stir in the audience to whom this *castrato* sound was now decidedly unfashionable and even scandalous. As the rage of London, Rossini was asked to many of the houses of the elite, for which he usually charged a fee of £50. He also gave singing lessons to the aristocrats of the day, among them, the Duke of Wellington. Another would-be singer was the King himself, and Rossini, already beginning to bulge, found himself in the company of this monstrously corpulent monarch, clinging to the tenor part of a *buffo* duet, while George IV wandered around hopelessly underneath in the bass. Thanks mainly to Rossini's singing he amassed a fortune of 175,000 francs during his six months stay in England, a fortune which enabled him to retire and—ironically—almost entirely give up composing.

Rossini was renowned for his generosity towards other musicians and about this time in Paris he was introduced to a young Irishman who had learned the violin as a child but had now developed a voice that he hoped was suitable for opera. Impressed, Rossini loaned him money for further singing lessons and subsequently arranged for his debut at the Théâtre des Italiens in *Il Barbiere.* Thus did Michael Balfe, future composer of *The Bohemian Girl,* not yet twenty, make his entrance into the important musical world of Paris in the early nineteenth century. According to contemporary reports Balfe possessed a voice of great sweetness and flexibility. One of his best roles was Don Giovanni which he sang *"con amore."* Balfe also appeared in several other Rossini operas including *La Gazza Ladra* and *Cenerentola,* the latter with the fascinating Maria Malibran, who also arranged for his engagement at La Scala. Ultimately Balfe returned to London to become manager of the Lyceum Theatre, for which he wrote a number of operas, largely forgotten with the exception of the sprightly *Bohemian Girl.*

About this time Hector Berlioz, sent by his father to medical school in Paris, had secretly begun to study music. When the medical training became unbearable Berlioz announced to his family that he was quitting in order to become a composer. Their classic bourgeois reaction was to cut off his financial support. Berlioz, who had already studied the flute and could sing at sight, applied for work at the Théâtre des Nouveautés. When an opening occurred for a chorus singer he was summoned for an audition. His rivals, he discovered, included a blacksmith, a weaver and a chorister from the Church of St. Eustache, each of whom sang a selection of his own choosing. Berlioz's turn came and when asked what he had brought to sing, the future composer re-

plied, "Nothing." Nothing? Had he no music with him at all—
not even an Italian vocal exercise? "Nothing," repeated Berlioz.
The next question was what operatic arias he knew by heart.
Berlioz's reply is characteristic of a man who never did anything
halfway. He had memorized the entire standard operatic repertory,
the Gluck operas *Orfeo* and the two *Iphigénies,* the Spontini
La Vestale, etc.

Dazed, the manager asked Berlioz to sing a selection from this
vast list and the next day the aspiring composer learned that he
had triumphed over the blacksmith, the weaver and the chorister
from the Church of St. Eustache, and was engaged at a salary of
fifty francs a month. Thus as a vaudeville singer did Berlioz embark on his extraordinary musical career.

Of the two towering operatic composers of the nineteenth century, Verdi and Wagner, no description exists of how Verdi sang,
but George Martin in his rich biography of this most vocal of
composers holds the theory that Verdi as he wrote most certainly sang, though not necessarily out loud. Or to put it another
way, Verdi responded within his own throat to his music as he
composed it. To support this idea, Mr. Martin points out that in
the years around 1844, Verdi, a man of excellent health and great
energy, was constantly beset by sore throats and hoarseness. It is
this period of his life that the composer with all the commissions
he could handle referred to as his "galley years" during which
he worked at an exhausting pace turning out one opera after another. Mr. Martin believes that as Verdi wrote, he unconsciously
sang or felt in his throat the many difficult roles that were pouring
out of him, and his sore throats and hoarseness were really the result of straining his voice by "over-singing." Later, when Verdi
slowed his rate of work, these throat ailments disappeared.

Of Richard Wagner it has been said that he would have been
the greatest singing actor in the nineteenth century but for one
deficiency: he lacked a voice. This did not prevent him from singing large sections of his music dramas, often taking all the parts,

Guiseppe Verdi by Caruso.

male and female, to stunned friends and admirers. Léon Carvalho, director of the Théâtre-Lyrique at Paris, gives us this description of Wagner's personal audition of *Tannhäuser:*

"I can still see Wagner, wearing a blue jacket with red braid, and a yellow Greek cap adorned with a green fringe . . . With a fire, an *entrain* that I shall never forget, he began by giving me the first part of *Tannhäuser;* then, dripping with perspiration, he disappeared, to return this time in a red cap decorated with yellow braid, his blue coat had been replaced by a yellow one embellished with blue braid. In this new costume he sang for me the second part of his opera. He howled, he threw himself about, he hit all kinds of wrong notes, and to crown it all he sang in German! And his eyes! The eyes of a madman! I did not dare to cross him; he frightened me."

Another of Wagner's famous performances was an audition in

Paris of the second act of *Tristan* in which he sang Tristan to the Isolde of the remarkable Pauline Viardot. Present was an audience of two, Madame Kalergis, a wealthy patroness of the arts, and Hector Berlioz. Wagner hurled himself into his role with his usual intensity while Viardot, who at that time had some reservations about the composer's music, "rendered most of her part in low tones," as Wagner sourly observed afterwards. It is typical of him to complain of her not doing justice to his music when she was reading her tremendously difficult role *at sight*. Of Wagner's singing, Berlioz could only find words of praise for the warmth of the composer's delivery. Nonetheless, whatever his voice lacked, Wagner's performances must have been thrilling and deeply moving.

Another celebrated operatic composer of this period, Charles Gounod, also liked personally to audition his operas. The comic actor, E. Got, heard Gounod sing and accompany himself through the entire score of his first opera, *Sapho,* and commented characteristically "no voice, but what charm!" And a worshipful fan, Marie Anne De Bovet, writing of Gounod in 1891, two years before his death, gives us this lavender description of the composer's song in old age:

"His tenor voice, once so sweet, which he manages with infinite skill, not of professional technicalities, but of intention and feeling, is now impaired by age; at times he can hardly sing at all." Nonetheless, she goes on to relate that "No one can sing Mozart as he does, it is with him a question of expression, of suppressed feeling, of intense vibration . . . With a voice that hardly carries beyond the piano, he will give Marguerite's appeal to heaven, 'Anges purs, anges radieux' or render the ecstatic triumph of Polyeucte after his baptism, so as to reveal beauties which the most applauded vocalization of a prima donna, or the highest notes of a fashionable tenor have never equalled."

Gounod seems to have understood well the nonsensical images awash in the average singing teacher's studio. Though Gounod never gave singing lessons, he pretended to let his daughter bring a friend to him for advice. "Child, you want to sing?" the composer is reported to have said with mock solemnity to the trembling young woman. "Well I'll tell you what to do. Place your bow (*archet*), let the urn of your voice pour out its contents and give me a mauve sound in which I can wash my hands."

Still another composer with a less than special singing voice was Georges Bizet, who maintained that he would have been a great singer if nature had endowed him with one. Bizet's father, Adolphe, was a singing teacher, also his mother's brother, the eccentric François Delsarte. An accomplished pianist, Bizet put singing before all. As his pupil Edmond Galabert recalled, "He . . . used the voice, particularly when he was playing an orchestral piece, to imitate by singing or humming the timbre of the different instruments, filling out or underlining the details and counter-melodies." Galabert also remembered Bizet's accomplished interpretations of various operatic roles in which Bizet would sing the female parts in a tenor voice, the male roles in a baritone or bass range. This prodigally gifted composer also suffered from throat ailments all his life. Was it for the same reason as Verdi—over-singing?

A little known, unfinished opera by Georges Bizet called *Don Rodrigue* was commissioned by the most celebrated baritone of his day, Jean-Baptiste Faure, who also composed himself. One song of his still survives, the well-known "Les Rameaux" ("The Palms"), a great favorite of baritones and basses. The Venezuela-born composer, Reynaldo Hahn, who wrote what might be described as slightly perfumed songs and operettas, was also an accomplished singer. His vocal art resembled his compositions, utilizing a slight, pastel *tenore leggiero* not unlike in quality that of Tito Schipa.

In modern times the relationship of the composer to his singing voice remains as powerful as ever. Poulenc, like Wagner or Gounod, used to give the world premières of his vocal compositions to friends with overpowering effect, even though he had no voice. Leonard Bernstein resorts instantly to his own limited voice to illustrate a passage in either his own or someone else's compositions. Samuel Barber, who writes so felicitously for the voice, is a trained singer and has even recorded his evocative "Dover Beach" for RCA Victor.

The composers of popular songs as singers are also many. Anyone who has heard Irving Berlin or Harold Arlen sing one of his own hits, quickly realizes that they cannot be interpreted more perfectly despite the limitations of the composers' voices. Still another pop singer-composer, even though she couldn't read a note of music, was Billie Holiday. An idea for a song such as "Bless the Child" would come into her head and she would then hum it to her accompanist who would pick it out on the piano. Billie Holiday shared in the writing of the famous "Strange Fruit." "La Vie en Rose," one of Edith Piaf's most famous numbers, was written by herself.

These are some of the more outstanding examples of composers as singers. It is obvious, however, that almost every composer at one time or another has had recourse to that most convenient and ready to hand of all instruments—the one in his throat.

The Amateurs.   Amateur singers come in many different varieties. Most common is the ordinary bathtub kind, booming and uninhibited in the privacy of his moist echoing chamber, usually shy and silent outside it. There are the amateur singers with little voice, who nonetheless regularly perform with choirs or choruses for love of singing. We have among us also amateur singers with beautiful natural or well-trained voices who for one reason or another never made professional careers, contenting themselves with singing for friends in the drawing room. Until the invention of the phonograph amateur music, including singing, formed an important part of an evening's amusement in homes both rich and poor.

Among the well-to-do of an earlier age one of the most desirable accomplishments of a young lady was her ability to sing, and voice lessons were given a high priority in her otherwise limited education. Natasha, heroine of *War and Peace,* possesses a lovely contralto voice and is studying when we first meet her. Elizabeth Bennet suffers agonies over the inadequacies of her sister Mary's singing at the Bingley dance in *Pride and Prejudice* and finally persuades her father to make Mary desist.

Amateur singing extended to royal circles as well. The Empress Maria Theresa is reputed to have been a gifted singer. While still princess, the contralto-voiced Victoria, a life-long devotee of opera, took singing lessons from the most renowned bass of his day, Luigi Lablache. It is on record that Her Highness performed the difficult duet, "Mira, O Norma," with her mother, the Duchess of Kent, taking the other part—but unfortunately not on a phonograph record.

Though *jeunes filles* of these and later times often took vocal instruction, there was usually no thought of doing anything so vulgar as going on the stage and making a professional career. An amateur, whose singing nevertheless gave her a fabulous career in the glittering salons of Paris during the 1850's and 1860's, was the amusing Lillie Moulton, born Greenough in Cambridge, Massachusetts. After studying in London with Garcia who said she reminded him of his sister, Maria Malibran—except that Lillie had brains and Maria did not—she moved on to Paris with a note from him to his younger sister, Pauline Viardot. "Do all you can to persuade her to go on the stage," he wrote. But in this project the powers of the fascinating Madame Viardot for once failed. Instead Lillie married the scion of a wealthy American diplomat and plunged into the rich and varied life of Paris in the Second Empire.

"This was a great occasion seeing and hearing Rossini, Gounod and Auber at the same time . . . I wonder that I had the courage to sing before them," she wrote home to her New England relatives.

Or, on another occasion, "I sang some of Massenet's songs, accompanied of course, by Massenet. Liszt was attentive and most enthusiastic. He said Massenet had a great future, and he complimented me on my singing, especially my phrasing and expression."

Or again, "Jenny Lind and I performed the duo from (Auber's) *Le Premier Jour du Bonheur* . . . She put her arm around my waist while we were singing, as if we were two school girls." How many professionals during the same period could have boasted of such performances before the musical elite of Europe?

Lillie's amazing penchant for being on the scene of an important musical event produced this interesting item written from Cambridge to her sister in June 1877. "There is also another invention, called phonograph, where the human voice is reproduced, and can go on for ever being reproduced. I sang in one through a horn and they transposed this on a platina roll and wound it off." On hearing the playback her reaction was similar to many people who hear their voices reproduced for the first time. "The intonation— the pronunciation—I could recognize as my own, but the *voice*— Dear me!" To Lillie de Hegermann-Lindencrone (she had remarried after the death of her first husband) must go credit for being the first person known to have recorded the singing voice.

Not generally known is the fact that James Joyce was the possessor, like his father before him, of a light, sweet tenor voice. Joyce grew up in an atmosphere of singing, as he recalled evenings in his childhood in *A Portrait of the Artist:*

"One by one the others took up the air until a full choir of voices was singing. They would sing so for hours, melody after melody, glee after glee, till the last pale light died on the horizon, till the first dark night clouds came forth and night fell."

In 1904, Joyce, discouraged in his attempts at writing and desperate to earn money by some means other than drudgery, decided to enter the Feis Ceoil, a musical competition held annually in Dublin. (The previous year it had been won by a nervous nineteen-year-old named John McCormack.) Joyce sang an aria from Sullivan's *The Prodigal Son* and an Irish air and would have won the contest but for the rules requiring each contestant to read a song at sight. Joyce refused, declaring grandly that it was not worthy of an artist to sing music unprepared. In fact he could scarcely read music and was near-sighted to boot. As a result Joyce only won second prize, a bronze medal which he is said to have thrown into the Liffey. On the strength of his appearance, the best voice teacher in Dublin offered to teach him for nothing, but the future author of *Ulysses* preferred to take the position of the great singer "who might have been."

Joyce continued to sing throughout the whole of his life, and a friend recalls him performing three ballads on his forty-sixth birthday "more beautifully than I had ever heard him, his voice charged with feeling." The author's love for singing illumines everything he wrote. "The human voice, two tiny silky cords," he once said, "wonderful, more than all the others."

In recent times when there has been no stigma attached to going on the stage, two amateur singers, and presidents' daughters, Margaret Wilson and Margaret Truman, attempted unsuccessfully to make professional careers. By means of the radio the whole country was able to gauge the essentially thin and tentative quality of Miss Truman's voice. Further study improved it and gave her more assurance in later appearances but she never really rose above the status of an amateur.

Over the years there have been aspiring amateurs, usually female, and very rich, who have tried to buy a singing voice and the ability to use it. One of the best known was Polish-born Ganna Walska, who by various alliances (her name was linked with Otto Kahn and the Chicago millionaire, Harold McCormick) as well as a couple of very brief marriages, gained a fortune. With equal ease she hoped to gain a voice as well, and engaged the soprano, Frances Alda, just retired from the Metropolitan "to sail with her to France, stay six weeks with her at her château, give her a lesson a day and, for this, accept ten thousand dollars.

"I did my level best in those lessons to teach Ganna Walska to sing," continues Alda in her amusing memoirs *Men, Women and Tenors.* "I demonstrated, I repeated, I praised wherever I honestly could praise. I scolded . . . But work as I did I could not teach Ganna Walska to sing.

" 'No, *No,* No!' I'd say to her. 'Not like that. You're singing like five million pigs.' "

One who sang like ten million pigs to the delight of her screaming fans was Florence Foster Jenkins, who annually would hire an auditorium in New York City's old Hotel Ritz and offer a program of songs and arias that she could perform scarcely even on pitch. The audience thought it wildly funny, and a record of one of these recitals—surely one of the cornerstones of camp—used to be produced at parties to provide a moment of mirth for the guests. At the risk of being charged with stuffiness, this writer's spirits, far from being lightened on hearing her, were agonized; but that was not a typical reaction. Did she herself know how comic her listeners found her? Did she realize how excruciatingly awful her singing was? These, of course, are questions which the amateur, if she is wealthy enough, does not have to raise.

As I have remarked, the era of the rich amateur singer who buys her audiences would appear to be dying out, but even at this writing the annual recital of one such soprano continues in New York City, a woman whose vocal endowments can scarcely be said to give pleasure to her audiences, yet who has done much to seek out unknown or unsung selections of modern vocal literature, as well as to commission the best contemporary composers. Thus, buried in the joke, is deep conviction and seriousness.

All around the world there are millions of amateurs who do not buy their audiences but love to have an opportunity to sing. They give up evenings to rehearse and perform with choral groups, and may surrender their Sunday mornings to the church choir as well. There are amateurs with shredded and patched voices, and amateurs who need to sing with others in order to keep on the pitch, but all carol away with as much joy as—possibly more than—the greatest opera star.

As Hugo von Hoffmansthal wrote: "Singing is near miraculous because it is the mastering of what is otherwise a pure instrument of egotism: the human voice."

The Mixed Chorus by Gluyas Williams.

PART FOUR

MAGIC:

THE ILLUSORY SCIENCE.

HOW IS IT DONE?

Have not poetry and music emerged, as it seems, out of the sounds the enchanters made to help their imagination to enchant, to charm, to bind with a spell themselves and the passers-by?

—W. B. Yeats

Out of Sight. Orpheus, the first great singer, was also a magician and often the spell that a singer casts upon his audience seems utterly magical. To a person watching and listening it all looks so easy. Singers simply open their mouths and a flood of tone comes pouring out capable of stirring up in us all kinds of emotions. We too can open our mouths and let forth a singing voice of a sort, but no such spell is engendered by our song—except sometimes a kind of self-hypnosis when the walls of a bathroom give back the voice in an enriched form. What then do great singers do that is different from when we sing?

Outwardly, our eyes detect nothing except perhaps an occasional odd, comic grimace on the face of a singer. At a piano recital we can see how a pianist holds his hands—with wrists held high, or, depending on his technique, with flattened wrists and fingers. In the same way our eyes can see a ballerina set her toe in a blocked shoe in a certain precise manner onto the floor of a stage, her arms held in various positions any of which again are demonstrable. But when it comes to singing it was God's little joke to place the larynx, the hard-surfaced kernel of the voice containing the vocal cords, *just* out of sight of any normal visualization of what is going on in the throat during vocalization. Ask a professional singer how he produces the easy flood of rich, powerful tone that emanates from his mouth and he may give an elaborate explanation of his sensations while singing. But he can only *tell* you—he cannot physically show you. And so we are in a world of mystery, where all is unbeheld sensation, and nothing apparent. No wonder that singing seems to be accomplished by magic.

When for the first time, in 1854, a human eye viewed living vocal cords vibrating in the throat of a human being it was believed that a basis for a scientific understanding of how the voice functions had finally been established. Before that much had been guesswork. In ancient Greece, Aristotle understood empirically that the larynx by some mysterious means played a part in the production of the voice, but thought that alterations in the length of the trachea (the windpipe) must control the changes of pitch of the voice, as though there were a set of organ pipes built into men's throats. (Aristotle also believed that the true source of the voice was the heart, and though this may have been scientifically inaccurate no one can gainsay its essential importance to great singing.) By the second century A.D., Galen, the Greek physician, had named and described the larger cartilages of the larynx. Hundreds of years later Leonardo Da Vinci made the first known drawings of the larynx in profile, including the vocal cords, though he did not realize their importance and still believed the voice to be produced by a column of air vibrating in the windpipe.

In 1636 by citing the laws of sound which were now understood, a French scholar gave the lie to this organ-pipe theory. Man would need to have a trachea or windpipe of giraffe-like proportions to produce a range of two octaves or more, he declared, and decided that the vocal cords, as revealed by dissection, must produce sound by vibrating.

A hundred years later another Frenchman, Antoine Ferrein, published the startling results of his experiments on a human larynx taken from a cadaver. By blowing air through the tiny organ he discovered that the two tweezer-shaped bands, joined at one end and attached to the front of the throat, but free to open or close at the back of it, could be made to come together and vibrate, thus producing a sound. He also showed that the greater the speed and the pressure of the air forced across these bands, the larger would be the volume of sound. Air playing on the vibrating ligaments, said Ferrein, had the same effect as the action of a bow on the strings of a violin and so he named them *"cordes vocales"* or "vocal cords" or "strings" a term familiar to us to this day.

(Frequently and nonsensically, however, they are referred to as vocal "chords." Present day laryngologists and vocal experts also feel that the word "cord" is inaccurate, since the wiry, immensely strong ligaments capable of crossing the larynx are really tapered membranes shot through with muscular fibers. They prefer to use the term "vocal folds.")

During the early part of the nineteenth century scientists worked in increasing numbers to establish somehow that the voice functioned on the basis of one of four types of musical instruments. At the same time attempts were made to see into the throat, particularly the fascinating glottis, the space within the larynx that contains the vocal cords or folds. All experiments to arrive at a means failed until curiously, not a doctor, but a grave, quietly charming vocal pedagogue with a scholarly turn of mind and a cracked singing voice succeeded in the fall of 1854 at Paris. This was Manuel Garcia II—a name held in reverence by many vocal teachers to this day.

Unaware of earlier unsuccessful efforts to see into the throat with a mirror, and with but one overwhelming desire—"If only I could see the glottis!"—Garcia went to a surgical supply place in Paris and happened on a new kind of long-handled dentist's mirror. Once home he warmed the instrument in hot water and placed it against the uvula at the back of his mouth and the top of his throat. (This operation, incidentally, must be performed with great delicacy, for the slightest excess of pressure will cause an instant reaction of gagging or even vomiting.) Taking up another larger hand mirror he stood by a window and caught a ray of the sun which he flashed onto the tiny mirror in the depths of his mouth. And there for the first time the glottis of a live human being containing its precious treasure—the means by which man communicates to his fellow man—was first beheld by the human eye. Manuel Garcia II had invented the laryngoscope. Now an exact science of voice production was at last assured.

Or was it?

At best the laryngoscope made it possible to view the top of the vocal cords only. Their undersides were, and still are, out of sight of the eye of the scientific observer. And then there was, and is, the vexing problem of the mirror inserted into the back of the mouth above the throat. Everyone knows what a dismal bleat emerges when a doctor places a wooden depressor on the tongue and asks us to say "Ah." How much more difficult then, to semi-swallow a mirror and be called upon to sing while the scientist makes his observations of the changes in the vocal cords. At best he sees only an approximation of their appearance during vocalization for the simple reason that there cannot be proper singing when the mouth is stopped up with bits of glass and metal. In more recent times we have had remarkable high-speed photographs taken of a singer's glottis in performance but even these had to be made with the ever-present mirror reflecting light down into the throat. Nor do these pictures show what is happening on the underside of the cords. Still more recently, in an untiring quest to see what occurs during the vocal process, laryngologists have considered the possibility of inserting electrode needles into individual muscles within the larynx and obtaining what are known as electromyograms. But as a doctor with a wryer sense of humor than some of his colleagues remarked of the idea, "This causes some discomfort to the subject, which he does not always recognize as necessary."

The invention of the laryngoscope, however, did corroborate certain principles either suggested in the dissecting room or arrived at empirically. A great wave of optimism combined with a surge of medical inquiry swept through the vocal world. This Victorian invention coincided with the belief that technology could solve all of man's problems and it now seemed certain that an exact scientific method of singing could be evolved. But following from 1854 no new race of vocal giants appeared in the musical world, only the usual fluctuating proportion of great singers that arrive on the scene with each new decade. Garcia, his simple little mirror always at hand, continued to produce a number of noted singers in his vocal studio; so did his sister, Pauline Viardot, and his pupil, Mathilde Marchesi. Though the laryngoscope might confirm certain theories about the changes in the vocal folds during singing and could reveal inflammation in a strained pair of vocal cords, the fact was that the instrument made it no easier to teach someone to sing. Confusion continued to exist concerning the vocal process and the arguments became, if anything, more heated than ever.

Indeed half a century later in 1909 an Englishman, Ernest G. White, published a book called *Science and Singing* in which he put forth the theory that the vocal cords did not produce sound at all. Illustrated with the skulls of snakes, sheep and giraffes, the volume gravely and apparently plausibly put forth the proposition that the tones of the singing voice are produced in the sinuses, with the result that a whole school of "sinus tone production" evolved in London and spread to the United States. White's book and several later volumes elaborating the theory remain in print even now awaiting the innocent voice student who might chance upon them, despite the comments of today's experts such as Elster Kay in *Bel Canto and the Sixth Sense:* "First prize in idiocy goes to the writer who said that vocal tone originated not in the vocal cords but in the sinuses. This particular book reached a very wide student public and was made the basis of an elaborate teaching method, which, hardly surprisingly, collapsed when after the passage of some years it produced no singers at all."

As late as 1950, not quite a century after the introduction of the laryngoscope, an emboldened Frenchman put forth a theory that rocked the laryngological world and set the scientists rushing to their sound laboratories. The larynx, maintained M. Raoul Husson, was not the sole vocal organ in the human body, but part of a system controlled from an acoustic center in the brain. Quite the opposite from the idea that a column of air rises from the lungs and pushes against the vocal cords making them flutter, this acoustic center sends nervous impulses—"coup par coup" as he put it—directly to the cords, which by their vibrations set in motion the column of air. This chicken-before-the-egg theory set up a tremendous fuss and was denounced by many as utter nonsense. However, to disprove it a considerable amount of research had to be accomplished with the result, as one noted voice doctor says, "we learned more about the physiology of voice in that decade than in any other, thanks to Husson's erroneously but sincerely conceived challenge."

The Theory.   Then what is really and truly known about the basic principles of voice production? Put very elementally, this much seems almost certain.

Air having been taken into the lungs is expelled back through the larynx. At the same instant the vocal cords come together, or, more accurately, approximate. Such is the pressure of the breath on these tiny ligaments that a portion, or the whole of them (depending on the pitch of the note being sung) is forced apart, letting through a tiny puff of air. This causes the cords or folds to vibrate, and since they are capable of changing their length and thickness these amazingly adjustable ligaments produce a series of notes ranging over two or more octaves. Resonators surround the larynx. These include the pharynx—the soft palate above the throat—also the arched roof of the mouth called the hard palate, and certain cavities that lie behind the nose. They vibrate in sympathy with the note giving it a special tone quality. It is believed that the larynx is also a resonator, and that in addition on certain notes the upper part of the chest also vibrates, though the idea of the chest as resonator has been disputed. The infinite varieties of these resonators, like the features of a face, give every voice a unique sound and character.

Battlefield Number One. "The voice," said Seneca, "is nothing more than beaten air." How right he was has now more or less been proven. Since there can be no singing without air let us examine the first of the basic factors in singing: that apparently simple and natural function called breathing. Immediately we are plunged into a battle in which the hue and cry is deafening. If nothing else, the vocal experts, those who set themselves up as absolute authorities on how to sing, are unabashedly vocal in their claims to know right from wrong.

Some vocal teachers pay no attention to a breathing technique, merely asking their pupils to take in air the way they ordinarily would. The subject is not raised. Other pedagogues believe that a good singing technique depends almost entirely on breathing correctly. But what is "correct" breathing? Here the bickering and strife break out in fearful force.

On one point only does there seem to be agreement: man can take breath in one of three basic ways. (He can also breathe in a combination of these ways, but for some reason dogmatism obtains in the manuals of singing, and the point is rarely stressed.) When we have been running and badly want breath, we take in air in a series of very short, quick breaths as our shoulders rise and fall. This is called clavicular or upper chest breathing, and though it feeds fresh supplies of oxygen to the lungs quickly it does not supply them with very much and only to the upper part of the body. Athletes mainly breathe in this fashion, but almost without exception the vocal experts condemn it as inadequate and unsuitable for singing. It should be pointed out, however, that a cunning singer falls back on this type of breathing when he cannot manage a very long phrase. Not wishing to break it, he takes a barely imperceptible half or "catch" breath.*

A second kind of breathing goes under such names as "lateral" or "intercostal." Air is drawn to the bottom of the lungs which are enclosed by the eighth to the twelfth ribs of the thorax or rib cage. Unlike the upper ribs rigidly attached to the sternum and back bone, these lower, so called floating, ribs make it possible for a large expansion of the lungs. If the abdomen is held in as a kind of base or support, this expansion will cause the ribs to push out in front and to the sides in the area just above the navel. Thus a fanatic believer in this type of breathing for singing, issues these exhortations to her students:

"1) Draw in the abdomen below the navel, as well as the navel itself, and keep them thus always, for the rest of your life." (In heavy black print.)

She also has a few other suggestions to the aspiring singer:

"2) Put yourself in the physical and spiritual state of one who is about to take a high dive into the sea, or is training for the championship in running, jumping, and so forth.

"3) Be happy, radiantly happy; please!"

Dividing the rib cage from the abdomen is a muscle known as the diaphragm which exerts an up and down force within the torso. Shaped like an inverted saucer, the diaphragm can be made to flatten out by taking a deep breath. This exerts pressure on the abdomen forcing it to protrude. The downward movement of the diaphragm creates a partial vacuum within the rib cage into which air rushes and we have what is known as deep abdominal, but sometimes diaphragmatic, breathing.

(Women who have taken courses in natural childbirth will understand well these three different kinds of breathing, particularly the intercostal, in which they learn to keep pressure off the top of

---

* Sometimes this gulp can be noisy, as in the case of Lotte Lehmann's singing— an idiosyncrasy she has passed on to her pupil, the mezzo-soprano, Mildred Miller.

the uterus during labor, and the upper chest, or clavicular, practiced during the last moments of birth.)

Assertions are made that intercostal breathing was the choice of the early great bel canto singers and of the wondrous *castrati*. The words of Manuel Garcia II that the chest should be lifted and the abdomen drawn up and in while taking breath are also frequently quoted by his fervent disciples in support of the intercostal breathing method. In 1855, however, one year after Garcia's discovery of the laryngoscope, a mettlesome doctor named Mandl, writing in the *Gazette Médicale,* published in Paris, dared to say that if the diaphragm was made to descend as deeply as possible more air would be taken into the lungs, providing always that the abdomen pushes out during this action. Soon after, his theories were taken up and taught by noted singing teachers in both England and America. The intercostal forces, uttering bel canto cries that *theirs* was the true method of the Italian master, rallied at once and the battle was conjoined. It continues to this day. Here is a section of a review published in *Opera* magazine by Rupert Bruce Lockhart in 1966:

"I once attended in Paris a meeting of the Union des Maîtres-Chanteurs and the subject for the evening discussion was 'Breathing.' In the auditorium were over a hundred professors of singing or speech and on the platform three doctors (throat specialists) and one physical-culturist. I was taken by one of the most famous musicians and singing professors in Paris. We laughed helplessly all evening. There was almost a free fight. No two people in the entire assembly seemed to agree on a method of breathing. Insults were hurled around and two of the doctors finally turned their chairs back to back and refused to speak to each other. The evening ended with the physical-culturist illustrating an entirely different method from anything that had been exposed by the singing fraternity."

Caught in this continuing fray is the student anxious to learn a correct breathing method that will enable him to take in three or four more times as much air as he uses in average quiet breathing. If this student turned to the literature, what might he find? I made a random survey of twenty-eight different books or manuals published in the last hundred years purporting to treat the subject of breathing authoritatively. (There are dozens and dozens more but these happened to be on my shelves.) I found that twelve experts advocated intercostal breathing with the abdomen drawn in, ten, abdominal breathing with a relaxed abdomen, three that counseled a kind of combination of the two, and three that advised breathing in any way that seemed comfortable but was at the same time supportive. Gentleness is simply not in most of the authors. J. C. Veaco announces his position with the thunderous title, *Why Abdominal Breathing is Fatal to Bel Canto.* Another declares that this kind of breathing may do dreadful harm to certain organs in the female abdomen. Herman Klein, in whose family's London house Manuel Garcia II gave singing lessons, declares that not only is abdominal breathing the only desirable method, but adds, "This I believe to be the old Italian system of breathing, as it was taught by Manuel Garcia II." What *are* we to believe?

The experience of great singers ought to reveal the truth. One book informs us that Melba, Eames, Nordica, the de Reszke brothers and Pol Plançon were all advocates of intercostal breathing, raising their chests high and restraining the lower and middle parts of their abdomens. On the other hand, a legend says that if Caruso stood next to a grand piano he could move it as he drew in breath and his abdomen pushed out. The celebrated coloratura soprano Marcella Sembrich is supposed to have built her vocal career on the use of half breaths, which suggests that she used the clavicular, high chest method of breathing. Sembrich studied with the noted teacher Giovanni Lamperti and tremendous squabbling goes on to this day as to whether he taught deep abdominal breathing or the intercostal system; if the story is true about the way Sembrich breathed, it suggests he taught neither.

Lilli Lehmann says that in the earlier part of her career she always had a sensation of taking in too much air and, feeling stifled, wanted to let some out before she sang a phrase. More recently the late, extraordinary Kirsten Flagstad is quoted as saying that the subject of breathing is "almost impossible to learn or understand and almost impossible to teach."

And yet it is breath and breath alone that makes it possible for singers to emit long, beautifully controlled phrases and sustained high notes that are part of the art of great singing. Singers can and do begin a note pianissimo, swell it out to a forte and then back again to its previous softness in a manner known as a *messa di voce* that leaves the audience, if only out of identification, literally breathless. All this is made possible by the support given their tones by breath (a support, by the way, that is far less needed in closely miked popular singing). Thus, because correct breathing is a necessity to fine singing, the experts continue to argue the merits of the various methods while students often undergo real physical torments practiced in vocal studios trying to learn how to breathe. Belts may be fastened around their waists or the lower part of their abdomens more and more tightly constricted. A pile of bricks or large books will be piled on the belly as they lie on their backs on the floor. Blanche Marchesi writes amusingly of a teacher who would make the student place a large tumbler of water on her chest while lying on her back. If the pupil breathed right the glass would remain in place. Most of the lessons, however, were spent in wiping up herself and the room. I had thought that by this time enlightenment might have put some of these barbarous teaching practices to rout, when to my amazement, on striking up a conversation with a student lyric soprano selling books at Schirmer's in New York, she said that she had left her previous teacher because *he had stood on her belly* to strengthen her abdominal muscles. And that was in December 1968.

It would be unsuitable—and highly dangerous as well—for this writer to enter the intercostal versus abdominal breathing battle, but there does seem to be one commonsense element to consider about the two methods. In the intercostal technique the abdomen is held in, creating a firm base for the air to spread out in a lateral way across the body just above the navel. People naturally wide in this part of the body would presumably find this method of breathing more congenial to the way they are built. Is this, as is well known, why women with their wide hips and abdomens containing organs that men do not have are naturally inclined to breathe in the intercostal manner? Equally a tall bass, say, with wide shoulders, a long torso and relatively narrow hips, might well find that deep abdominal breathing would provide him with a powerful, vertical column of air to sustain his tones. Could this be the reason, as has been established, that men take more instinctively to abdominal breathing?

Another smaller but vexing point of dissension exists among the breathing experts: is it preferable to take in air through the nose or the mouth when singing? "Whenever possible, breathe through the nose, as that ensures a deeper breath as well as being kinder to the throat." "Breathing through the nose is inefficient because 1) it is stilted and awkward, 2) it prohibits the swift and quiet inhalation of requisite amounts of air, and 3) it is inclined to lead to a high chest position, which induces throatiness." These two opinions written within six years of one another in the 1950's show that as with almost all aspects of vocal technique, concord and peaceful agreement is unknown among the experts. The advocates of nasal breathing point out that not only is it natural, but also ensures that outside air, which may be cold and contain particles damaging to the larynx, will be warmed and filtered before being drawn into the lungs. The mouth-breathing exponents emphasize the impossibility of taking in air through the nose quickly enough to meet the ordinary demands of singing. Certainly it is true that if air is drawn rapidly into the nose the resulting sound can only be described as a sniff. (This was a noise that marred the singing of the volatile, red-haired soprano Ljuba Welitsch.) Herbert

Witherspoon, a bass of some renown at the Metropolitan during the early part of this century, advises the readers of his manual to take breath through *both* nose and mouth.

Is there then one proper breathing technique? I can only cite the result of tests made to determine how eight important famous singers breathed which was published in 1948. Dr. E. Froeschels, a prominent laryngologist, found that *each one of the eight singers breathed differently.*

Attack! Up from the lungs rises the breath, having been taken in whatever fashion. Hurtling into the trachea, or windpipe, it encounters an extraordinary nut-sized organ known as the larynx which is the Greek word for "throat." Though we have come now to think of the larynx as the "voice box" there is every reason to suppose that while earliest man possessed one he had scarcely any voice at all. If one considers the matter, speaking and singing are not absolute requisites for survival, though many of us, once having known them, would not be much interested in an existence that did not include the use or the sound of the voice. A number of years ago the Doctors Jackson, professors of bronco-esophagology at Temple University, listed some of the truly important uses of the larynx that enable us to live.

1) Regulatory. The larynx is not just a passageway through which air flows into and out of the lungs. This tiny organ, a skeleton of cartilages bound together by ligaments and membranes, exerts a "delicate and co-operative" effect on the regulation of the interchange of carbon dioxide in the bloodstream, so that the level remains constant during all phases of breathing. The precision that the larynx possesses in controlling our respiration is vital to our survival.

2) Circulatory. Working like a valve, the larynx maintains a control of lung pressure. This in turn exerts a pumping action on the blood flowing through our thin, elastic vessels as well as on the heart itself. Another absolutely vital function.

3) **Fixative.** The next time you lift something slightly heavy, note how the larynx, probably quite unnoticed by you, locks air in your chest cavity. Try lifting something of comparable weight while continuing to breathe in and out and it will readily be seen what an important aid this fixative function of the larynx is to man's physical actions. Studies show that persons who for one reason or another have had their larynxes removed and with them the power to lock air within their bodies, are practically incapacitated for manual labor. This same fixing ability of the larynx also works during defecation, enabling straining at the stool.

4) **Protective.** Day and night the larynx keeps vigilant watch against the entrance of any matter into the air passage. In the event that a large crumb should enter the windpipe instead of the esophagus (the second pipeline in the throat down which food descends to the stomach), the tiny folds within the larynx instantly snap shut, blocking any further descent of the unwanted crumb. At the same time air pressure builds up in the thorax below the larynx. With equal rapidity, the tiny little ligaments now fly apart and the compressed air rushes out, blowing the crumb before it with a sound we describe as a cough. Without the vigilant larynx our lives would be in constant danger of "swallowing the wrong way" or of death by choking.

5) **Emotional.** Not everyone can sing and we all have to learn to speak. The larynx however provides a basic means of expression of our more animal emotions such as grief or terror through its ability to make a noise of sobbing or moaning or of crying out in delight.

Only this far down on the list of essential functions of the larynx do the Doctors Jackson place the voice, which they, while admitting that it has become rather vital in modern times, still say is not "an absolute necessity under ordinary circumstances."

To return, however, to the singing process, expelled breath, as has already been said, rushes into the versatile larynx. At the same time, solely by direction of the brain, wedge-shaped folds within the larynx dart out from either side and all but block the passage of the breath up to the mouth. Such is the pressure of the air that the ligaments are forced to give way in all or part of their length and a puff of air escapes through. In what is known as the "Bernoulli effect" the ligaments immediately resume their former position until the pressure of the air rising from below once again forces through a minute puff. This breath, chopped up at an incredible rate of speed, becomes sound. (Certainly it is no longer air. A properly trained singer can stand before a candle flame, and having taken a deep inhalation of air will expel it in the form of a wave of lovely sound; the flame close to the singer's mouth does not move.) The vocal cords or folds which have shut like gates across the glottis must however swing together smoothly, firmly and at the *exact* instant that the air strikes them in order to achieve what is known in singing as a perfect "attack."

"It was not an attack at all. She just opened her lips, and the tones dropped out like the pearls from the mouth of the princess in the fairy tale," wrote the vocally astute W. J. Henderson of the way Nellie Melba began a vocal phrase. "Or one might liken an attack of this kind to the beginning of a flow of water when a faucet is turned." Critics at the time that Melba was in her prime seem to make more of the attack than they do today. (Henderson says in the paragraph following his description of Melba, that the attack of the fabled, all but legendary Lilli Lehmann, "was imperfect throughout her career.") Possibly, vocal authorities of that time had become preoccupied with the attack because of another violent controversy that had broken out due to a confusion that has plagued the singing world ever since.

When in the middle of the nineteenth century Manuel Garcia II wrote in French a manual describing the mechanism of the singing voice he called the coming together or approximation of the vocal folds, "le coup de glotte" or in English, the "stroke" or worse still "blow of the glottis." To explain more clearly what he meant, he wrote, "By slightly coughing we become conscious of the existence and position of the glottis, and also of its opening and shutting action." The inevitable conclusion seemed to be that the great Garcia, inventor of the laryngoscope, god of vocal pedagogy, had advocated a method of attacking notes with a hard "h" sound like a very quick clearing of the throat. Immediately a whole school of teaching arose around this idea and pupils were instructed to strike their tones with a tiny edge to them. Nothing could be more disastrous for the voice. In order to make this sound like a catch in the throat the vocal cords have to bang together tightly an instant *before* the air from the lungs reaches them. The pressure then literally blows them apart. Such a violent process injures the vocal apparatus in a very short time. Yet this kind of attack was solemnly taught in the name of Garcia.* Actually when a note is correctly attacked a singer should have no feelings in his larynx at all.

Certain languages, however, demand this forceful, ejaculated way of striking a note. In good German a kind of rough click is imposed on vowels that begin words—for instance *"aber"* or *"echt."* As a result German voices often have a harsh quality from the violence with which the vocal folds are treated by the language. Spanish also calls for a sound like the soft clearing of the throat. Careful listening to the singing of Victoria de los Angeles and Monserrat Caballé will reveal this characteristic little Spanish clutching sound when these sopranos attack certain notes.

An "h" placed before a tone that is sung on a vowel will give the note a certain focus that it might otherwise lack, and we often hear a series of "ha-ha-has" rising from the throats of baritones and basses when, lacking agility, they come to grips with some of the florid music devised for them by Bach, Handel or Mozart.

Another faulty kind of attack also exists, less dangerous to the vocal apparatus, but scarcely welcome in the art of fine singing.

---

* Later, Garcia, appalled, was to write: "The meaning of the term, 'stroke of the glottis' which was invented by the author . . . has been seriously misrepresented and its misuse has done a great deal of harm."

In this case a tiny volume of air escapes past the edges of the vocal folds *before* they have come together. The result is a breathy tone as though the note being sung had been preceded by a tiny whisper. This kind of soft, aspirated singing we often expect to hear from sexy pop singers of today.

A Voice That Trembles. Air rising from the lungs forces its way through the gate-like folds across the glottis. Because of the tremendous pressure that blows them apart the number of vibrations of a note that a singer intends to hit rises fractionally higher than the precise frequency of the note. As the folds snap back to their original approximated position, the number of vibrations sinks a tiny bit below the true frequency of the note that is in the singer's mind. This deviation of frequency in the human voice, occurring with lightning-like speed, is known as vibrato, and means that in fact no singer sings precisely on pitch. Because this slight swerving to each side of the true pitch is small and, ideally, regular most ears hear the tones produced by a fine singer as being in tune.

Responses of people to vibrato in a singing voice are as varying and subjective as tastes in physical types. There can be no doubt that a vibrato invokes an atmosphere of the sensual, the voluptuous, though why this should be so is difficult to say. Witness this passage in George Moore's *Evelyn Innes,* a novel about a Catholic soprano, who, remorseful over the sinfulness of her career and her love affairs, seeks to return to the Church:

"Evelyn hummed the plain chant under her breath, afraid lest she should extinguish the pale voices and surprised how expressive the plain chant was when sung by these etiolated sexless voices. She had never known how much of her life of passion and desire had entered into her voice and she was shocked at its impurity . . . Her voice, she felt, must have revealed her past life to the nuns, her voice must have shocked them a little; her voice must have brought the world before them too vividly. For all her life was in her voice, she would never be able to sing this hymn with the same sexless grace as they did. Her voice would be always Evelyn Innes—Owen Asher's mistress."

Of singers in earlier times there is the usual speculation which voice buffs seem to find so enjoyable as to whether they employed vibrato in their singing. Some musical historians claim that the vocal music of the Renaissance was sung with a so-called "straight" tone, but that the vibrato was cultivated and used to ornament or embellish music. Today, when this music is re-created for us, singers who possess relatively vibrato-free voices or the ability to make them so, usually perform it, though there is no actual proof that the early voices sounded in this manner. Writing of singing in the eighteenth century, no less an authority than Mozart has this to say about vibrato in a letter to his father: "Meissner, as you know, has a bad habit in that he often intentionally vibrates his voice . . . and that I cannot tolerate in him. It is indeed truly detestable, it is singing entirely contrary to nature." Then he adds, "The human voice already vibrates of itself, but in such a degree that it is beautiful, that is the nature of the voice."

Mozart lived in a relatively relaxed time when it came to sexual mores. A century later with Victorian morality the dominant influence in parts of the Western world, there is much inveighing against the vibrato. It was sweeping "through Europe like the influenza" complained the young music critic, George Bernard Shaw, who was not without his prudish side. "I have the voice of a choirboy," Nellie Melba once proudly proclaimed, comparing her silvery tones to those piping singers who lack pulsations to their tones. Phonograph records of Melba and other singers of her time attest to the fact that many used much less vibrato than we are accustomed to today. "The vibrato is popular among the Latin races, while the Anglo-Saxons will not tolerate it." Dr. Holbrook Curtis, a noted American laryngologist, who treated the throats of many singers at the Metropolitan, wrote this in 1909, adding, "No great singer has ever succeeded in securing recognition in the

United States . . . who has attempted to secure his effects with a vibrato quality." Given the time he was writing and his familiarity with the artists at the Metropolitan, it was an odd statement to make. If ever there was a singer who secured "his effects" with a glorious vibrato quality it was Enrico Caruso, then in the prime of his adulation both in New York and London. Even as late as 1923 the singing teacher and authority on voice, Herman Klein, denounced vibrato as a "sin."

Oddly enough it was in the American mid-West where "sin" does not go unremarked, that a psychologist at the University of Iowa attempted to make "an objective analysis of artistic singing" during the late 1920's and into the thirties. Among Dr. Harold Seashore's discoveries was the fact that "individual differences in the capacity for hearing vibrato are very large In a normal population one individual may be 50 or 100 times as keen as another in this hearing . . . Each individual has his own illusion," he adds, "and his individual sense of the vibrato determines what shall be good or bad for him." This statement renders arguments between the fans of various singers over the tone quality of their favorites absolutely ludicrous, since it appears that *no two people hear the same voice the same way.* Measuring an aesthetic response is a dubious undertaking at best, but Seashore declared that a voice to sound beautiful should possess a smooth, regular vibrato of between five and a half to eight pulsations a second—the ideal being about six and a half. Such a conclusion, presumptuous as it may seem to measure beauty of tone, is given credence by the analysis of the vibratos of a number of famous singers of the time made by another investigator. Here are a few of the results:

Singer	Rate of Vibrato per second
Galli-Curci	7.4
Caruso	7.1
Martinelli	6.8
Gigli	6.3

He also found that when these singers performed concert selections and were not fighting a large-sized orchestra, the rate of the vibrato usually dropped by as much as one full vibration per second. Equally in climaxes or long-held notes, the swing either side of the true frequency increased to almost as much as a whole tone and the rate picked up to anywhere from eight to ten per second. Most ears interpret this wider swerve and increased rapidity of vibration as greater brilliance and excitement in a tone and applaud all the harder when the singer has left off.

A really wide swinging vibrato of a whole tone or more, when sung correctly goes by another name—the trill, or the more old fashioned word "shake." In this case our ears actually do make out the whirring of two distinct pitches, a half tone or whole tone apart, unlike an ordinary vibrato in which we hear a synthesis of the varying pitches. Coloratura sopranos have a particular fondness for the trill and may sometimes hold one for what seems like hours to the ears of an astonished and delighted audience.* Because the lower voices have longer and thicker vocal cords they take less readily to the trill, but the ability can be acquired through practice, though few low-voiced singers seem to have the patience to learn it. There are more trills for men's voice in opera than is perhaps generally realized. Walther von Stolzing in his Act One aria "Am stillen Herd" in *Meistersinger* has a whole measure's trill; Verdi writes a trill for the manly Rodrigo, friend of Don Carlo in the Third Act aria "Per me giunto." Handel and Rossini did not neglect to write trills for the bass voice as well, but these usually emerge as blobs of sound when performed by today's artists. Among those able to trill there is often discussion as to how to begin one—whether from the top note to the lower one, or the other way around. Not the least of the many amusing scenes in the memoirs of Lillie (Moulton) de Hegermann-Lindencrone

---

* A singer named Bernardine Hamaekers, who appeared at the Paris Opéra between 1857 and 1870, is supposed to have sung a trill at the end of "Caro Nome" that lasted one minute.

is her morning call on Jenny Lind-Goldschmidt, living in retirement at a villa on the French Riviera. The two ladies fell to discussing singing, and eventually the Swedish Nightingale asked the gifted American amateur to sing her a trill.

"I looked about for a piano to give me a note to start on," writes the ubiquitous Lillie. "But a piano was evidently the thing where the Goldschmidts had drawn the line. I made as good a trill as I could without one.

" 'Very good!' said she, nodding her head approvingly. 'I learned my trill this way.' And she made a trill for me, accentuating the upper note.

"Pointing her finger at me, she said, 'You try it.'

"I tried it. Unless one had learned to trill so it is very difficult to do; but I managed it somehow . . .

"Twelve o'clock sounded from a cuckoo-clock in the next room, and I felt that my visit, fascinating as my angel was, must come to an end. I left her still standing on the verandah in her white brocade, and as I walked off she made the trill as an adieu."

A trill can be learned and some of the great singers have taken the trouble to do so. John McCormack was the possessor of a beautiful trill and even a soprano with the immense voice of Kirsten Flagstad could trill, as a record she made of the aria from Weber's *Oberon* "Ozean zu Ungeheur" attests. She was less successful with the sustained high F' sharp trill that Wagner demands of Brünnhilde in her enormously difficult opening "Ho-jo-to-ho" at the beginning of Act Two of *Die Walküre*. Indeed though one usually thinks of a trill in association with the florid music of Donizetti or Rossini, Brünnhilde has to sing several trills in the course of the *Ring*, particularly in *Siegfried* where the tenor is supposed to join her in these rapidly vibrating notes of ecstasy during the Awakening Scene.

Producing a wide vibrato, that is a trill, can be learned by deliberately acquiring the agility to alternate two notes in the voice. It is also possible to gain the skill of taking vibrato *out* of a tone, though oddly this is not a vocal exercise but a mental one. The singer has to think dead center of the note and then imitate it with his voice. William Vennard, a distinguished voice teacher, makes the interesting suggestion that singers who wish to obtain a perfect vibrato-free tone should apply to the public relations department of the Bell Telephone Company for their record of baritone computer singing, "Daisy, Daisy give me your answer do." À propos of the machine's performance he adds dryly that automation seems to be "less a threat to the arts than to any other profession."

Unlovely and Unwanted.   So far we have discussed the vibrato, which, except by those who might almost be accused of prurience, is considered a virtue in today's singing voice. High on the list of what constitutes bad singing is that quality of tone which resembles a quaver, or the slow turning over of a car motor on an icy morning. This unattractive, undesirable effect goes under various names, most commonly, "tremolo," but also "wobble." (I have seen the word "judder" in a British manual of singing, though it does not appear in the shorter version of *The Oxford English Dictionary*.)

Here again we are caught in a tangle of confused semantics. It was Dr. Seashore's idea to do away with the term "tremolo" and call it "bad vibrato," since each listener has a varying concept of what is "bad" vibrato to his ears. A later writer on the subject declares that "there is no such thing as having a 'bad vibrato' and the term is self-contradictory." In his *Bel Canto,* Cornelius L. Reid states instead that the term vibrato stands for exactly one thing, a cycle that "is completed about six and a half times each second with absolute consistency." The tremolo, which some people refer to as excessive vibrato, often has as many as eight pulsations per second; the slow moving wobble is made up of four vibrations per second. What makes these sounds unattractive to the ear is the fact that the pulsations are irregular and the swerve to either side of the pitch uneven. Just as a singer works to achieve a smoothness of tone quality throughout his range, in the case of the vibrato, evenness of periodicity and frequency fluctuation is essential.

As I have mentioned elsewhere an intense vibrato or shiver seems to be innate to the voices heard in eastern Europe and Russia, nor does it offend the ears of audiences. In Western climes the voices of Negro singers like Leontyne Price often have a pronounced vibrato, a quality which some people find not to their taste. But then vibrato *is* a matter of taste. The tremolo or wobble, however, must be accounted a distinct vocal fault caused by too little breath support, nervousness, which of course affects the breath, or old age, which diminishes it. Muscular tensions within the throat, a kind of tensing and clutching at the tones may also be a cause of tremolo. A mainly involuntary vocal fault, it is not an easy one to correct. Sometimes the more the unfortunate vocalist struggles to eliminate a tremolo, the more likely he is to make it worse. Breathing exercises, singing pianissimo and above all trying to establish in the singer's mind the idea of a tone free of tremolo or wobble are some of the means of correcting this unlovable, unwanted sound.

Another Battlefield. Within the tiny cave of the larynx, breath expelled from the lungs is chopped up by the pulsating vocal folds, creating a basic sound. Curiously, that sound, though born of muscular action, is "thought" into being. That is to say, the brain directs the cords to produce the tone of every note sung in whatever infinite variety of tone color and loudness. Even more curious is the fact that while singers experience a number of different sensations as they perform, they do not, or at least *should* not, feel them in the larynx, where in fact their song is being produced. Most vocalists, except for light sopranos, are aware of vibrations at the base of the neck and the top of the chest while singing low notes. Tones in the middle of the range produce a feeling of fullness at the back of the mouth and the top of the throat. And in the top part of the compass singers have very real sensations that their high notes are proceeding from somewhere behind the nose or eyebrows or even out of the top of the head.

The most uninformed amateur can feel these basic changes of sensation by singing "ah" up the scale from a note comfortably situated in the middle of his voice. If he tries to maintain this same comfortable feeling as he continues higher and higher, he will find it increasingly difficult to keep his original vocal position. Moreover the sound that he makes as he attempts to force his way upward will become "shouty" and unpleasant. Finally, if he continues to push on in this same vocal position there will be a sudden sound like a truncated cackle and his voice will have "broken." Let him repeat this experiment, however, but at the note which begins to strain his voice, make an adjustment to the level of his larynx, letting it sink back very slightly, and he will then be able to continue up the scale feeling a different set of sensations, much more, now, in the head. The tones too, particularly if he is an amateur, will have a different timbre.

The most uninformed amateur can also hear the sharply differing tone quality of the husky chest tones in women's voices, just as they recognize the fluty, comic sound that men can make known as falsetto. In both cases different sets, of sensations accompany the singing of these odd types of tones. The variety of physical feelings that a singer experiences when producing a variety of different kinds of tone quality brings us to the phenomenon of registers—a subject over which rages full scale warfare.

As far back as the seventeenth century the singing voice is mentioned as having two basic qualities of tone. Since within the voice two sets of notes had a distinctive quality they came to be called registers like the registers of an organ with its series of pipes that make tones resembling one another in quality. In an early manual on singing, Giambattista Mancini wrote in 1774: "The voice in its natural state is ordinarily divided into two registers,

one of which is called the chest, the other the head or falsetto."
In his use of the term falsetto, Mancini unwittingly stirred up
the most frightful turmoil among those seeking to understand the
registers of the voice, for to others, falsetto meant not the ordinary
top part of a singing voice, but an artificial voice, higher and ludicrous sounding (to most ears) when sounded by a man, and eerie
and unhuman when emerging with a peanut whistle sound from
the few sopranos who have ever managed the trick of producing
it. As a result, even modern manuals of singing emulate the use of
the Mancini term and divide up the voice into chest and falsetto
registers, leaving those who understand falsetto as completely
different, utterly confused.*

Even before his invention of the laryngoscope Manuel Garcia
II had defined a register of the voice as "a series of consecutive
homogeneous sounds produced by one mechanism, different essentially from another series of sounds equally homogeneous . . ."
A view of the cords seemed to prove this; they could be seen to
take on a specific shape and density and vibrate during one section
of notes or "register" in the voice and change quite definitely
when the singer used another set of tones with a different quality.

In the early 1880's, Emil Behnke, a voice teacher with a sound
knowledge of anatomy, succeeded in obtaining the first photographs of the glottis in song, in this case his own. These showed
that at the bottom of the range the edges of the vocal folds were
thick, dense and impenetrable to light; also that they vibrated
throughout their entire length. Singing the middle notes of the
compass caused the folds to lengthen slightly and become thin,
tense and translucent. In this phase they still continued to vibrate
for their entire length. When Behnke sang his top notes the vocal
folds did something extraordinary. A portion of them came to-

---

* Viktor Fuchs relates that at the Third Congress of International Society for
Logopaedia and Phoniatry in Vienna in 1920 a professor gave a talk on "The need
for a generally acknowledged nomenclature for the physiology, pathology and
training of the voice. Unfortunately it was impossible to please all the members of
the Society and the fine plans were abandoned."

gether at one end and locked tight, so that the breath could only pass through a partial aperture between the folds. This had the effect of shortening the vibrating lengths and raising the pitch of the note being sung. In addition Behnke was able to observe that if he attempted to sing his high notes while retaining the position of his middle register, the folds, usually a pearly white or pale pink in color, turned bright red in anger at such abusive treatment. Behnke also confirmed a theory of Garcia's that there were two subdivisions to the lower and medium registers of the voice. In partnership with a distinguished laryngologist, Lennox Browne, he published his findings in a book called *Voice, Song and Speech.* To enrich the brew of confusion, however, these men along with several others changed the nomenclature to read for Garcia's chest register, "thick reed"; for the medium, "thin reed"; and the head, "small." To the subregisters they gave the names, "lower thick" and "upper thick" and "lower thin" and "upper thin." This book setting forth their scientific theories with a relative amount of clarity sold widely (an undated secondhand copy in my possession is marked "Twenty-third edition") and the "method" was taken up and taught on both sides of the Atlantic.

Unfortunately the glottis as seen by the camera settled absolutely nothing. In the first place, disclaimers asked if these were accurate pictures of the folds in normal singing, considering that the singer had to vocalize half choking over an object in his throat. They also pointed out that they were pictures of a vocalist who sang by a certain method. Would photographs of the glottis of a singer who sang in another way be the same? And what of the great teachers and singers of the past, demanded those ever wistful for the golden age of bel canto? They had described only two registers. Why now were there thought to be three?

The threats and denunciations mounted. Investigations continued and scientific manuals poured from the press propounding new theories illustrated by vaguely obscene looking drawings and photographs of the vocal apparatus. All claims were put forth with absolute authority and conviction that brooked no contradiction nor any other possible explanation.

Well over a century after the invention of the laryngoscope, that supposed shiny key to a scientific understanding of the voice, how do we stand today in our knowledge of the registers? Here are excerpts from important manuals on the technique of singing, almost all of which have either been published for the first time or re-published from older editions *within the past twenty years.*

"Register changes are no more inherent in the anatomy of the vocal cords than they are in the construction of a violin . . ."

"According to natural laws the voice is made up of only *one* register, which constitutes its entire range."

"As Mancini categorically stated, 'all voices divide themselves into two registers,' the first duty of the teacher is to recognize this condition and to take proper steps necessary to establishing them in their divided form."

"Most teachers and singers now believe that both men's and women's voices consist of three registers—chest (lowest), middle and head (highest)."

"There are altogether four resonance walls and consequently four registers."

"All five registers are usually present in the contralto voice."

". . . it is not surprising that some pretend to tell us that there are two, three, four or five registers. It will be much more correct to call every voice by the name of a new additional register, for in the end every tone will and *must* be taken in a different re-lation."

"As the whole conception of voice registers is a hazardous one it is best to disregard their existence altogether."

Of two authoritative *medical* manuals on the voice published in the last two decades, one ducks the entire question of registers altogether, while the other gives this tentative advice: "Use the terms *upper and lower register* to refer to the two vocal ranges . . .

In some cases we might sub-divide to upper, middle and lower registers. One is thus committed to no theory of function."

This little survey omits the scorn and vituperation heaped upon one expert by another for enumerating the registers differently, or for declaring or denying their existence, nor does it convey the often astonishing amount of self-praise that rises like heavy scent from the pages of these books. *"I have proved that there is but one continuous register in a voice—any voice,"* triumphantly proclaims the author (italics hers) of one such manual, finishing up her treatise with a paean to the "youthful freshness, quality and power" of her voice for more than forty years, not to speak of her praiseworthy musicianship.

On the subject of registers, G.B. Shaw with his superior insights into matters of singing had this to say:

"The laryngoscope has proved that the old tradition of three voices coming from the chest, the throat and the head respectively, had, in the registering mechanism, a foundation of physiological fact; but as to how many registers can be made, how many *should* be made, whether any at all ought to be made, whether the old names should be retained, which is which and what practical conclusions the singing master should draw; on all these points there exist not only differences of opinion, but feuds—deadly, implacable vendettas—in which each party regards all the others as imposters, quacks, voice smashers, ignoramuses, rascals and liars."

Shaw's words are as fresh and pertinent today as when he wrote them eighty years ago.

Tell Me No Lies. Then what, if anything, are we to make of this mass of contradictions? Ever hopeful of enlightenment, let us review these conflicting theories of the registers in more depth beginning with perhaps the most complicated one, that every note of the singing voice is a register unto itself. It is a concept that contains more than a little truth. Certainly with the sounding of each note in the range of a human voice, subtle, tiny muscular changes must take place within the larynx. No two notes of a different pitch, quality or volume are produced exactly alike. Therefore in one sense every note *is* a register. The idea, however, begs the question of the obvious basic changes in the vocal mechanism, as high speed photographs have shown of some of the different positions that the vocal folds take during singing.

Next, there are those who believe that there are only two registers to the singing voice: the chest and the head. Some, tradition-bound to "bel canto" theories, even cling to the old terminology and refer to the normal top of the voice—not the strange, artificial one sounded an octave higher—as falsetto. The two-register advocates point out that the major break in the male voice, when it goes into a head tone, and the female voice, when it changes to a chest tone, occurs within the same range: approximately D to F above middle C, *on exactly the same pitches*—not, as might be supposed, an octave apart. In the main, the male voice uses the chest register up to this break, after which it goes into the head register. The head quality, however, can be brought down and imposed on notes lower than where the break occurs, creating a nice blend of the two kinds of sound.

The two-register believers also assert that the higher women's voices use the head register for the top two-thirds of their compass and pass down through the break into the chest tone. They contend that this head quality can be brought into the chest tone, smoothing over the break or disparate quality of the two registers. It is *universally* agreed that for both men and women to take the chest register up beyond its natural range will be fatal to the voice, causing the high notes to go flat or be lost altogether. Finally the disciples of the two-register theory point out that the tenor and the contralto, who share a goodly number of the exact same pitches, will have the most difficulty in adjusting their two registers as they pass over the area of the break and attempt to make all their notes sound with an equalized quality.

The three-register school, to prove their theories, will point to photographs of the vocal folds, showing how they are thick and comparatively slack when the chest register is being sung, how they become thinner and tense looking in the medium register, and how only part of the ligaments vibrate in the top register. To prove their thesis they might also take as an example an untrained dramatic soprano. This young woman may possess heavy contralto-like tones, joined to a veiled, weak middle part of her voice in which she finds it uncomfortable to sing. On the top will be a high soprano of a light, almost fluty quality; in short, three distinct vocal sounds. Three voices, three registers say the supporters of this school. Three voices or three registers which must somehow be made to melt into one another to produce an evenness of quality throughout the compass. Even in a well-trained dramatic soprano these separate qualities of tone are sometimes exposed. One of the best arguments for the three-register theory I know of is to listen to the three different qualities of tone in the voice of the dramatic soprano Ina Souez singing *"Come scoglio"* in the old Glyndebourne recording of *Così fan Tutte*. This also explains why the dramatic soprano is such a difficult voice to train.

Those who opt for the three-register idea are merely saying that beside the basic break which the two-register devotees acknowledge, there is another one approximately an octave higher in the woman's voice, when she goes into her head tone. Some who subscribe to this idea also say that a man has only two registers, and this is why the woman's voice is more difficult to train in general. Others believe that the male and female voices both have three registers and the break in the male voice occurs anywhere from A, to C,. If a man wants to produce a true chest tone he can do so by using a kind of belch—rather the way a female can sound her chest tones by imitating the quacking of a duck. Otherwise the male chest tone merges more simply with his medium register than does that of the female.

Those who assure us that the singing voice has five registers are in fact closely allied with the three-register school. By subdividing the chest and medium into "upper" and "lower" registers they maintain that it is possible to sing the same note in two different positions, so that the singer experiences different sensations when he does so. Hence the upper chest overlaps the lower medium, and the upper medium merges with certain notes of the head register. This more elaborate concept is aimed at smoothing out the *two* breaks they claim exist in the voice, which are the bane of many student singers.

The four-register man is rather a loner compared to the multitudinous disciples of some of the other theories. He allies himself with the three-register idea but points out that we are forgetting a fourth—the strange, unnatural sound of the falsetto. In the male it is a quality of tone easy to recognize and one that usually brings forth laughter. His sensations when singing falsetto are entirely different than when producing tones in his other registers. There is an odd feeling of letting go and blowing through the open glottis, which then creates this curious hooty sound. (Other men, of course, may feel entirely different sensations. I am describing my own.) Whatever they may be, this series of notes exists as an entity, and therefore may legitimately be considered another register in the male voice.

The odd sounding fourth register at the top of a man's voice is useful to the tenor, who when diminishing his pianissimo high head tones, if he is skillful, can merge them into a falsetto without most ears being able to detect the change. For this reason the falsetto is sometimes referred to as the "tenorino" register. Overuse of these high, crooned falsetto tones, however, may be dangerous to the tenor's low tones. Richard Crooks, the much admired somewhat stolid American lyric tenor, who sang at the Metropolitan during the thirties, is supposed to have been a casualty to an indulgence in falsetto.

Not so much is made of the fourth "whistle" register in the female voice that is the equivalent of the male falsetto. The highest notes in the voice of Lily Pons, her F″ and G″ above high

C'' which required that the Mad Scene in *Lucia* be transposed *up* for her convenience, were not produced in the same way as the tones around high C''. To sing these highest notes, far from opening her mouth wider as do most singers when emitting their top tones, Pons half closed her mouth and let out her pure, if thin altitudinous sounds, looking slightly startled as if she didn't quite know where they were coming from. Indeed in the opera house they seemed to emerge from somewhere behind her. The production of this whistle-like tone has been compared to the violinist's technique of playing a harmonic, which he does by not pressing a particular string down the whole way so that it vibrates an octave higher.

At the Sistine Chapel in Rome, the great soprano Emma Calvé heard a Turkish *castrato* named Mustafà utter "strange, sexless tones, superhuman, uncanny" which he called his fourth voice. "You have only to practice with your mouth shut for two hours a day," he told her when she asked how to sing these tones. "At the end of two years, you may possibly be able to do something with them." Determined, Calvé went to work and after three years mastered the use of this fourth voice. Its notes, as one listener commented, were "very sweet with a noticeable difference in timbre from the usual tones of the singing voice, and with a distinct bell-like quality—a reflection, delicate and evanescent, rather than an echo of the other voice." In her memoirs Calvé admits that she was never able to pass on the secret of producing this falsetto or fourth register to any of her pupils.

And what of the idea that there is only one register in the voice? This is often put forth by authorities who agree that there may be changes in tone quality in different parts of the voice, but don't want singers, particularly novices, to become selfconscious about these so-called breaks. It is certainly true that some singers from their student days on have no trouble in knitting up changes of tone quality so that the voice seems to possess only one register. Others have to work hard for years smoothing away these abrupt transitions of tone that are considered aesthetically displeasing in the art of song. Therefore the one-register idea has validity if only as a teaching method: if no attention is called to the mechanism that produces changes of tone quality in the voice, then hopefully, the notes will emerge naturally equalized. Viktor Fuchs quotes Professor Martienssen-Lehmann, a teacher of singing, as writing: *"One register is not a starting point but a goal."*

"There are rare examples," writes Mancini, "in which one has received from nature the most unusual gift of being able to execute everything in the chest voice." It all depends what he meant by "everything." Many female pop singers belt out their songs entirely in the chest register, which makes them one-register vocalists, but the range of the music they perform is not great. The extraordinary Kirsten Flagstad with her warm, voluminous lower tones, produced them by bringing down her medium or head register (depending on whether we go by the two- or three-register theory) deep into the region where an ordinary dramatic soprano must use the chest tone if the notes are to project. Flagstad, then, under the two-register theory, was a one-register singer.

And finally there is the no-register concept. But surely this is another way of saying that every note is a register unto itself; and we have come full circle.

Vibrations of Sympathy. Two basic factors then, breath and the vibrating vocal folds, produce tone within the larynx. These, however, are not enough to produce the beautiful sounds of a singing voice as we ultimately hear them. In experiments on patients about to undergo removal of the larynx because of cancer, an incision was made in the windpipe just above the voice box and they were then asked to phonate. The resulting sounds were small and weak. Access had been cut off to the third essential factor in the singing process—the resonators.

This term refers to cavities that surround the larynx and which vibrate in sympathy with the basic tone set up by the fluttering folds. Of these resonators one of the most important is thought to be the cavity above the throat known as the soft palate, or pharynx. Also influential is the mouth with its bony arched roof and rows of teeth having hard resonating surfaces. Below the larynx lies the trachea, a cartilaginous tube believed by some to add sympathetic and enriching overtones to the voice. Finally there is the larynx itself. A number of authorities think it may be an even more important resonator than the pharynx.

In the past, a good deal of attention has also been paid to the chest, the nose and the sinuses behind the nose as important resonators, simply because singers feel vibrations in these areas when they perform. But the chest or top of the thoracic cage where the vocalist has definite sensations when he sings low notes contains a kind of insulating material which far from adding richness to the tone would seem to deaden it. The nose too, is lined with soft unvibratory membrane and we are all familiar with the unlovely sound it can produce when we direct vocal resonance into it. The nose is the last place that a singer wants to sing to produce a lovely tone. Some evidence exists that the various sinuses behind the nose and under the eyes may vibrate fractionally with the note that is produced in the singer's throat. But though the singer may have pronounced sensations in his head (the feeling of singing his so-called "head tones,"), there is strong reason to believe that he hears these vibrations by conduction to his ears, and that *the audience does not,* as these vibrations have no way of getting out and mixing with the tones emerging from the singer's mouth. This is one of the explanations why singers, and of course non-singers as well, are often surprised and shocked when their recorded voices are played back to them.

It is the singer's resonators then that add the final beauty and power and quality to the tone produced. Much is written of the importance of "placing" a voice. This term refers to these all-important resonators which vary in shape and size in every person, thus creating the infinite diversity of tone that singing voices possess. In placing his voice, a singer learns mainly through sensation to use his resonators to their best advantage, so that they add brilliance—"ring" is a word frequently used—to his tones. Paradoxically, though he feels sensations in resonators which contribute little or nothing to the emergent sound, they nonetheless seem to set off vibrations in other parts of his mouth and throat which produce the desired quality of voice that he wants. Thus these sensations, if physically illusory, are important to a singer's vocal technique.

I have used the word "illusory" once again. Looking back on this little survey of the theory of voice production, we can now perceive of what stuff "vocal science" is actually made. Almost everything to do with the technique of singing seems to be unclear, guessed at or not understood at all. Even the act of singing is commenced by a mental concept and controlled by illusory sensations.

No wonder then that singing seems like a kind of magic—for that is almost what it is.

PART FIVE

THE AGES

OF VOICE

I

.........At first the infant,
Mewling and pewking in the nurse's arms.

They tell a lovely tale in the world of the singing voice that the
first cry of the newborn Adelina Patti was a perfect F″ above
high C″. Less gifted newborn babies utter their first cries at a
pitch of around A′ or B′ and do so to rid the glottis of that curse
to all singers, an accretion of mucus. For this reason the first
human sounds are apt to be hoarse in quality. Immanuel Kant
devoted a long chapter of his *Anthropologie* to the first cry of an
infant, declaring that it may well have been a dangerous characteristic in primitive man, since these first sounds would betray
the mother weakened by childbirth and her helpless infant to
beasts of prey. Actually the cry is a sign that the infant will live,
for with the viscous phlegm cleared from his throat he can now
take a proper breath.

Experts, as usual, disagree over the length of the vocal folds of
the newborn infant, though all admit that they are very tiny indeed—anywhere from three to nine millimeters long. At between
two and four weeks old, according to one authority, Dr. Paul J.
Moses, an infant emits "about six to eight half tones in the middle
soprano range . . . interspersed with high notes, occasionally as high

as high C″." At fourteen weeks he starts to make sounds not unlike singing. Over the next months his range develops mightily, and another scientist in a paper with the delightful title, "An Acoustical Study of the Pitch of Infant Hunger Wails" declares that by the time a baby is nine months old it can produce sounds ranging between 207 to 2631 vibrations per second—a compass calculated to excite the envy of the most richly endowed coloratura soprano. In addition, he breathes perfectly and has a faultless vocal technique, so that he never develops hoarseness nor other flaws of tone quality that mar the song of older singers. In later life vocalists sometimes have to learn to "throw" their voices, so that they project to the back of theaters and auditoriums in which they sing. Not so the infant—as we all know. His voice, with its unforced vocal production, carries perfectly.

I I

And then the whining schoolboy, with his satchel
And shining morning face . . .

At the age of four, the same year that Freud has stated that a child's sexual impulses are at a heightened state, the voice loses something of its infantile piping quality and begins to strike a slightly more personal and sexual note. There is little if any differentiation between the male and female tone or range. From this age children can be trained to sing and by the time they are seven will have a compass of anywhere from ten to thirty-one half tones. Besides continuing to develop, the vocal folds are constantly subjected to shouts and shrieks and other violent shocks inflicted by their youthful possessors. For this reason the voices of pre-adolescent boys and girls will sometimes be heard to "break"; but this is not the true mutation that comes with puberty. Children, particularly by the time they have reached eleven or twelve, often have extensive ranges and love to squeak out very high notes as a kind of game. The rare, extreme top tones or "whistle register" heard occasionally in sopranos (whose voices often have a childish quality anyway) is thought to be a left-over from these pre-adolescent days.

Sometimes if children possess naturally beautiful voices, especially boy sopranos, they are trained, particularly in England. Most authorities seem to think, however, that except for instilling musicianship into a child, to impose extra strain on the delicate, still developing vocal apparatus may ruin it forever. Occasionally, as a result of training the pre-adolescent voice, nodes, the wart-like growths on the vocal folds that all singers dread, have been found in the throats of boy sopranos.

Aside from one or two boy singers who have soared to a limited amount of fame in England—often singing selections such as "O for the Wings of a Dove"—vocalists who became celebrated while they were pre-adolescent are practically non-existent. In the thirties when child movie stars were the vogue, Shirley Temple piped her untuned ditties in a "cute" but scarcely inspiring voice. We also had a boy soprano movie star named Bobby Breen. As his contemporary I remember hating him, for not only was he a goody-goody but I was certain that my voice was much better than his. On the whole, children's lungs (whatever our experience to the contrary) simply do not have the capacity to sustain the line and volume required for good singing. One exception, however, did exist, if we can believe the mass of astonishing material written about her.

The Diva.   In the spring of 1850 at a charity concert in New York City, a seven-year-old girl with round brown eyes stood on a table and with the same self-assured manner that never left her throughout fifty-five years of appearing in public, sang "by ear" the enormously difficult "Casta Diva" from *Norma*. Moreover she gave it with all the interpolated ornaments and embellishments fashionable at the time. For the next five years Adelina Patti made a successful and lucrative career as a child soprano touring the United States and Cuba, sometimes performing alone, or jointly with the celebrated pianist Louis Gottschalk, or the equally well-known violinist Ole Bull. Charming audiences wherever she went, she was most charmed, we are told, by her dolls waiting for her in her dressing room. "Correct breathing, scales, shakes, ornaments, fioriture of every kind, all came naturally to her," writes Patti's contemporary, Herman Klein, and whatever she needed to be taught, "thanks to a marvellous ear, she could instantly repeat." These were the P.T. Barnum years and in a country inclined to applaud the prodigious more than the artistic, one wonders how childish in quality little Adelina's voice actually was. Obviously a musical marvel and a born imitator the way most prodigies are, did she have the physical strength to sing plausibly the long, sinuous phrases of the "Casta Diva" that have exhausted in their time the sturdiest of prima donnas?

Yet here is part of an account by another contemporary, the conductor and composer, Luigi Arditi, who with his musical friend Bottesini, received a call from the little girl in the company of her mother and her doll. After the child had "demurely placed her music on the piano," she asked him to accompany her in the Rondo of *Sonnambula*.

"How am I to give an adequate description of the effect which that child's miraculous notes produced upon our enchanted senses? Perhaps if I say that both Bottesini and I wept genuine tears of emotion, tears which were the outcome of the original and never-to-be-forgotten impressions her voice made when it first stirred our innermost feelings, that may, in some slight measure convince my readers of the extraordinary vocal power and beauty of which little Adelina was, at that tender age possessed. We were simply amazed, nay electrified, at the well-nigh perfect manner in which she delivered some of the most difficult and varied arias without the slightest effort or self-consciousness."

Remarkable she certainly must have been—which makes one

wonder how many other "mute inglorious" Pattis have existed in musical history unheard and undetected because they were born into non-musical families or backgrounds. Both Patti's parents were in fact singers: she was born at Madrid an indecently short time after her mother had sung the role of Norma at the Royal Opera House. Her sister, Carlotta, also sang professionally. (A rival prima donna of Adelina's is not reluctant to declare, "if the truth must be told, many people found Carlotta the more satisfactory singer of the two.") At any rate the little girl was surrounded by musicians who were there to "discover" her when she sang her first phrase.

They were also there five years later to advise on what was probably the most important single step she ever took in her extraordinary career. At the age of twelve Patti "retired" from the public for two years presumably because her astute and vocally experienced family forbade her to sing during the most dangerous of vocal ages—adolescence.

SINGING FAMILIES

One thinks of a beautiful singing voice as an accident, a very rare occurrence. And yet there have been several in one family. Here are a few instances.

Emmy Strömer-Ackté—mother of Aino Ackté, soprano, and her sister the mezzo-soprano, Irma Tervani

Andrews—three famous sisters

Carl David Bjoerling—father of three singer sons including Jussi whose son Rolf is also a singer

Boswell—two sisters including Connie

Castagna—two sisters

De Reszke—two brothers and a sister

Willi Domgraf-Fassbänder—a daughter, Brigitte

Garcia—father, mother, son, two daughters

Judy Garland—daughter, Liza Minnelli

Giannini—father, two daughters including Dusolina

Gigli—father and daughter

Grisi—two sisters

Homer—mother and daughter both named Louise

Selma Kurz—and her daughter Desi Halban

Konetzni—two sisters

Karl August Lehmann—a tenor married to Maria Theresia Lehmann-Löw, also a singer. They were parents of Lilli and Marie

Anton Ludwig—a tenor married to Eugenie Ludwig-Besalla, a contralto, had a daughter whom they named Christa

Manski—mother, Dorothee, daughter, Inge

Marchesi—father, mother, daughter

Nevada—mother and daughter

Patti—father, mother, two daughters including Adelina

Pickens—two sisters, including Jane

Pinza—father, Ezio and daughter, Claudia

Ponselle—sisters Rosa and Carmela

Ravogli—sisters Sophia and Giuglia

Rysanek—sisters Leonie and Lotte

Frances Saville—and her niece Frances Alda

Sinatra—Frank and his son and daughter

Tetrazzini—sisters Eva and Luisa

Van Zandt—Jennie, mother of Marie (the first Lakmé)

Weber—sisters Josepha and Aloysia

Fritz Windgassen—a tenor married to the mezzo-soprano Vally van Osten, the parents of tenor Wolfgang. His aunt was soprano Eva von der Osten

Albert Wagner—oldest brother of Richard was a light tenor and father of the celebrated Johanna Wagner, a soprano

III

> ....*And then the lover,*
> *Sighing like a furnace, with a woeful ballad*
> *Made to his mistress' eyebrow.*

The awkward age—all arms and legs, stumbling over things, gawkiness—and the voice with its unexpected cracked tones, one

note that of a child, the next of a man. During adolescence a youth's
vocal folds grow with the same astonishing rapidity as his body.
Within six months they may lengthen a whole centimeter, as well
as thicken. Is it any wonder that the bewildered adolescent presented with these new, seemingly enormous ligatures, "trips" on
them much as he does over the newly acquired length of his hands
and feet? Just as with his members, he has to retrain or even
develop a whole new set of muscles to control the odd, new
sounds that now arise from his throat.

Aurally the process is less evident in the female whose speaking voice, which sounds slightly husky during the period of mutation, drops only two or three tones in pitch whereas a boy's will
usually deepen a whole octave. This is because the vocal folds of
the adolescent girl lengthen only three or four millimeters. Nonetheless she too has to learn to manage the changed apparatus of
her speaking and singing voice, and mutation for her—a process
which in the female usually takes place two years earlier than the
male—is also a critical vocal age, lasting the same length of time,
a minimum again of two years.*

What high school anywhere in the Western world is without
its choral group or glee club? Considered wholesome and bene-
ficial, group singing brings together confused adolescents trying to
sort out a hundred different identities and gives them a communal
one in a shared love for singing and music. Ironically, there is
good reason to suppose that this same much approved activity may
mar or even destroy many incipient fine singing voices; ironic
too, to consider that the average high school music teacher in discovering an attractive or interesting voice, singles it out for attention and (quite naturally) piles extra strain upon it, rather
than asking its possessor to keep silent until the process of mutation has definitely taken place. Various books have been written,

* During her voice change in her early teens, Luisa Tetrazzini, who had sung
soprano as a child, thought she was a contralto. She always had a pronounced
break in her voice.

usually by choirmasters reluctant to lose years of training to the inexorability of nature, explaining how the young male may sing through the time of his voice break supposedly by simply singing the old boyish top tones, now cracked, an octave down in his new man's register. But with the exception of one or two whose passion for the boy's voice blinds them to good sense, all the authorities warn, even thunder against adolescents singing during mutation. Of course boys and girls have sung while their voices were changing and developed into fine singers. It is interesting to note, however, that in England where choirboys are frequently urged to continue singing after the breaking process has begun, a study showed that out of a selected number who had sung well as boys about two per cent turned into good adult singers, a fact "attributed to the irreparable damage contracted in adolescence."

The strange change that takes place in the human throat confirms how directly connected are the singing voice and sex. As most people know, if a boy fails to mature sexually or is castrated before adolescence he will retain his child's small larynx coupled with a man's body; surgery which prevents a female's sexual development will cause her to retain her "little girl's" voice too. A woman's menstrual cycle also appears to be connected with her voice. Swelling often occurs in the turbes at the back of the nose causing the voice to sound husky just before the onset of a period. For this reason women singers may have clauses in their contracts excusing them from appearing during these times, a practice, however, more common in Europe than the United States. Sometimes this swelling adds resonance to a voice and it will sound enriched.

The sexual characteristics and the voice that young men and women develop during pubescence very often are directly linked. Thus women with deep contralto voices may have large bodies, heavy features and excess facial and body hair, while men with high tenor voices frequently turn out short, fleshy and without much need of a razor. The eunuch-like Pardoner in Chaucer's tale was one of these:

> A voys he hadde as small as hath a goot.
> No berd hadde he, no nevere sholde have,
> As smothe it was as it were late y-shave.

"In both sexes those who mature early have high voices, and those who mature late are inclined to have low voices," writes an authoritative laryngologist, Irving Voorhees. But it must be pointed out that he uses the word "inclined" and that there are definite exceptions to his statement. He also tells us that "nearly all boy sopranos become baritones or basses," * but again there is that qualifying "nearly" which makes this a general rule rather than a fixed one. Sometimes, indeed, boys' voices don't turn into anything at all, but keep their treble quality. This may be due to some kind of pubescent atrophy of, or accident to the testes. Very rarely, a web of membrane stretched across the glottis allows the breath to pass but inhibits growth of the vocal ligatures. When this membrane, an accident of birth, is divided or removed, the voice will develop properly.

For one who has a pleasing voice as a child and has begun to dream of becoming an adult singer, waiting through pubescence to see what kind of voice will develop adds yet another agony to these frequently tormented years. "All last winter I could not sing a note. I was in despair; I thought I had lost my voice," the thirteen-year-old Marie Bashkirtseff, never one to conceal her feelings, reported to her journal. "Now it has come back again, my voice, my treasure, my fortune . . . I said nothing but I was cruelly grieved. I did not dare to speak of it. I prayed to God and he has heard me! What happiness. What a pleasure it is to sing well!"

But in fact if there is a voice and talent to go with it the pains of adolescence are nothing compared to those of making a career.

* The voice of the celebrated Luigi Lablache is said to have dropped overnight from high soprano to deep bass.

IV

. . . . Then a soldier.
. . . .
Seeking the bubble reputation,
Even in the cannon's mouth.

What are the necessary basic requirements for an aspiring singer to go out into a treacherous world to fight for fame and fortune? Rossini is said to have answered, "Voice first, voice second, voice third." (This plump, neurasthenic composer much given to *mots* is also reported to have said of Adelaide Kemble, one of England's first international singers "To sing as she does three things are needed: "this"—touching his forehead,—"this"—touching his throat, "and this"—laying his hand on his heart.) Surprisingly, the doyen of singing teachers, Manuel Garcia II, who might be thought to have put voice before all, gave his three basics for a singing career as, "First character, secondly character and thirdly character."

Voice, heart, mind, character—the list grows,* and to it must be added several more fundamentals. The most beautiful voice in the world is nothing without a basic ability to sing in tune and at least some kind of musical ability. The most beautiful voice in the world combined with acute musical sensibility is still little or nothing if these are contained in a body that is diseased or frail. Still another element enters into the careers of singers, one which they are intensely aware of—luck.

It is the voice that basically fascinates, however, the element that stands out and attracts attention thus conjuring up the idea of a career. The great soprano Rosa Ponselle, while singing in her Connecticut school chorus, gave annoyance as a teenager because she sounded too loud and was asked to soften the tones of her voice that a fanatic admirer once compared to "warm alabaster."

---

* Caruso's requisites included "A big chest, a big mouth, ninety per cent memory, ten per cent intelligence, lots of hard work and something in the heart."

"Natural" voices, that is those that need no training, are a great rarity in the operatic field, though found among pop singers (Frank Sinatra never took formal singing lessons) where an assured vocal technique is less essential. One who definitely appears to have been a "natural" was Ponselle, who had only heard two operas in her life (let alone sung in any) when she made her debut in the long, demanding role of Leonora in *La Forza del Destino* opposite Caruso at the Metropolitan. She paid for her fabulous gift by having to acquire a more conscious technique while appearing in public, and throughout her long career nervousness never relaxed its grip on a single appearance.

An earlier "natural" was the afore-mentioned Patti. It is said that she took singing lessons from her stepbrother but these were probably mere exercises to increase the brilliance and flexibility of her voice. When throughout her long career she was sometimes questioned as to what method she used in singing, she would smile disarmingly and say, *"Ah, je n'en sais rien"*—"Ah, I know nothing about it."

Obviously the possession of a naturally beautiful singing voice is the greatest incentive towards making a professional career. Few singers have been born with voices that required no training at all, and even the naturally beautiful ones usually have defects in part of the range. A naturally lovely female voice is becoming still rarer because of the taste for baritone-like chest tones in pop singers which adolescents admire and therefore imitate. A few months of singing entirely in the chest register and carrying it recklessly up the scale will quickly end any beautiful voice that a young girl of today might possess.

What about a young person in the grip of an absolute passion to sing but not born with an unusual voice? In other words, is it possible to make a voice? Let us turn to the pre-phonograph years where all is speculation—always a great pleasure to the voice buff— and study the careers of the two remarkable Garcia sisters.

A Chain and a Silk Thread.   Surely in all of musical history no one can have been more obsessed, more fanatic about the singing voice than a handsome, curly-haired, violent Spaniard—some say of gypsy descent—named Manuel del Popolo Vicente Garcia. He was born in Seville in 1775 the illegitimate child of a mother who died when he was six. Fate in the form of a pretty singing voice and musical talent saved him from the beggar's lot of an orphan of those times and he entered the choir of a cathedral. Thereafter singing was all. Garcia grew up to become one of the leading operatic tenors of his day and the first Count Almaviva in Rossini's *Il Barbiere*. When in the course of time three children were born to the singer, Manuel (1805), Maria (1808), and Pauline (1821), with a zealousness that seems almost to border on the insane, he determined to make singers of them too, whether they possessed naturally good voices or not.

The fate of Manuel II was irony itself: forced by this fanatic and at times cruel father to sing during the voice change, his vocal career was lost forever. Of the charming, highly strung, impulsive second child, Maria, there is the oft-repeated story of two friends passing under the window of the Garcia house in Paris and one expressing alarm at the screams issuing from it. "It is nothing," says the other; "just Garcia beating trills into his daughter." When reproached later by his daughter's friend the Countess de Merlin for his harsh treatment of Maria, Garcia replied that she could "never become great but at this price: her proud and stubborn spirit requires [it] . . . to be bound by a chain."

Garcia had already subjected the highly gifted dragonfly of a little girl to rigorous musical studies before beginning to train her voice seriously when she reached the age of fifteen. Here, according to the same Countess de Merlin, who was about the same age as Maria and often sang duets with her, was the material that the obsessed father had to work with:

"Maria Garcia's voice was at first feeble. The lower tones were harsh and imperfectly developed, the upper tones were indifferent in quality and limited in extent, and the middle tones wanted clearness. Her intonation was so false as to warrant the apprehension that her ear was defective . . .

"One evening Maria and I were practicing a duet into which Garcia had introduced some embellishments. Maria . . . was vainly endeavoring to execute a certain passage and at last uttered the words 'I cannot.' In an instant the Andalusian blood of her father rose. He fixed his large eyes upon her and said 'Did I hear aright?' In another instant she sang the passage perfectly. When we were alone I expressed my surprise at this. 'O!' cried she, clasping her hands with emotion, 'such is the effect of an angry look from my father, that I am sure it would make me jump from the roof of the house without hurting myself.' "

Thus Garcia through tyrannical domination turned his daughter into the most celebrated singer of her time. Indeed, more than a singer, she represented the impetuous, impassioned force of Romanticism itself that brooked no limitation until the welcome release of death. A creature of the moment, Maria Garcia (or Malibran as she came to be known after her married name) would become so carried away in a performance that her acting bordered on what might be described as the sensational. Another apostle of the romantic movement but a critical opera-goer, Eugène Delacroix, remarked to his journal after witnessing Malibran rip up her handkerchief and tear her gloves to shreds as the despairing Maria Stuarda in Donizetti's opera: "That, again, is one of those effects to which a great artist will never descend: they are of the sort that delight people in the loges and win an ephemeral reputation for those willing to indulge themselves in that way."

There is no reason to suppose that the voice which Manuel Garcia managed to wrench from his daughter's throat ever possessed the beautiful quality of that of, say, Monserrat Caballé. The astute English music critic Henry Chorley recalled that it was a mezzo-soprano stretched in both directions, so that it ranged over

two and a half octaves and was weakest in the middle. Her daz-
zling rendition of ornaments and embellishments, her ability to
leap from the highest to the lowest notes in daring fashion, together with an almost exhausting conviction with which she sang,
seemed to completely distract her adoring audiences from the
deficiencies of her vocal quality. Thus showmanship, musicianship drilled into her by her father, sensibility (it is said that on
hearing Beethoven's Fifth Symphony for the first time she had
to be carried unconscious from the hall) combined with great
charm of appearance if not classic beauty, all aided in building one
of the most sensational careers in musical history of a woman
who had quite literally "made" a voice.

A story is told that Maria Garcia Malibran was standing talking
to a friend on a Paris street when a carriage drove by containing
her sister, Pauline, thirteen years younger, who leaned out the
window and blew kisses to her. The friend asked who the little
girl was. "That child is someone who will eclipse us all," replied
Malibran.

"That child" was completely different from her sister; calm,
contained, highly intelligent as her brother, Manuel Garcia II,
had to admit that Maria was not. From an early age Pauline showed
precocious musical talent and when eight years old could play the
accompaniments for her father's teaching sessions. The daughter
of much older parents, she seems in fact never to have been a
child, possessing from very early on a kind of grave assuredness
that when she sang was transformed into a quality of nobility.
Of his three children the elder Garcia treated only this last one
gently and with tenderness. The disparity which must have been
difficult for the older children to accept he explained to the
same Countess de Merlin: "Towards [the] younger sister, on the
contrary, I have never had cause to exercise harshness, and yet
she will make her way," adding that she could be led as easily as
"though by a silken thread."

Pauline was just short of eleven when her father died in June

1832, after which Malibran became the bountiful provider for the family. By the time Pauline neared her fifteenth birthday she was studying with Franz Liszt, her mind firmly set on a pianist's career of her own. Occasionally she accompanied her sister in concerts. In a biography of Pauline Viardot, as she afterwards came to be called, April Fitzlyon says that on Pauline's fifteenth birthday her mother shut the case of her piano and told the astonishingly plain girl with heavily hooded eyes and a long, arching upper lip that she was to become a singer. Pauline Viardot was a woman of tremendous character and will and one wonders what might have ensued between mother and daughter over this choice of a musical career to be imposed on the latter. Two months later all possibilities of conflict were removed: Maria Malibran while out riding in the early stages of pregnancy fell from her horse and died shortly after, at the age of twenty-eight. There was now only one Garcia left to sing. This strange, sacred trust had been handed to Pauline and she took it up.

No contemporary account exists of the raw material with which this second Garcia sister diligently went to work to make a voice. The descriptions of the end result tell enough. "Unevenness," "harshness," "feebleness," are some of the words used to describe its quality. Even at her London debut, aged seventeen, it was never a "young" voice, according to Chorley. Camille Saint-Saëns had this comment: "Hers was not a voice of velvet or of crystal, but a voice just a trifle harsh and occasionally was compared to the flavor of bitter-sweet oranges." The twenty-five-year-old Turgenev fell under the spell of this plain, magnetic young woman when she came to sing at St. Petersburg and became enmeshed in a *ménage à trois* that lasted all his life. Seeking at one point to escape the enslavement of it, he fired off this little poem to Pauline Viardot which speaks eloquently of the beauty of her voice and face:

> *Corbeau, corbeau*
> *Tu n'es pas beau*

Mais tu viens de mon pays
Eh bien! retournez-y.

(Crow, crow
You are not beautiful
But you come from my country
Well—go back there.)

Yet her career was as remarkable as her sister's short-lived one
and, though less sensational, founded on far deeper artistic principles. How then did she do it, without voice, without physical
beauty? One explanation was her unremitting capacity for hard
work. Her friend, George Sand, modelled a rather preposterous
novel called *Consuelo* after her, in which however the author
observes of the heroine singer: "Consuelo enjoyed one of those
rare and happy temperaments for which labor is an enjoyment, a
sort of repose, a necessary condition and to which inaction would
be an effort." Charm and fascination we know she possessed in
abundance. In addition to magnificent musicianship and conviction one final element must have been movingly apparent in her
singing. Her admirer, Alfred de Musset, put it this way:

"She possesses, in a word, the great secret of artists: before expressing something, she feels it. She does not listen to her voice,
but to her heart . . ."

Can a voice be made then? These two instances are, of course,
most extraordinary. Overshadowed always by the will of another,
the self did not have to provide the entire impetus toward making a career. Yet it is apparent that much can be done and a
career made, provided that the singer has the force of personality
and musical temperament to triumph over what nature failed
to provide. The usual puritanical price will be exacted however. Gounod described Pauline Viardot at the age of thirty
"as already nearing her end" and a musical paper of the same
period declared that "every note that comes from her voice is an
ear-splitting cry." Such "made" voices fare infinitely better in the

intimate spaces of the concert hall where they do not have to fight a heavy orchestra. While Viardot's operatic career was cut short at a relatively early age, she was still able to perform with telling effect in small auditoriums and at private parties, including her own.*

The Singer as Musician. "Voice first, voice second, voice third," Rossini may have declared to be the requirements of a sing-ing career, but he was much given to facetiousness. Obviously the most beautiful voice in the world such as the one possessed by Trilby in George du Maurier's novel is of little use to the world if the singer can't stay in tune, as poor Trilby could not except by the aid of hypnosis. In the matter of faulty intonation it is interest-ing to note how much more tolerant were our forebears. Giuditta Pasta, the first Norma and often conceded to be the greatest sing-ing actress of the nineteenth century † was evidently much given to off-pitch singing. "Never before have we had a Tristan able to sing the declamatory music . . . with correct intonation, to say nothing of the duet of the second act," wrote the critic Henry Krehebiel of Jean de Reszke's first Tristan. That was in 1895. A great star of the 1910's and 1920's was Amelita Galli-Curci with her ex-quisitely pure tones which her most extravagant admirers declared were always in tune. Less loyal ears, however heard her tendency to go flat, undoubtedly due to a goiter growing in the soprano's throat. Nowadays, almost without exception, any singer who does

---

* Madame Viardot's "musical parties are rigidly musical and to me, therefore, rigidly boresome especially as she herself sings very little. But when Mme Viardot does sing, it is superb. She sang last time a scene from Gluck's *Alcestis*, which was the finest piece of musical declamation, of a grandly tragic sort that I can con-ceive." Henry James in a letter to his father, April 11, 1876.

† Madame Catalani "is the first of the queens of song I have seen ascend the throne of popular favor in the course of sixty years, and pretty little Adelina Patti the last; I have heard all that reigned between the two, and above them all Pasta appears to me pre-eminent for musical and dramatic genius—alone and un-approached, the muse of tragic song." Frances Anne Kemble: *Records of a Girl-hood.*

not have a sure sense of pitch is almost certain to displease his listeners.

As to actual musicianship, this is obviously extremely important too, though singers have a reputation in the musical world for being self-indulgent and sloppy exponents of their art. Certainly there have been great stars who counted on the beauty of their voices to gloss over the fact that they hadn't bothered to learn their music properly nor interpret it with distinction. Neither Tetrazzini nor Pinza, for example, could read music; their parts were simply drummed into them by a diligent répétiteur until they knew the words and music—for life. And yet it would not be accurate to say that either of these great stars was "unmusical." Both possessed an innate flair for singing and that was enough. Naturally, it is no aid to a career for a singer not to be able to read music and surely only those with the feeblest mental capacity cannot learn if they wish to. Being "musical" or "unmusical" is often a question of exposure. Tetrazzini, for example, came from a family to whom Italian opera was as familiar as Mass. Her much older sister, Eva, was a well-known opera singer married to the equally distinguished operatic conductor, Cleofonte Campanini. In this family and musical atmosphere little Luisa grew up. One hates to think how many great singers may have been lost simply because they were raised in surroundings where music was not heard nor cherished, though of course all the various music media that we now have makes this less possible today.

Musicianship can however be drilled into those who do not possess the gift altogether naturally. A tough coach can stand over a vocalist and make him dot a quarter note as the composer has written it or teach him to count through the two measures of rest until his next entrance. Some singers have been what is known as a "slow study," artists who have had great trouble in committing to memory the words and music that they must perform.

"High ideals and application"—a motto that any aspiring singer might well adopt—were the watchwords of one of the first great American sopranos, Lillian Nordica. Her career was an interesting one. Endowed with promising basic material, she had to undergo long, extensive vocal training before her voice emerged in its full richness and beauty. The first American to sing all three Brünnhildes at the Metropolitan, she was an immensely slow study. To learn her long, difficult roles, the Maine-born diva with her sparkling eyes and determined chin would work six hours a day with a coach, going over the scores two pages at a time. Sometimes when she felt it physically unwise for her to continue she would lie down while the coach continued to play the passages under study over and over again. This gluttony for hard work enabled her to endure the daily grind of learning Elsa at Bayreuth under the supervision of the dragon herself, Cosima Wagner. But Nordica was the first Bayreuth Elsa and the first American to sing there. She also managed to learn some forty other operatic roles besides.

Curiously, the next American soprano to sing the three Brünnhildes at the Metropolitan, Helen Traubel, also had the same slow approach to learning her roles and throughout her career worked three hours a day with her coach, painstakingly going over every phrase in the music. In total contrast was her counterpart, Kirsten Flagstad, who learned the long, arduous part of Kundry in *Parsifal* in eleven days.

Some singers then are innately musical. Many, such as Lily Pons or Leontyne Price, are proficient at a second instrument, the piano. The much beloved Polish coloratura soprano, Marcella Sembrich, was accomplished on the piano and the violin as well. When the operatic career of Sembrich came to an end, not surprisingly she moved effortlessly and most successfully into a career of lieder singing.

Mens Vox, Mens Corpus. Given a lovely voice (or the ambition to make one) combined with basic musical talent, there is still one other absolute requisite the hopeful singer must possess before considering a career. I speak of good health and a strong, even ironclad constitution. The human body is the case of the singing voice and if there be any cracks or weaknesses in it the voice no matter how lovely will not endure. Singing is a mental process too, with the voice highly responsive to imagination and nerves. So there must also be good mental health. In an attempt to sing against poor physical health, the nervous tensions can become stretched so that the psyche and soma interact, precluding all possibility of a career. Such was the case of Mark Twain's beloved first daughter, Susy.

"Madame Marchesi said she had a grand opera voice—'Marvellous voice' was one of her expressions," Mark Twain wrote proudly in his notebook of the famous old teacher's pronouncement on Susy's singing. Mathilde Marchesi's daughter, Blanche, also a voice teacher, concurred with her mother's opinion, saying that Susy's "voice was competent for the parts of Elsa and Elizabeth in *Lohengrin* and *Tannhäuser;* and later she added Isolde . . ." Susy, however, with her poignant eyes and poetic, nervous sensibility, had always inclined to frailness. Earlier that year at a previous audition Blanche Marchesi had detected a formidable tremolo in her voice "which did not only come from forcing the high notes, but which seemed to have its source in a physical weakness." She had suggested a treatment of baths in Austria and Bavaria which Susy, eager to become a singer in her own right and not merely the daughter of a celebrated author, underwent. Returning to Paris, she began her training with high hopes only to have them immediately destroyed.

"After the second lesson what she [Blanche Marchesi] calls my 'general anemia' took hold of my breathing power and ever since, my breath has been so short and weak that all my volume of voice has gone," Susy wrote to her sister Clara, later to become the wife of the pianist and conductor Ossip Gabrilowitsch. "I am frightened to death for fear this will last, in fact, I am entirely broken hearted. Cold douches, eating, walking, sleeping, *nothing* helps . . ."

Blanche Marchesi blamed Susy's lack of strength on her poor living habits. "I found that she slept very little and ate next to nothing, and her education, as is frequently the case in America, seemed to have been taken in hand by the girl herself, the question of food being thrown aside as very uninteresting. Here was a case of voluntary self-starvation, and she laughingly confessed to have lived chiefly on mixed pickles, ice cream, candies and similar foods." Mournfully, in her next letter to Clara, Susy wrote, "For the present I'm stopping all the hard exercises, and everything, and may have to stop the lessons . . . I'm paying now for my past sins."

Eventually she allowed herself to be thoroughly examined by a doctor in Paris in the hope that medicine might come to her aid. Of this, Mrs. Clemens wrote to her husband who was in America trying to repair his broken fortunes: "He says that one great trouble with her is that she is not sufficiently developed, particularly her chest. The doctor prescribed gymnastics and massage. I hope now she will be soon on the road to health. It has been very pitiable to see her look so miserable."

Mark Twain, who could spot a fool at a hundred paces but was always ready to believe in some magical solution to the problems of life, soon after became convinced by Mrs. William Dean Howells that hypnotism was the answer to Susy's health. "The very source, the center of hypnotism is *Paris*," he wrote excitedly to his wife. "Dr. Charcot's pupils and disciples are right there and ready to your hand . . ."

But of course it was hopeless. Nothing could give Susy the physique and stamina required of a singer. Finally she faced the truth and returned to America where shortly afterwards to Mark Twain's unassuageable grief, she died unexpectedly in August 1895 of meningitis. On her deathbed she imagined that she was singing again.

Some indications as to who should and should not attempt a singing career for physical reasons are given by the basic body types as categorized by Dr. W. H. Sheldon. There is the plump, jolly endomorph, particularly happy at the dinner table, rather simple and elemental away from it. He laughs easily, doesn't mind playing a comic role and basks in the attention of it when he does.

There is the husky, muscular mesomorph, vigorous, outgoing and usually an excellent athlete. This type, according to Dr. Sheldon, is often highly ambitious and, in his desire to achieve his aims, likely to be self-centered.

The third type is the tense, narrow-shouldered ectomorph, a bundle of nerves and sensitivity. Often this type lacks physical strength, has a small, unresonant voice and is likely to be self-critical and inhibited.

Of these various shapes of body obviously the possessor of the third body type, the ectomorph with his narrow chest and shrinking ways is least suited to a singing career. Having a generous covering of flesh to pad his nerve endings, the endomorph will be happy before his public and know no fear of it. The burly mesomorph may be subject to nervousness but will overcome it in order to accomplish his ends. And of course his excellent physique will be a bulwark in sustaining the athletic rigors of a singer's life. What a pity though, that neither type possesses in such marked degree the ectomorph's sensitivity. On the few occasions when this third body type have become singers, they are usually artists of rare subtlety and insight.

Of course most people are a mixture of body types, but in the case of a pronounced ectomorph here is the baleful advice of Judith Litante, who takes Dr. Sheldon's theories very seriously in her *A Natural Approach to Singing:*

"If the ectomorph clings to the idea of being a singer let him do it for his own pleasure and that of his friends. He would be far wiser to choose some other lifework, and that as early as he can. Otherwise he may suffer the painful awakening of finding himself a square peg in a round hole too late to remedy the tragic error. *Worse, he could become a candidate for a mental institution."* (Italics mine)

Singers often seem to come in standard sizes—short tenors, tall basses etc. There are of course exceptions in anything where the laws of nature are concerned. Very rarely does a big, dramatic voice proceed from a petite woman or a slimly built man. There have been dramatic singers of small stature but not girth. Giulietta Simionato with her large, opulent voice, was very short but built like a bubble. A big chest and accompanying lung capacity are inevitably associated with a big voice. Kirsten Flagstad points out in her memoirs how as she progressed from the light, lyric soprano roles to the heavy Wagnerian ones, which she did not undertake until she was close to forty, her body enlarged and seemed to thicken, as the photographs in the book attest. Weight, therefore, a subject so much on the modern mind, is a necessary adjunct to the big voice, literally shoring it up like a bulwark. Take away this support through a drastic weight loss, the result will be vocal disaster. This seems to have been the case with Maria Callas, who began her career as a corpulent young woman with a large, well supported voice and has apparently ended it a thin middle-aged woman having scarcely any voice at all. A pity that she did not read the sensible little manual, *Hints to Singers,* written by Lillian Nordica close to seventy years ago:

"With progress in one's career, and when one has a reputation to sustain, the nervous strain becomes increased, and one evidently needs one's nerves covered with fat to shield them. Singers who have banted or taken medicine to reduce their flesh have more frequently paid for it dearly. One of my colleagues told me that she had banted for six weeks, and could not sing for three months; she had no strength."

Sheer physical endurance is also required of singers who have to stand for long periods of time during rehearsals and performances, sometimes for several hours in the case of those who sing

Wagner. A story is told of an aspiring dramatic soprano who on being introduced to Flagstad gushingly asked this great artist if there was any particular advice that she could give out of her experience of singing Wagner. "Yes," Flagstad replied calmly, "a sensible pair of shoes."

What about physical appearance as an essential for a career? Obviously beauty is a great help, especially in the field of popular singing. In former times audiences in the opera house seemed to have been able to accept the ludicrous and not be put off by the homeliness combined with mass of, say, Teresa Tietjens, the nineteenth-century soprano, or in later years the much admired Luisa Tetrazzini. Today we demand (and usually get) singers of more prepossessing face and figure, and managers may even insist that an artist shed a certain amount of weight for a forthcoming season. If a visage or body shape be markedly odd or comic, this obviously will limit an aspiring opera singer to humorous or character roles. Such was the case of Thelma Votipka who sang only *comprimario* parts at the Metropolitan for twenty-five years, despite the fact that she possessed a voice of outstandingly beautiful quality. Lack of stature limited the career of the Roumanian tenor, Joseph Schmidt, to concert and later, film appearances: he was simply too short to meet even the undemanding credulousness of operatic audiences. Another who might have made a fine operatic career, the baritone Emilio de Gorgorza, was prevented by another physical reason: he could not enact operatic roles because of short-sightedness.

Though glamor and beauty are much emphasized in the field of popular singing, Fanny Brice with her tragic-comic "funny face" made in her younger years a marvelous singing career. Edith Piaf, with looks generously described as *"gamine,"* became one of the most successful popular singers of her time.

Not very long ago the combination of a beautiful singing voice and a black skin used not to be a total invitation to embark on a singing career. Against obstacles that had nothing to do with the

Tetrazzini by Caruso.

way they sang, such great artists as Bessie Smith, Ethel Waters and Billie Holiday made it to the top. Black so-called "classical" singers had to wait longer for acceptance. Marian Anderson with one of the most remarkable vocal instruments of this century was repeatedly denied important appearances because of the color of her skin and only made her debut at the Metropolitan under the aegis of Rudolph Bing when not quite fifty-three—the first Negro ever to sing there.

With an enormous figure that an earlier age might have found acceptable as it would have objected to her complexion, a black twenty-four-year-old soprano competed in the finals of one of the recent National Opera Auditions at which the writer was present. She revealed a large, rarely beautiful voice and musicianship besides, but only received a scholarship for further study. Nonetheless she seemed born to sing in opera. I couldn't help wondering whether she was handicapped not, happily, because of the color of her skin, but by her exceptional girth. Today's audiences would find it difficult to accept her as Aida or Tosca or the Marschallin, all roles that she gave evidence of being able to sing most effectively. In time she might certainly grow into the heavy Wagnerian repertory in which with the help of abundantly draped costumes combined with Wagnerian concepts of character, girth would not seem such a problem. But here is a case where physical appearance might proscribe an operatic career, though not one made in the concert hall.

Voice, musical aptitude, a strong constitution—even these elements would not be enough to make a career without overriding ambition to accompany them. Many a fine potential singing artist has existed who for one reason or another refused to take on the rigors of a professional life—and perhaps rightly so. It is an unnatural, arduous and not always rewarding existence. But for those with the necessary qualifications, who cannot stop themselves from attempting a singing career, the next step is one of the most vital—but potentially horrendous—moments in the vocal ages: the choice of the right teacher.

Svengalis. Fresh, pulsating with youthful vitality, the female voice at seventeen or eighteen, the nineteen or twenty-year-old one of the male, is now ready to go out into the world to find fulfillment. But what a perilous, sometimes cruel world it is. For each sensible, intelligent, above all judicious teacher of singing there is his regrettable counterpart, lurking spiderlike in a studio, door wide open, awaiting his victims who are for the most part young men and women with little money at their disposal, desperately anxious to believe that the master—for he is literally that—to whom they have committed their vocal destinies possesses the "true method" of producing a beautiful voice. The embittering fact is that anyone—the singer of bit parts with the Riga Opera Company in 1931, a Texas church soloist, young singers studying themselves

Felia Litvinne

...AND ABSURDITIES

Liff-Stuart Collection

Liff-Stuart Collection

Albert Alvarez

Edouard de Reszke

Therese Tietjens

Lifj-Stuart Collection

Enrico Caruso

Mrs. Kennerley Rumford
(Clara Butt) and
Master Roy

Collection of author

Luigi Lablache

Victoria and Albert Museum

Liff-Stuart Collection

Reynaldo Hahn

Gioacchino Rossini

Collection of author

Kunsthalle, Hamburg

Jean-Baptiste Faure by Manet

The Singer and the Listener. From a painting by Edgar Degas.

and trying to pick up extra money on the side, failed singers, not even singers at all but the maid or valet of a famous opera star, coaches, hack accompanists, ex-instrumentalists, throat doctors, out-and-out charlatans—anyone can hang up a sign and claim to be a teacher of singing. No license has to be displayed, no qualifications produced. The only requirement is faith which at this vulnerable moment the student singer unwittingly gives because he *wants* to believe.

Because of this unwholesome situation that leaves open the field of vocal pedagogy to any and all comers, singing teachers as a group have scarcely enjoyed a very good reputation. As far back as 1906 a number of thoughtful vocal instructors in New York City banded together (an unusual occurrence in a profession where one self-proclaimed expert is often inclined to snub or vilify another) and formed an association to establish certain standards of teaching and a code of ethics. In addition it began a lobbying operation at Albany in an attempt to have legislation passed requiring all singing teachers to be licensed. By 1924 when nothing had come of this effort, the New York Singing Teachers' Association decided to ask its members to register with the Association in answer to a questionnaire their qualifications for teaching. The questions were simple and logical enough. What, where and with whom had the teacher studied voice and for how long? Had he a thorough musical education? Could he play an instrument? And so forth. Out of the hundred odd members about half chose to register their qualifications; the others abstained—presumably because they lacked them.

1944 saw the founding of a national organization with similar aims. Called the National Association of Teachers of Singing, it accepts as voting members voice teachers who have completed five years of continuous teaching and, as affiliated nonvoting members, teachers who have not yet completed their five-year stint. Applicants have to set forth their qualifications in full, together with recommendations from two other NATS members.

In addition they pledge in writing their adherence to the code of ethics of the Association. Accusations of malpractice by three NATS members against another, if substantiated by the Board, can force a teacher's resignation.

At this writing the organization has about two thousand qualified members around the United States, most of whom belong to regional chapters. NATS sponsors summer workshops at various campuses throughout the country that offer recitals, lectures, coaching and all that can further a knowledge of the art of singing among both students and teachers. An annual convention is also held every year that includes a song contest among young finalists for an award known as "The Singer of the Year." In addition NATS issues teaching outlines for its members, "A Statement of Laws and Precepts upon which Vocal Pedagogy may be Based" together with a plump quarterly bulletin that contains articles such as "An Investigation Concerning Vowel Sounds in High Pitches" and reports of the various activities of the Association. A book column also appears regularly written in what must be regretfully described as characteristic "singing teacher's" prose. A typical review, this one of a book called *The Science of Vocal Pedagogy*, begins:

"One's initial reaction to studied perusal of this multi-faceted approach to ultimate attainment of a sound vocal technique is apt to be that of absolute amazement, the more so, if and when diversity of investigative procedures leading up . . . etc."

The idealistic aims of the National Association of Teachers of Singing are of course extremely commendable, but in summing up the organization's first twenty-five years of existence a former president, Bernard Taylor, sounds a trifle rueful over what NATS has accomplished in that time: "Members and non-members are certainly more aware of what a code of ethics means to the profession," he writes in the October 1968 bulletin, "altho' [sic] I would not, nor indeed could not say that there has been a complete and unqualified adherence to the ethical code on the part

of even our own membership." As to the NATS objective of establishing and maintaining "the highest standards" of teaching
principles he is silent.

Nevertheless, the aspiring singer who chooses to study with a
member of NATS knows that he is going to a person with certain
important qualifications for teaching and a minimum of five years'
experience in the profession. Otherwise the fact remains that a
chiropodist or a masseur each requires a license to practice, but
not so a voice instructor, even though he is concerned with a highly
delicate and complex mechanism of the body. And yet were legislation to be passed, what would be the criteria to obtain a license?
A previous professional career in singing? The experience of having studied singing? Thorough scientific knowledge of the vocal
process? Historic knowledge based on vocal "methods" set down
by great teachers of the past? Experience gained from having long
been connected with singers and their world? At this time there
are teachers who believe they are qualified to teach singing and
who fit each one of these categories.

On the face of it singers who have made long, successful careers
founded on a secure vocal technique should make the best voice
teachers. Though the analogy is inexact, this does not work out any
more than that fine authors should be able to impart a fine style
of writing to their students. Out of the many great stars at the turn
of the century only a handful chose to teach: Jean de Reszke and
Emma Calvé (neither of whose pupils made a stir), and Lilli Lehmann and Marcella Sembrich. But not Patti, Eames, Mary Garden, Fremstad or Farrar,* all of whom lived on to become very
old ladies with nothing much to occupy them after retirement.
From outward evidence, Lilli Lehmann appears to have been a
very good teacher, perhaps because she didn't subject the voices of
her students to the drillmaster routines, hours of singing even
when hoarse, through which she put her own. Sembrich, a superb

* The last two studied with Lilli Lehmann.

musician, was also a fine teacher, though judging from her records her voice was not equalized in the lower part of its range.

Nor have the great stars of more recent years turned to teaching. Flagstad never considered it, nor has Melchior. Giovanni Martinelli "coached"; Lucrezia Bori never made any attempt to impart her vocal secrets to the generations that succeeded her. Neither have Lily Pons and Bidu Sayão. Two outstanding exceptions are Lotte Lehmann who opened a studio on the West Coast and Rosa Ponselle, teaching at her home just outside of Baltimore.

It is the opera singers of slightly less stellar quality, the ones who lacked the ultimate opulence of voice and sweep of personality to make them great stars, who seem more likely to teach after retirement, and often with very good results. In this category we might put Margaret Harshaw and Rose Bampton, each currently teaching at universities with fine music departments. Both, oddly enough, were mezzo-sopranos who made the difficult and not altogether successful change to sopranos; both made careers distinguished by intelligence and musical discrimination. Others in this category have been Queena Mario, Dorothee Manski and Mack Harrell, each deceased within the past few years. All could add "formerly of the Metropolitan Opera Company" after their names, a claim glamorous enough to attract probably as many students as they could handle. In England the former soprano favorite, Joan Hammond now teaches. To facilitate the flow, this kind of "name" teacher often employs assistants, many of whom are either unknown singers or not even singers at all and who often give the entire lesson into which the teacher may drop in or not at his pleasure. Such was the practice of Mack Harrell, my first so-called singing teacher, who paid a call on exactly one lesson during a summer term at the Juilliard School of Music, though ostensibly I was studying with him. (Perhaps he was only sparing himself needless pain, for to be sure after auditioning for admission to the fall term the school turned me down.) Sometimes these assistants go on their own using the name of the well-known Metropolitan Opera singer with whom they have once worked, as a magnet to draw in students, though they themselves may have had little or no voice training.

Then there are singers who turn to teaching after a short and not particularly notable career. Probably the best example is Manuel Garcia II, who sang in his father's opera company—he was America's first Figaro in *Il Barbiere*—but too much too soon with the result that he had "not the ghost of a voice." Another to fit into this category of the one-time professional singer who enjoyed a limited career is Mathilde Graumann Marchesi, a pupil of Manuel Garcia II. As a mezzo-soprano she sang concerts for a few years on the Continent and in England before settling down in Vienna to impart the methods of Garcia at the Conservatory. In a second incarnation she opened up a school in Paris. Marchesi accepted only women and her classes were unique for being just that—classes. She rarely gave private lessons, only to the most advanced students or the miraculously gifted such as Nellie Melba, who did not have to make her way up from the beginner's classes as did Emma Eames, much to the latter's annoyance. This method of having to sing before their fellow students and (naturally) most merciless critics wiped away any inhibitions at appearing before people. In addition the pupils could easily be taught ensemble singing. It is a system having considerable merit but little practiced today.

The list of Marchesi famous pupils, almost all sopranos, is impressive indeed: the eccentric coloratura, Ilma di Murska, who always toured with a menage of animals and birds; Etelka Gerster who broke down mentally during a marvelous career, and Gabrielle Krauss, "the most compelling dramatic soprano who ever existed," according to Mathilde Marchesi's daughter, Blanche. There were the two American coloraturas, Emma Nevada and Sybil Sanderson, the latter possessing the extremely rare soprano *acuto sfogato* range. Nellie Melba is probably Mathilde Marchesi's most famous pupil, but the latest biographer of this flamboyant prima donna believes that much more credit for Melba's flawless technique should be given to her teacher of six or seven years in Australia, an Italian tenor named Pietro Cecchi. Emma Calvé is always listed as a Marchesi pupil, but she left her after six months because the aging woman had lost her voice and gave her pupil nothing to imitate. Another pupil, the beautiful blue-eyed Emma Eames, with her flaring nostrils, writes coldly of Marchesi as being an "ideal Prussian drillmaster" who "fortunately did not attempt to change my natural singing voice, and as my voice was a healthy one, she did it no harm, but neither did she show me the absolute vocal security which I was to gain for myself later."

The personalities of Marchesi—"an old, curt, haughty woman who came forward like an empress and just deigned to bow to you"—and the young Mary Garden completely failed to mesh, particularly as the famous teacher then in her seventies wished to make Garden into a coloratura soprano, the last thing the young girl wanted. After a few lessons she wrote to Marchesi that she would not continue. "Mary Garden," came a note in return, "A rolling stone gathers no moss. Don't cry till you come out of the woods. Mathilde Marchesi." In her eighties, Marchesi taught Frances Alda, her last pupil, whom she called "her Benjamin." Alda, not known for her graciousness, leaves a generous portrait in her memoirs of "a czarina . . . who altered the course of my life."

Inherent in the authoritarian, parental role of the singing teacher is the often desperate dependence on the part of the pupil not only for vocal, but total personal approval. It is this interaction in the teacher-student relationship that perhaps explains why a teacher is successful with one pupil and fails with another. Marchesi evidently mothered her girls or as Emma Eames puts it "got a hold over them." She criticized the way they dressed, made sure they lived in a suitable section of Paris and generally oversaw their deportment even though they might have with them their own mothers as chaperones. Mary Garden, a strong-willed young woman, could not accept the domination of the older one and so the teaching attempt quickly proved a disaster. Alda, orphaned at an early age, and indeed brought up by a grandmother, fitted into the psychological climate of Madame Marchesi and there was rapport.

A good example of the "motherly" tone frequently adopted by a teacher toward her student is conveyed in this chiding letter from Erminia Rudersdorff, who was a pupil of Manuel Garcia II, to Emma Thursby, one of America's earliest sopranos. (Thursby, who in turn taught Geraldine Farrar for a time, held views against the stage and never appeared as an opera singer.)

"My naughty little speranza, after heartily thanking you for your ready assistance yesterday, I am going to scold.

"My child, you did *not* sing well yesterday. That was not the singing of a faithful student and a great artiste. It was very unfinished, often downright blurred—and—the worst—out of tune. The last cadence was so and you finished quite a quarter of a tone flat.

"That must not happen again. You have no excuse, you had all your changes and cadences written three weeks ago, and you owed it to yourself to have studied them faithfully. You have not had so many engagements as to render study impossible, moreover to those who *want* to study, study is *always possible*."

In more recent times Florence Kimball has also adopted a motherly attitude towards her "girls" such as Leontyne Price and Veronica Tyler, counseling and grooming them in matters far exceeding the vocal.

Lacking the magic title "formerly of the Metropolitan Opera Company" or "Covent Garden" the teacher who can describe himself more vaguely as the internationally famous "Madame X" or "Signor Y" still has a fly of sorts that can be cast on the water to hook students. Just where and how the fame of Madame X and Signor Y has been achieved is usually rather vague and the student in all probability too intimidated to ask.

HIERARCHIES OF TEACHERS

Here are a few examples of a teaching "method" being handed down over the years:

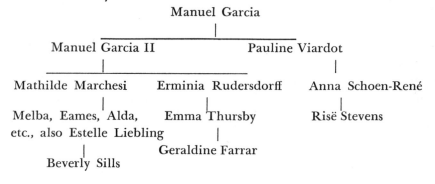

Manuel Garcia
|
Manuel Garcia II   Pauline Viardot
| |
Mathilde Marchesi   Erminia Rudersdorff   Anna Schoen-René
| | |
Melba, Eames, Alda,   Emma Thursby   Risë Stevens
etc., also Estelle Liebling |
| Geraldine Farrar
Beverly Sills

Francesco Lamperti
|
Marcella Sembrich
|
Florence Page Kimball
|
Leontyne Price

Then there are singer-teachers who have no "name" at all. Sometimes they are young and studying themselves while they pick up extra money by passing on to beginners what they themselves are still trying to learn. Such were two young women on the faculty of a well-known music school in New York which the writer entered after his Juilliard rejection. I began lessons with one of them because her fee was half what the "names" on the faculty charged, and also because the "names" may well not have been interested in teaching anyone who produced the sounds I was making at that time. My teacher proved to be kind, young, extremely musical and pleasant to be with. Her voice, a soprano, sounded attractive enough, though I was aware that she had trouble with her top notes just as I did. In my case "trouble" was a euphemism. I didn't *have* any top notes. Not too long out in the winter I began to realize that I really wasn't making very much progress with this agreeable and always encouraging person. The magic key that would unlock the "beauty" of my voice in which all students have to believe simply wasn't in her possession. And yet, not knowing what else to do or who to go to, I drifted on with her—and two years passed.

Common sense would seem to dictate that the person who teaches singing should have studied voice for a number of years and have knowledge of the sensations of the vocal process—even if they have never made careers. There are however, many, many teachers who never attempted to learn voice. Often they are coaches or répétiteurs, who after a number of years of being around singers and drilling them in repertory, diction and so forth, feel that they understand enough about vocal technique to teach it. Some go to the manuals and give vocal instruction by the Porpora or Garcia method, simply putting their students through the course of exercises left behind by these great pedagogues, certain that they will benefit each and every student. Throat doctors or men and women who have acquainted themselves as best they can with all the physical intricacies involved in singing also set themselves up as teachers without ever having sung themselves, using a strictly "scientific" approach to the achievement of a beautiful singing voice. Still another kind of non-singer teacher is one who has assisted in the studio of a celebrated teacher and now carries on that great antecedent's "method."

Strangely, to this last category belonged my next teacher, a middle-aged man with a leonine head and a belly that pushed out his shirt tautly over the top of his trousers. I had been sent to him by a handsome, gifted dramatic soprano who believed that he could help me as he had her. By this time I was in a desperate state. I had discovered that under the G.I. Bill I could qualify for several thousand dollars worth of free vocal training if the American Theater Wing which supervised the program considered me to have sufficient promise. The Theater Wing after hearing me audition did not. But they were prepared to give me one more chance in three months' time, if by some fluke my new teacher could make something of my voice.

I cannot remember much of the first half hour with this somewhat awe-inspiring figure except the usual terror that accompanies all such moments in the life of a would-be singer. Almost all voice teachers sing, or at any rate make noises of some sort, however distasteful. Imitation is one of the basic elements in vocal instruction. To my amazement this teacher was silent. He looked as if he was going to sing: that is, he fixed me with purposeful, glaring little eyes and then quickly dropped his jaw so that I could see into the rosy interior of his mouth. But no sound came forth. I was told to do as he had done, except to sing, which I did, and for the first time sang the F sharp, G, and A flat, the high notes of the baritone range which I did not believe were in my voice. How or why this alchemy was accomplished I shall never understand. At the end of two lessons a week for six weeks I returned to the Theater Wing for another audition and was promptly accepted. It was, one of the judges remarked, the greatest piece of teaching he had ever heard.

"There is nothing more strange than this question of voice teachers," writes Sydney Homer, who followed his wife around from two teachers in Paris until she found the third that shaped and polished one of the most remarkably beautiful of vocal instruments. "I have long made up my mind that when a pupil does not make progress it is not necessarily a reflection on his teacher. Another pupil will do wonderfully under his care and the unsuccessful pupil will get on famously under another master. There is an alchemy about it, a reaction of personalities, a mysterious mutual helpfulness, an unexplainable sympathy."

One of the most celebrated singing teachers of the nineteenth century was François Delsarte, uncle of Georges Bizet. Delsarte turned to teaching after his own voice had been ruined in training at the Conservatoire. That delightful reporter Lillie (Moulton) de Hegermann-Lindencrone who went to study with him, has left an account of his methods.

"He is not a real singing teacher, for he does not think the voice worth speaking of" she writes; "he has a theory that one can express more by the features and all the tricks he teaches, and especially by the manner of enunciation than by the voice . . ." On Delsarte's walls "were hung some awful diagrams to illustrate the master's method of teaching. These diagrams are crayon-drawings of life-sized faces depicting every emotion that the human face is capable of expressing such as love, sorrow, murder, terror, joy, surprise, etc.

"It is Delsarte's way, when he wants you to express one of these emotions in your voice, to point with a soiled forefinger to the picture in question which he expects you to imitate. The result lends expression to your voice."

The method of a total charlatan one might suppose, and yet it evidently proved effective. One of his last students was the young Lillian Nordica who felt that she learned much from him. Here again is a connection of magic with the singing voice. "Svengali" has become a commonplace in today's vocabulary. We should not forget that Svengali was a singing teacher, who by using the highly irregular vocal method of mesmerism was able to make "Trilby, the tone deaf, who couldn't sing one note in tune! Trilby who couldn't tell a C from an F" into a marvelous singer. George Du Maurier's story is absurd, of course—

"Well, we both taught her together—for three years—morning, noon and night—six—eight hours a day. It used to split me to the heart to see her worked like that! We took her note by note— there was no end to her notes, each more beautiful than the other —velvet and gold, beautiful flowers, pearls, diamonds, rubies— drops of dew and honey; peaches, oranges and lemons! . . . She could run up and down the scales, chromatic scales, quicker and better and smoother than Svengali on the piano, and more in tune than any piano! and her shake—ech! twin stars, monsieur! She was the greatest contralto, the greatest soprano the world has ever known!" Though the story is ridiculous the fantasy of the singing teacher who by some magical means can elicit the most beautiful voice in the world from his pupil is a very real one in the mind of almost every student who steps hopefully across the threshold of a teacher's studio.

What Am I? Unless his family happens to move in musical circles the aspiring singer looking for a voice teacher is as defenseless as the newly hatched baby turtles on the Galapagos Islands, making their frantic dash to the safety of the sea while frigate birds hover relentlessly above waiting to snap them up. Who can the incipient singer turn to for advice? His high school music teacher will probably be interested and sympathetic, but in a small town will have little experience or information. One possibility is to enroll in a music school or a college with a good vocal department and then move on from there to private instruction. More impatient students who want private instruction from the outset but do not know to whom to go, sometimes boldly write a favorite singer and ask for advice. Others simply contact a teacher on the strength of his label "Formerly Metropolitan Opera Company," or his claims to have taught a number of celebrated singers.

An application to even the humblest teacher involves an audition (for which in most cases a fee is charged). The nervous student brings out his music—a song, an aria that brought down the house in high school, while the teacher, wondering if an exciting new talent has happened into his studio, slips to the piano—unless he employs an accompanist. The introduction sounds and at the moment of entrance, like plunging down the first fall of a great roller-coaster, the hopeful singer utters his opening note. Now there is no going back . . .

The last note dies away. An anxious silence follows. Will the teacher ask to hear more? "Have you something else? Something a little simpler?" come the welcome words. And then, "Will you sing me this scale slowly up and back down again?"

In the case of an aspiring singer who manifestly could never make a career, how difficult for all but a truly kind teacher to say the truth. And even the most experienced judgment could always be at fault. Easier to say, "I'm not accepting any more pupils at the moment—but if you want to call me in six months' time . . ." The more unscrupulous teacher given such a prospective pupil will delve immediately into his victim's ability to pay, murmuring in a prophetic way, "There is potential. It will take work, a great deal of work. But there is definite potential."

"You don't have a voice anymore," was Manuel Garcia's comment to the eighteen-year-old Jenny Lind when she auditioned for him in Paris in 1841. Already a famous singer in her native country she had sung herself into a state of vocal fatigue through incorrect methods and performing too much. Shattered, she begged Garcia to help her, to which he replied doubtfully that if she went away and rested her voice completely without speaking for six weeks, it might be saved. Jenny Lind, always a hard worker, used the six weeks' enforced silence to teach herself French and Italian. All the world knows the result, but contemporary reports of Jenny Lind's voice always speak of a veiled, husky quality in the middle of its range, suggesting that in fact she had done it permanent harm. How many teachers would prescribe such treatment today, one wonders, or indeed students endure it?

If the young hopeful shows promise and the teacher has time as well as interest, the new pupil will be accepted and an hour appointed for the first lesson. Before leaving the audition the gratified student may ask eagerly, "What kind of voice do you think I have? My music teacher always said I was a contralto but I have some very high notes as well."

Unless the classification is a most obvious one such as a deep bass or a high, light coloratura, a scrupulous teacher will reply that this must remain to be decided, perhaps only after several

months of lessons. The classifying of a voice can be most misleading and tricky and even experienced teachers have been known
to make mistakes. I know of one gifted singer who started off
her training in her 'teens as a coloratura soprano, though there
were rich contralto tones in her voice as well. Later she went to
Europe to study with the noted contralto, Sigrid Onegin. One of
the pitfalls of working with celebrated singers is that they tend to
think of their pupils as images of themselves, so that the former
coloratura soprano was turned into a contralto. In the end her
voice was correctly classified as a dramatic soprano. With some
voices the quality and range will make it perfectly obvious what
they are: with others, it is more difficult. In all cases the note on
which the singer must change into a different register is a helpful
clue. If a man, for instance, can sing an open "ah" no higher than
E flat, and possibly not even this, it suggests that he is a baritone
or bass. If on the other hand he can carry the "ah" up to an E
natural or F, this arouses suspicions—however rich and baritone-
like his voice may sound—that he could sing tenor.

There is another, by no means certain, but intriguing clue.

A friend of mine engaged the noted German baritone, Hermann
Prey, to sing a private recital at his house in Philadelphia and
asked me to drive down from New York to hear it. Prey sang
beautifully a program of lieder in a lyric, not overly-rich baritone
slightly weak and without fullness of tone at the bottom. On the
other hand the baritone's transition note of E flat he sang openly
and with consummate ease and it seemed to me that he could
have easily gone higher in this same register without having to
make the requisite change for his high notes. The intimacy of a
beautiful reception room in a private house made it possible to
study the shape of Prey's face closely: it is round, not long, with
wide-spaced eyes, prominent cheek bones, and a short space between the lower lip and chin.

The next day my host asked me if I would give the singer and
his wife a lift back to New York, and in the car somewhere along

the New Jersey Turnpike I realized that I felt under compulsion to ask Mr. Prey a question which at best might be construed as rude, and at worst insulting. From observations over the years I had long held the theory that the shape of a singer's face gives a clue to the range of his voice. It had struck me that a face which was wide across its top half, often with knobby cheekbones, and then tapered sharply to a chin set not far beneath the lower lip produced a high voice in either sex—soprano or tenor. These faces were also likely to be convex. Baritones and mezzos were inclined to have longer faces, and the low basses and contraltos an oblong shape to their heads. Catching sight of Mr. Prey in the rear view mirror and remembering his vocal quality of the previous evening, also the ease of his high tones, I could contain myself no longer. "Mr. Prey, do you think by any chance you're really a tenor?"

"Oh yes," he replied calmly. "I could sing tenor."

"Then why—?"

"It would mean studying again." I saw in the mirror the reflection of his smile and a shrug. "Why should I?"

Soon after, much to my delight I came upon medical confirmation of my totally empirical theory. In his highly informative *Keep Your Voice Healthy*, a practicing oto-laryngologist, Friedrich S. Brodnitz, quotes from the writings of a fellow throat expert, Dr. Deso A. Weiss. Dr. Weiss "who examined a large number of successful singers believes that a definite body type can be associated with the high and low voices. According to him, singers with high voices have: round faces with short noses, a convex profile with small delicate details, short necks, round or quadratic chests, high palates with delicate soft palates; while the deep voices are characterized by: long faces with long noses, straight line profiles with massive details, long and narrow necks, long and flat chests, broad palates with massive soft palates. A flat palate or a sharp angle between the floor of the mouth and the neck was rarely found in a singer with a good voice." * To which I would add, again totally from observation, that one does not see a singer with a decidedly undershot jaw or what might be described as a "weak" chin.

Here is another description of a classic tenor face. "The depth, width and height of the roof of the mouth, the broad cheekbones and flat even teeth, the wide forehead above wide-set eyes—that spacious architecture gave him his deep resonance of tone." Thus Mrs. Caruso describing her husband. Naturally, the theory that the shape of a face tells what kind of a singing voice is behind it cannot be expected to operate with one hundred per cent accuracy. An exception that comes instantly to mind is Joan Sutherland, long of face and long of jaw, scarcely typical of a soprano. Nevertheless just as the soprano *acuto sfogato* is most often doll-like and petite, and the bass tall and commanding, the shape of the face is one more guideline to vocal identification.

AAH-OOH-AAH.   Excitedly the student singer arrives for his first lesson eager to learn the secrets of his new teacher's method. This will have one of several definite orientations.

Most common is some kind of physical approach, though as has been pointed out a demonstration of how to sing is perforce very limited. Still there are certain muscular actions that a student can learn to control and regulate. It is possible, for instance, to slightly raise or lower the level of the larynx while singing, thus increasing or decreasing the size of the resonating pharynx at the back of the throat. There have been teachers who made the pupil stand with the back of his head forced hard against a wall and by this extra pressure push down the larynx in his throat. The result, as anyone can find out by doing so, will be a dark, thick tone, which may also sound lugubrious and lacking in vitality. Then there are teachers who demand that the student bring the tongue forward,

* Caruso could hold an egg in his mouth without anyone realizing it was there and the teacher of Kathleen Ferrier declares that "one could have shot a fair-sized apple right to the back of her throat without obstruction."

which has the effect of raising the larynx. The resulting tone is usually a "white," bleaty kind of tone. (I have seen the adjective "chicken" applied to it.) Somewhere between these extremes lies the best level of adjustment. But one must ask where? And isn't it possible that a desirable level will vary from singer to singer?

Some teachers emphasize the shape of the mouth and going back to the early song manuals cite Mancini, for example, that the mouth should be in the shape of a smile. W. J. Henderson gives this confusing report of various singers in the golden age at the turn of this century: "Some teachers and some singers believe that the secret of good tone lies in pushing forward the lips. The mouth is resolutely opened in the form of the letter O, the lips being compelled to protrude somewhat. Sbriglia of Paris is the most ardent advocate of this style, and Jean de Reszke who studied with him for a time * discarded it in the very beginning. Madame Nordica employs it and is a firm believer in it. Madame Sembrich, on the other hand, employs the horizontal oval, or letter O laid on its side. This lip formation, the old masters asserted, gives the tones a beautifully soft sonority, suitable for the expression of feeling."

Other teachers lay great stress on the tongue. Should it be humped—or flattened? Blanche Marchesi writes in her *A Singer's Pilgrimage* of mechanical devices used to control this organ, the action of which most of us take perfectly casually. She mentions in particular a kind of mouth cage that the teacher sold to each of his pupils. Smaller at the back and flaring out in front, it was supposed to flatten the tongue. This unpleasant contrivance came in but one size—which certainly cannot be said of the human mouth. She relates another story of a teacher in Dresden who made the pupil balance a large round piece of lead on the tip of the tongue, thus forcing it down. Fear of swallowing the lump of metal naturally caused the mouth to dry out and the muscles

* Sbriglia is generally given credit for training Jean de Reszke from baritone to tenor.

in the larynx to tense. The lead did slip down the throat of one unfortunate student whose life was despaired of until the metal was ultimately retrieved. But such ordeals and worse are often the lot of those who strive to achieve a beautiful singing voice.

Still other teachers have evolved often mad-sounding theories concerning movable parts of the face, the mouth and the throat over which we have some control. "Cause the cheeks to become hollow from without inwards, pout the lips as far out as possible in trumpet formation. This will add to the resonance of the voice, as the space between the teeth and the lips is the real resonator." Try it!

Or, "Lie crosswise on your bed. Let the arms hang down on one side and your feet on the other until the body feels well stretched. Extend the arms in the shape of a cross. Let the mouth open by letting the head fall down instead of lowering the jaw. Sing AH! This will send the voice in the head, take the strain off the throat, widen the chest."

Or here is an injunction from a well-meaning authority claiming to impart the secrets of Elisabeth Schumann's vocal technique: "With teeth closed, lips pressed firmly against them and cheeks well raised (the upper teeth will be clearly visible), the singer must blow on to a lowish note through the consonant sound 'v,' taking care that only the diaphragm and not the throat does the pushing. After a time he must release the teeth just sufficiently to make a real note instead of merely a buzzed hum. This will be 'a small note' and will as yet have no vowel shape."

The great tenor, Jean de Reszke, when his voice began to fail turned to teaching, and the result was another muddle that seems so often to beset singing and its instruction. Together with the American laryngologist Dr. Holbrook Curtis they concluded that the aforementioned "coup de glotte," which Garcia had so unfortunately named, was fatal to a proper singing technique and that the only way to avoid the quick striking together of the vocal folds or lips within the glottis was by preceding each tone with a kind of hummed "n" sound. This was conveniently demonstrable to the most inexperienced student, but it also had the effect of putting the tone undesirably in the nose. De Reszke retired from the stage, taught this method for years in his studio at Nice, in which the composer Reynaldo Hahn was for a time répétiteur, but from which no pupil of any international distinction emerged.* Meanwhile in 1909, Dr. Curtis, a doctor but never a singer, brought out his manual *Voice Building and Tone Placing* in which we find this excerpt: "On welcoming my dear friend Jean de Reszke to my house after his fourth return to our shores I said to him: 'Jean, have you any new facts for my poor book? Have your studies during the past year taught you anything which may be of use to me?' 'Yes,' he responded. 'I find that the great question of the singer's art becomes narrower and narrower all the time, until I can truly say that the great question of singing becomes a question of the nose—la grande question du chant devient une question du nez.' "

There remain a few other demonstrable movements of the face which may also be called on in the struggle for a beautiful voice. Hopeful students are frequently instructed to flare their nostrils as though an offensive odor had been thrust beneath them, or perhaps to lift the eyebrows in an effort to "think high." The position of the head can obviously be varied so that for every would-be singer who is taught to lift his chin and throw back his head in order to obtain a high ringing note, there is another instructed to bow his head in what is known as a "goose-neck" position, which some believe aids in placing the high notes.

Finally there are the physical devices to which teachers will resort in the hope of training the voice to ring with all the resonance that is inherent in it. Thus to prevent singing in the nose, a teacher will force a pair of corks up the nostrils of the student. And though it would seem that in our supposedly en-

* The lyric-coloratura soprano, Bidu Sayão, is often regarded as his last pupil, but she only studied with him in a limited way.

lightened age such artificial methods might be harmful, there is a singing manual written only ten years ago and available in shops specializing in music which advises the beginner to place "a small, *clean* [italics mine] cork between the front teeth, separating them one half to three quarters of an inch," so that he may learn how wide apart the jaws should be when singing.

Absurd and ludicrous as these instructions may sound, strangely enough there is always a chance that they may be of help, and some muscular action, however little related to the vocal process provide a singer with a kind of crutch towards reaching a desirable tone quality.

Another kind of teacher will decry this physiological approach to vocal instruction, believing that it makes the student self-conscious about the muscles used in singing, and ultimately tense. Instead he advocates a psychological approach. The voice is all in the mind, he declares; if one simply conceives a pleasing tone mentally, the proper muscular action will result automatically. In the studio of this type of teacher images and metaphors shower down like petals blowing off a fruit tree that has just given up flowering.

"Think of the tone as a ping-pong ball riding on a jet of water."

"Make a foolish face in order to relax. Then place the hands behind the back, bend, and chase an imaginary dove around the room."

"Think of *stinking fish* to produce the head voice."

"Sing high notes with a *black snore*."

Caruso is said to have been much amused by a vocal teacher of whom he said, "He knows more than me. When he teaches he takes an umbrella and when he opens it the pupils sing 'EEE-EEE-AAAA' and when he closes it slowly, slowly they go 'AAA-AAA-EEE.' "

Students are frequently instructed to think of a "pear-shaped" tone, to lift their upper jaw (impossible, as it is rigid), or to feel the tone coming out of the roof of the head (where it is not nor ever

THE AGES OF VOICE

could be). The relentlessly disciplined Lilli Lehmann provides a scary looking chart in her book *How to Sing* of a head in profile with red lines flying out from the skull to indicate all the different places where a singer must feel his head tones—again all fantasy. In certain cases this chart has actually been helpful to singers in extracting the marrow, as it were, from their resonators; to others, Frau Lehmann's manual, a miasma of the sensations she felt when she sang, is incomprehensible to the point of nonsense. Here is a characteristic excerpt:

"As I have said before in speaking of the attack, in order to make the vowel sound ā, the larynx is with energy brought in closer relation with the nose. By dilating the nostrils a preparation is made. The sensation is then as if the larynx were under the nose in the chin. If we then sing ā energetically we soon become conscious of an inherent strength which is created partially by the energetic opening of the epiglottis in the pronunciation of ā and partially by the position of the larynx which makes possible the attack of the breath on the hard palate," etc.

Making desperate attempts to bring out resonance in the tones of their students, the metaphors of teachers sometimes exceed the hallucinations of a "trip." Elster Kay in his *Bel Canto* gives this splendid example of metaphor run riot.

"One is required to think of a ladder (two ladders) in one's head, a biscuit-mold and Hoover in one's mouth and a chimney in one's throat . . . The upper jaw has to be thought of as a pointed bird's beak which, during singing, stabs into an apple. And of course, during singing one must relax completely body and soul."

And yet again these images, strange and ludicrous as they may seem, can perhaps have meaning to one person, and that person translate them into the tones of a lovely singing voice. Many a singer has produced his song within the realm of his own vocal fantasies, feeling sensations to which he gives names or comparisons that have no meaning to another person.

Another approach is the "natural" one. A runner doesn't think how his leg muscles are functioning as he sprints for the finish line—so there is no talk of anatomy. Emphasis is placed on the involuntary and spontaneous, with no thought to any kind of muscular control. Such teachers often liken singing to speaking and put much emphasis on the pupil's speaking voice; if the speaking voice is perfected, they believe, the singing voice will automatically follow.

Whatever the approach (or combination of them) the student will eventually, if not right away, be asked to vocalize during his lessons. Some teachers give their pupils scales and exercises only, believing that when technical mastery is gained over the voice then and only then can it be applied to the art of singing. These pedagogues divide up still further. Some believe that the same set of exercises, perhaps as prescribed by Manuel Garcia II or Mathilde Marchesi, will invariably benefit every voice that practices them. Others, perhaps wiser, tailor the various scales, arpeggios and *vocalises* to the individual voice of the student and its problems. This type of teacher may keep his beginner student singing scales and exercises and nothing else for a number of months, or he may start the pupil off right away on a song used as an exercise. The various "Arie Antiche"—Italian seventeenth- and eighteenth-century songs with long, flowing lines and accommodating open syllables—are particular favorites of teachers in this respect. Over the decades how many multitudes of hopeful singers have attacked the Giordani "Caro mio ben" or the charming "Nina," supposed to be a lament by Pergolesi for his cat—but now, in this age of disillusion declared to be neither by him nor for his pet.

The Making of a Singer.   And so time passes—time which the aspiring singer quickly comes to feel as a nemesis to his career, insistently there and having to be overcome, only later to be held back. With each lesson questions bedevil the student's mind. Am I making progress? Am I on the right track? If the temperaments of teacher and pupil mesh and there arises a strange, almost mystical comprehension between them, and if the teacher is an experienced and intelligent one, then one day, magically, the student may suddenly feel his voice ring out free and easily in a way that it never has before. Here at last is a kind of breakthrough. Excitedly he returns for the next lesson but now this exhilarating, soaring tone is lost. At the next lesson it returns briefly, only to disappear again. I have found no better description of the manic-depressive life that a student singer leads than this passage from the memoirs of Clara Doria Rogers, an English singer who studied in Milan almost a hundred years ago:

"There is no ecstasy like that experienced at the sound of one's own voice when it fulfills one's ideal, as there is also no depression so profound as that induced by the loss of it—even when one believes that loss to be temporary! I was frequently and painfully subject to these fluctuations, and my alternate spells of ecstasy and misery cannot be gauged by any ordinary standard of human emotions. I was constantly seeking for a way to clinch my triumphant tone. The word which expressed it for me was 'it.' Yesterday 'it' was mine to keep forever, as it seemed; today 'it' was gone and I as helpless as an owner of a pet bird that had flown from its cage! In vain did I plead with my teacher for help. 'If you could only give me some advice what to do, how to practice to get a permanent tone-emission! If you would only tell me why I have no voice—no breath—no anything today, when in the last lesson I had all of these and you were so pleased with me!'

"All I could expect from him was a kind, sympathetic smile, and 'You are tired; you have been overdoing and have exhausted your vitality; stop singing and you will find your voice again.' He was invariably right! Still I was not satisfied. I ached to discover the why and wherefore of this tantalizing state of things. I went searching—searching—day after day. I shut myself in a little studio, trying every sort of experiment with my voice—all in vain, till I would bury my face in my hands on the keys of the piano in utter despair.

"There my poor dear little mother would find me and in anxious tones say, 'For God's sake, Clara, don't work so hard. Do you know that you have been singing for four hours? You will kill yourself if you go on in that way!'

"To which I would answer, sobbing, 'Oh I have lost my tone-emission; I have lost 'it.' "

Melodramatic and typically nineteenth-century as this may sound to those who have never studied voice, it is an all too agonizing and true experience to those who have. As a result, in the quest for "it" many students leave one teacher for another, and that one for a third, taking up a nomadic life which for some never becomes settled.

In desperation some students try to teach themselves and turn to the manuals of singing. These exist by the hundreds and range from a 95¢ paperback (*A Short Course in Singing* by C. R. Thorne) to thick volumes filled with complicated, often disgusting looking diagrams of the throat and head, strange symbols such as might be used in a calculus problem and of course vocal exercises. The pages are thick with interjections: "ee!" "aw" "OH"—and the prose denser still:

"By means of the tongue thus raised, the closely but flexibly held larynx, and the free and slightly covered nose, the two bright vowels partially remain, and combine with them the dark vowel, thus making a complete singing tone . . ."

Or: "Thus an increased tension of the abdominal muscles causes the vocal cords to vibrate at greater amplitude horizontally, the greater adduction of the vocal cords means that less breath volume is needed to vibrate the same depth of vocal cord vertically."

Or: "Be it noted: If the singer *thinks* 'back of the vertical,' at a certain angle, the throat obeys the thought, releasing the parts concerned and assuming the right shape; whereupon the sound beam will *of itself* soar upwards into the head cavities at the correct angle with respect to the vertical. It is really all very simple."

Presumably publishers wouldn't go on printing these books unless there was a market for them among people to whom they have meaning. Again it is a question of a word, a suggestion, an image striking the student-reader's sensibility in such a way as to help him.

Students also attempt to teach themselves by imitating records of famous singers. This was the method of Amelita Galli-Curci who claimed to be self-taught, as does Franco Corelli. There is a so-called "private" recording of Maria Callas singing "Tu che invoco" from Spontini's *La Vestale* which is a ghostly imitation of Ponselle's rendition of this aria, suggesting that the one diva learned from the records of the earlier one.

Let us assume, however, that our hypothetical student is making excellent progress with his or her teacher. By this time a rapport will have inevitably grown up between them. The pupil feels the teacher's backing and confidence in his emergent voice and art, while the teacher grows more and more involved in the promise of this particular student.

To his growing knowledge of vocal technique other skills must be acquired by the student to make a singing career. As the voice develops the teacher will recommend that the pupil study one or more of the three languages that are a requisite—Italian, French and German. Here again, background plays such an important factor in the life of the would-be singer. If for one reason or another he has heard one of these languages spoken at home he is that much ahead of the game. Perhaps he has had good instruction in French in high school, or simply possesses a facility for languages that others do not. These factors will be of immense help. Many English-speaking singers never do become fluent in all three languages, content to go over the words of their repertory with coaches who drill them in the pronunciation and meaning of the texts.

Another essential soon needed in the pursuit of a singing career is an accompanist. Some teachers, afraid that beginners will go on repeating mistakes in vocal technique, do not allow them to practice except under their own supervision or possibly that of an assistant. Others expect them to practice outside the studio but not seated at the piano—a position less conducive to good singing than standing up. Therefore an accompanist is required. As the voice develops and can undertake more difficult music an accompanist (a good one is perhaps even more of a rarity than a good singer) becomes yet more of a necessity. Only the most musical voice students can play for themselves the quick, dancing accompaniments of a Mozart aria or make their way through the complexities of a song by Richard Strauss.

The finest vocal technique properly only serves musical art, and a conscientious teacher will eventually recommend that his promising pupil go to a coach, who will supervise points of interpretation, or work on tricky ensemble passages in the various operatic roles that by this time he has begun to study.

Having to work privately with all these different mentors puts a crushing load of expense on the student singer. Well-known teachers charge fifteen or twenty dollars an hour—sometimes more. A good coach asks ten to fifteen. Accompanists may vary from piano students who charge three or five, right on up to the professional accompanists whose fees are commensurate with their experience. The fee of the language teacher will also depend on his specialized knowledge of song and operatic literature in his particular tongue. Thus an aspiring singer may find that he is spending a hundred dollars a week before he has taken up a forkful of food or put his head down on a pillow. In addition he must have a room with a piano where he can practice; he has the expense of purchasing necessary scores and sheet music and he also should attend as many live vocal performances as he possibly can.

How to finance the study of the singing voice thus becomes a major problem. One often hears the complaint that singers don't study as long as they ought to, that they should remain in the studio on the average several years longer than they usually do. What forces them out prematurely is this overwhelming financial pressure that causes them to take a job singing in the chorus of a musical or as hard working church soloists when their voices are not yet ready to undergo the strain. Yet how else are they to support their studies? If they are lucky they may find a patron, as did Leontyne Price from a Mississippi family for whom her mother was a domestic. Geraldine Farrar borrowed money from a wealthy woman in Boston and proudly displays a photograph of the debt marked "Paid in Full" in her memoirs. The sum came to $30,-000—and that was at the beginning of the century!

Another solution, though an arduous one, is to take a full time non-vocal job, which necessitates dashing for lessons in the lunch hour or after work and practicing and studying in the evenings, a killing schedule but in some cases the only possible one. Sometimes success in a job and the resultant security will weaken and eventually undermine the ambition of an aspiring singer and he abandons the idea of a career altogether. Louise Homer saw the dangers of this as she became more proficient and better paid as a court stenographer in Philadelphia. Eventually she threw over her well-paying job and the dangerous safety it offered in order to go to Boston to study.

There are also many stories of kind and generous teachers who have waived their fees or at least reduced them for promising pupils without the ability to pay. There are equally unpleasant tales of pedagogues who make the student sign a binding contract that he will pay a percentage of his future earnings—sometimes *for the rest of his life*.

HOW THEY BEGAN

In order to support themselves while studying singers have held a wide variety of jobs. Others were already equipped for an entirely different profession before discovering their voices.

Albert Alvarez, tenor, was leader of a military band.
Peter Anders, tenor, was an accountant.

Francisco d'Andrade, baritone, studied law.

Hendrik Appels, a Dutch tenor, was first a practicing dentist.

Salvatore Baccaloni, the *basso buffo,* studied architecture.

Alfred von Bary was a qualified neurologist before his tenor voice was discovered. He returned to medicine for a time after failing eyesight terminated his musical career.

Don Beddoe, a Welsh tenor, was first a miner.

Eugenii Belov, baritone, started out as an engineer.

Erna Berger, coloratura soprano, was a governess.

Ingrid Bjoner, soprano, worked in an apothecary shop.

Beno Blachut, a Czechoslovakian tenor, was an ironworker.

Alessandro Bonci, tenor, was a shoemaker's apprentice.

Kim Borg, bass-baritone, began as an engineer.

Giuseppe Borgatti, a tenor and the first Andrea Chénier, started out as a mason.

John Brownlee, baritone, worked as a bookkeeper.

Aloys Burgstaller, the German tenor, studied to become a watchmaker.

Florencio Constantino, tenor, was a ship's engineer.

Régine Crespin, soprano, studied to be a pharmacist.

Charles Dalmorès, a noted French tenor, was also a horn player.

Peter Dawson, Australian bass-baritone, began as a professional boxer.

Nelson Eddy was a reporter.

Kathleen Ferrier was a telephonist.

Mario Filippeschi, bass, started as a police official.

Miguel Fleta, tenor and first Calaf in *Turandot,* was a miner.

Alfons Fügel, German tenor, began as a tile-setter.

Beniamino Gigli worked in a pharmacy.

Alexander Girardi, a popular Austrian operetta tenor, was a locksmith.

Apollo Granforte, the celebrated Italian baritone, began as a shoemaker.

Joseph Hislop, Edinburgh-born tenor, was a press photographer.

Samuel Hybbinette, Swedish tenor, was principally a surgeon, directtor of the Seraphiner Hospital in Stockholm and physician to the King. He appeared frequently in concerts and was said to have the most beautiful tenor voice in Scandinavia.

Morgan Kingston, English tenor, was a miner.

Walter Kirchoff, German tenor, began his career as a cavalry officer.

Dorothy Kirsten worked as a telephone operator.

Mario Lanza was a truck driver.

Emanuel List, Austrian bass, learned the tailor's trade.

Cornell MacNeil, baritone, was a machinist.

Emilio de Marchi, tenor and first Cavaradossi, began as a lieutenant.

Queena Mario, soprano, was a journalist.

Alfred Piccaver, the tenor idol of Vienna, worked in the laboratory of
Thomas A. Edison before his voice was discovered.

Ezio Pinza was a professional bicycle rider.

Charles Rousselière, French tenor, began as a smith.

Leo Slezak, the great Austrian tenor, was a gardener and a locksmith.

Thomas Stewart, baritone, worked in a government laboratory doing
mathematical-physical research.

Martti Talvela, bass, was a school teacher.

Jess Thomas, tenor, started out as a child psychologist.

Jacques Urlus, the Wagnerian tenor, began as a metalworker.

Walter Widdop, English tenor, began as a wool-dyer.

Erich Zimmermann, a *buffo* tenor, painted porcelain at the Meissen
factory.

And so these difficult, intense studies continue—training the
voice, developing musicianship, improving memory and concentration, learning how to act, to project, to move on the stage, and
all this accompanied by—God willing—an unfolding of the soul
without which there can be no great singing.

How long do the studies last? A purist would reply, as long
as the career itself, for a true artist never ceases to continue to perfect his technique and his art as long as his career endures. As I
have said, nowadays laments go up that young singers do not study
long enough and by singing in public with an imperfect technique
soon throw away their voices. There are the usual references to the
golden age of bel canto when one *castrato*, Niccolo Porporà, taught
another, Gaetano Caffarelli, the same set of exercises for six years,
at the end of which he is supposed to have said, "Go, my son, you

have no more to learn. You are the finest singer of Italy and of the world."

Tetrazzini in her memoirs claims that she studied only one year, though she grew up in an atmosphere that exposed her to opera throughout her childhood. She also was unable to read music.

The bass, Jerome Hines, seems only to have studied two years before he made his operatic debut. Mary Garden had two teachers and three years of training before her dramatic substitute debut in Paris as Louise on Friday the thirteenth of January, 1900. Eames studied about five years. Melba worked six or seven with a teacher in Australia before coming to Mathilde Marchesi, who seems to have done little more than polish her. Flagstad credits three teachers over a six-and-a-half-year span for her flawless vocal technique, though in addition both her parents were musicians. To train her enormous, sumptuous soprano voice, Helen Traubel declares that she studied seventeen years with one teacher, her "second mother," Madame Vetta-Karst, performing the same scales and exercises throughout this entire span of time. There seems no ready answer then, to the question of how long a singer should pursue his studies before appearing in public, since it depends much on his original vocal endowment, together with his musical background, education and general aptitude.

Meanwhile as the training progresses, the feelings of a fine teacher who succeeds in molding a lovely voice and vocal art, can readily be imagined. This voice becomes his creation, like a child whom he has come to love and whose every need he understands perfectly. Because the teacher-student relationship is such a close one, it can be subject to all the strains of intimacy itself, but with one difference; at any time a promising student with a voice that the teacher cannot help feeling he has created, may take that voice away and never bring it back, leaving the teacher to feel as betrayed as a rejected lover. A number of reasons can bring about this for the teacher disillusioning and embittering defection, the simplest being that the student decides after several years that the demands of a career are too great. Or perhaps the money for his training has run out with no possible source of any more. Female students marry and give up the idea of singing professionally in the interests of a husband and a family. Impatient students may develop their voices to a point and then leave the teacher for easy money in show business. Such is the close relationship between teacher and pupil that an ill-judged criticism, a tactless personal comment can send a sensitive pupil in flight from the studio never to return. Every singing teacher of any merit will have his stories of students who might have been a glory in the singing world, but who betrayed or were lost forever through pressure of outside circumstances.

Spending several hours each week in a fervent joint search for a vocal technique and art, it is not surprising that the closely closeted teacher and pupil often develop a strong personal relationship. As has already been pointed out, some women teachers tend to play a motherly role with their students. In the case of the male pedagogue, he too may be cast in an authoritarian paternal image, but he can also enact another part. In Mr. Reginald Peacock's Day Katharine Mansfield has left a biting portrait of a vain, unctuous, but lecherous voice teacher presumably drawn from her first husband who taught singing. Sometimes, however, out of this situation a meaningful and lasting relationship can arise. One thinks in recent years of Mary Curtis-Verna who married her teacher, and Astrid Varnay, who married the late Hermann Weigert, her vocal coach.

MARRIAGES BETWEEN SINGERS AND TEACHERS, COACHES, CONDUCTORS, ETC.

Singers often choose mates who are in some way connected with their careers but are not vocal rivals. These marriages would appear to be particularly felicitous, but obviously not always.

Adelina Agostinelli (soprano)
Emma Albani (soprano)
Frances Alda (soprano)
Rose Bampton (soprano)
Fedora Barbieri (mezzo)
Louise Beatty (mezzo)
Xenia Belmas (soprano)
Cathy Berberian (soprano)
Teresa Berganza (mezzo)
Lillian Blauvelt (soprano)
Theresa Brambilla (soprano)
Jean Browning (mezzo)
Muriel Brunskill (mezzo)
Marion Claire (soprano)
Isabella Colbran (mezzo)
Hedwig von Debicka (soprano)

Anton Dermota (tenor)

Blanche Deschamps-Jehin
  (contralto)
Ludmilla Dvořaková (soprano)
Minnie Egener (soprano)
Elise Elizza (soprano)
Cato Engelen-Sewing (soprano)
Birgit Engell (soprano)
Dietrich Fischer-Dieskau
  (baritone)
Thérèse Foerster (soprano)
Helena Forti (soprano)
Amelita Galli-Curci (soprano)
Marguerite Giraud (soprano)
Alma Gluck (soprano)
Marie Gutheil-Schoder
Marilyn Horne (mezzo)
Maria Ivogün (soprano)

Giuseppe Quirolli (teacher)
Ernest Gye (impresario)
Giulio Gatti-Casazza (impresario)
Wilfred Pelletier (conductor)
Maestro Barzoletti (impresario)
Sydney Homer (composer)
Alexander Kitschin (conductor)
Luciano Bero (composer)
Felix Brambilla (accompanist)
Alexander Savine (composer)
Amilcare Ponchielli (composer)
Francis Madeira (conductor)
Robert Ainsworth (conductor)
Henry Weber (conductor)
Gioacchino Rossini (composer)
Pietro Stermich de Valcrociata
  (conductor)
Hilde Berger-Weyerwald
  (pianist-accompanist)
Léon Jehin (conductor)

Rudolf Vasata (conductor)
Louis Hasselmans (conductor)
Adolf Limley (teacher)
Henry Engelen (impresario)
Hans Erwin Hey (teacher)
Irmgard Popper (cellist)

Victor Herbert (composer)
Walter Bruno Iltz (*régisseur*)
Homer Samuels (pianist)
Albert Carré (impresario)
Efrem Zimbalist (violinist)
Gustav Gutheil (conductor)
Henry Lewis (conductor)
Michael Raucheisen
  (accompanist)

Helen Jepson (soprano)
Barbara Kemp (soprano)

Auguste Krauss (soprano)
Annelies Kupper (soprano)
Frida Leider (soprano)
Zélie de Lussan (soprano)
Maria Malibran (soprano)
Lucille Marcel (soprano)
Edith Mason (soprano)
Susan Metcalfe (contralto)
Zinka Milanov (soprano)
Audrey Mildmay (soprano)
Caroline Miolan-Carvalho
  (soprano)
Anna Moffo (soprano)
Agnes Nichols (soprano)
Elena Nikolaidi (mezzo)
Lily Pons (soprano)
Delia Reinhardt (soprano)
Jane Rhodes (soprano)
Leonie Rysanek (soprano)
Therese Schnabel-Behr (contralto)
Grete Schneidt (soprano)
Elisabeth Schumann (soprano)
Irmgard Seefried (soprano)
Maria Stader (soprano)
Hanny Steffek (soprano)
Giuseppina Strepponi (soprano)
Joan Sutherland (soprano)
Tarquinia Tarquini (mezzo)
Viorica Ursuleac (soprano)
Astrid Varnay (soprano)
Galina Vishnevskaya (soprano)
Carolina White (soprano)

George Possel (flautist)
Max von Schillings
  (composer-conductor)
Anton Seidl (conductor)
Joachim Herrmann (accompanist)
Rudolf Deman (violinist)
Angelo Fronani (pianist)
Charles De Bériot (violinist)
Felix Weingartner (conductor)
Giorgio Polacco (conductor)
Pablo Casals (cellist)
Ljubomir Ilic (teacher)
John Christie (impresario)
Léon Carvalho (impresario)

Mario Lanfranchi (régisseur)
Hamilton Harty (conductor)
Tanos Melos (teacher)
Andre Kostelanetz (conductor)
Georges Sebastian (conductor)
Roberto Benzi (conductor)
Rudolf Grossmann (teacher)
Artur Schnabel (pianist)
Jacques Stückgold (teacher)
Karl Alwin (conductor)
Wolfgang Schneiderhan (violinist)
Hans Erismann (conductor)
Albert Moser (impresario)
Giuseppe Verdi (composer)
Richard Bonynge (conductor)
Riccardo Zandonai (composer)
Clemens Krauss (conductor)
Hermann Weigert (coach)
Mstislav Rostropovich (cellist)
Paolo Longone (teacher)

The years have passed. A fine teacher has been found and a vocal technique mastered, so that the voice is free and ringing and beautiful. The singer now possesses some knowledge of three languages different from his own. He has committed to memory the words and music of a number of operatic roles, as well as a quantity of songs and labored to interpret them persuasively and with sensitivity. He may even have found time to fit in lessons in acting and stage deportment as well. And most miraculously, he has been able to lay his hands on the money to pay for all this expensive training. One would now suppose his troubles were over. The sad fact is—the battle has not even been conjoined.

Just One Break.   We are in London. A performance of *Madama Butterfly* has been announced for that evening in the fine old opera house that stands amid an aura of vegetable smells at Covent Garden. That afternoon the General Administrator and his staff have been listening to auditions, among them one by an unknown American whom I shall call Lucy. Lucy has a well-trained lyric-*spinto* soprano and unusual dramatic talent, but she has discovered how thin are operatic opportunities in America. She auditioned for the New York City Opera and they were most encouraging, but since they already had two *spintos* on the roster and a repertory with only three operas calling for this type of voice, they proffered no contract. And where else? Lucy herself realizes that she is not ready for the Metropolitan. She has no experience whatsoever and at best, if they liked her voice, she might be taken on in *comprimario* parts, a potentially dangerous dead end. The National Metropolitan Opera Company would have been ideal but that has folded for lack of money. Of the other companies around the country, they generally engage established stars for the leading roles in their not frequent productions, so again there would only be the prospect of singing say, the few lines of Leonora's companion in *Trovatore,* instead of Leonora herself.

So Lucy has somehow saved her pennies and with the blessing

of her teacher started on a round of auditions in Europe. She might have tried to obtain a Fulbright scholarship, but that would require her to take a full year of study in Europe before accepting engagements. Both Lucy and her teacher felt that with her excellent Italian (her mother was in fact Milanese) and her more than adequate German which she has picked up quite easily, Lucy is ready for an engagement now.

At London, her first stop, she has chosen to audition Leonora's last act aria in *Trovatore* to show off the lovely, limpid high pianissimi that her teacher has given her. Evidently everything has gone well, for a voice out of the shadowy auditorium has asked Lucy for another aria. In contrast, this time she picks the *Butterfly* "Un bel di" which gives her a chance to display dramatic intensity as well as the beauty of her voice. When this is sung, the same polite British voice thanks her and asks her to leave an address where she can be reached. Nothing more. Gathering up her music, Lucy reminds herself in her disappointment that she is American; with a growing wealth of fine English singers, as in every country, native talent must be served first. But the thought is poor consolation. Returning to her hotel, which is cheap and smells vaguely of mutton fat, she contemplates a lonely dinner, not knowing anyone in London. On the following day there is the prospect of setting out for the Continent and the unknown. Weary from the strain of auditioning, she kicks off her shoes and stretches out on the bed. . . .

In the semi-darkness a telephone is ringing and ringing, mixed with the clack of shoes on the sidewalk below the window. For a moment Lucy cannot think where she is. Then the now strong, permeating smell of the fat rushes into her nostrils: London, and the sound of tapping feet. It must be the rush hour . . . *My* telephone? . . . But no one knows me in London. A vaguely familiar British voice speaks her name in inquiring fashion. "Yes. This is Lucy—" The voice is identified as belonging to the assistant General Administrator of Covent Garden. He was much impressed by her audition that afternoon and wonders—"Yes?"—the soprano scheduled to sing Butterfly that evening at Covent Garden has been struck down by flu. Her "cover" so far cannot be reached; no one seems to know where she is. The only other soprano in the country at the moment who knows the part is unfortunately committed to a concert in Manchester. The management wondered if by any chance Miss —"But I—" would consent to fill in. "But I—" It is now close to six with the performance announced for seven-thirty. The curtain could be held for at least a quarter of an hour.

"I'll be right there."

On the stage of the opera house she is shown the first act set and where she must make her entrance singing Cio-Cio-San's difficult music that rises sequentially higher and higher. Photographs of the second and third act set—fortunately the same—are handed to her together with blocking outlines of her positions onstage throughout the opera. Also she is shown her props, her fan, the few possessions that Cio-Cio-San brings with her on her wedding day, and the knife with which she will eventually stab herself.

Time begins to run short. The costume of the ill soprano—unfortunately a woman larger than Lucy, who still commands a shapely figure—have somehow to be fitted to her. A man in American naval uniform comes up and says in broken English that he will whisper to her where she must go and what she must do whenever he can. For a moment in the daze of it all Lucy wonders how the United States Navy has come to hear of her plight and send rescue until she realizes that this is her Pinkerton for the evening. A friendly Suzuki with a brisk British accent appears to wish her luck and say that she too will give guidance whenever she can.

The nervous opening music of the opera strikes up and before she knows it, as if time had accelerated, Lucy hears the tremulous high strains of the violins that signal the entrance of Cio-Cio-San. She nestles behind the other girls with their parasols as slowly they begin to move out onto the stage. Still in the wings Lucy takes breath:

"Madama Butterfly" by Caruso.

"Ancora un passo or via . . ."

Next morning she is the talk of London. All the newspapers on the Continent and in America have carried accounts of her triumphant feat. She is launched, on her way to a fabulous career . . . stardom. . . .

A crash, a tinkle of glass of two taxis colliding in the rush hour. The clack of heels on the paving stones and from far off the sound of Big Ben striking the hour. Our student stirs on her lumpy bed. Of course it was all a dream.

Many years ago in Paris, Mary Garden did just what Lucy dreamed, and went on without a rehearsal in the third act of *Louise* as an absolute unknown never having appeared on the operatic stage before. But now in this age of the jet such dramatic substitutions are almost unheard of. In London recently, when Josephine

Veasey became ill just before a performance of *Carmen,* the management was able to fly in an experienced singer from Paris who had performed the role countless times before; there was no need to try out an inexperienced unknown quantity. And only the other day when Jon Vickers, scheduled to sing the name part of *Peter Grimes,* came down with a throat infection, the Covent Garden management resorted to the BBC to find his "cover." Ronald Dowd, motoring in the country with his car radio on, heard the special announcement asking him to contact the opera house immediately—and an unknown who might have stepped in and made his way to stardom was done out of the opportunity.

Today, the way up is slow, frustrating, intensely competitive and very, very difficult. For each who succeeds, numbers fall back and are never heard by the general public. As I have already said, opportunities for the aspiring young opera singer in a vast country like America to get a break, are severely limited. For a dispiriting prognosis of the young American singer's chance to succeed the reader is referred to excepts from an editorial in the NATS Bulletin, February/March 1970 to be found in the appendix. Aside from auditioning for the pathetically few companies that have any length of season at all—these include the Metropolitan, the New York City, Chicago and San Francisco Opera Companies, and the summer seasons at Santa Fe and Chautauqua—one of the best ways to further operatic ambitions is to enter the well organized National Opera Auditions. Hopeful singers in the section of the country from which they hail first appear before regional judges and then, if successful, gradually work their way up to the semi-finals and finals. These are held in the Metropolitan Opera House before an audience that has contributed financially to this valuable enterprise of discovering new singers. Some finalists obtain immediate Metropolitan Opera contracts. In 1961 the young Negro tenor, George Shirley, won hands down with his exciting rendering of "Nessun dorma" from *Turandot.* The house went wild and everyone felt that they had participated in a great discovery. On the same afternoon a young mezzo-soprano who billed herself as Shirley Verrett-Carter sang an aria from *Carmen*. She failed to win a contract but was awarded one of a number of scholarships available to help promising students finance further studies. Today, of course, as Shirley Verrett, she is a big star.

NAME CHANGES

Many singers with unpronounceable or merely prosaic names have changed them. Also in years gone by American singers often felt it necessary to italianize their names in order to succeed in opera. Here are some of the more drastic mutations.

Lucy Armaganian	Lucine Amara
Eleanor Broadfoot	Eleanora de Cisneros
Richard Bunn	Richard Bonelli
George Burnstein	George London
Archer Cholmondeley	Mario Chamlee
Alfredo Cocozza	Mario Lanza
Francis Dinhaupt	Frank Valentino
Reba Fiersohn	Alma Gluck
Frances Gumm	Judy Garland
Ilse von Güntler	Maria Ivogün
Elisabeth Elfriede Sigrid Hoffman	Sigrid Onegin
Lebrecht Hommel	Lauritz Melchior
Maria Jedlitzka	Maria Jeritza
Jon Edwin Johnson	Eyvind Laholm
Maria Kalogeropoulos	Maria Callas
Emmy Kittl	Emmy Destinn
Praxede Marcelline Kochánska	Marcella Sembrich
Werner Krzywonos	Werner Alberti
Clara Lardinois	Blanche Arral
Elisabeth Letzergroscher	Elise Elizza
Marie Louise Martin	Louise Edvina

Antonietta Meneghelli	Toti Dal Monte
Helen Mitchell	Nellie Melba
Lillian Norton	Lillian Nordica
Jacob Pinkus Perelmuth	Jan Peerce
Ernestine Rössler	Ernestine Schumann-Heink
Olivia Rundquist	Olive Fremstad
Françoise-Jeanne Schütz	Felia Litvinne
Apollonia Stoscus	Polyna Stoska
Giovanni Titta	Titta Ruffo
Marian Toucke	Marian Telva
Sarah Jane Layton-Walker	Mme. Charles Cahier
Hugh Whitfield	Riccardo Martin
Florence Wilson	Florence Austral

A Norwegian soprano whose career spanned the first two decades of the twentieth century appears never to have known who she was. She sang first under the name Borghild Bryhn, then Borghild Langaard, then Borghild Bryhn-Langaard and after that as Borghild Lindvig. Not content with all these identities she made guest appearances in Milan as Borghild Brunelli!

If opportunities in America seem insufficient to the promising would-be opera singer, he has the chance, thanks to the excellent system of Fulbright scholarships, of obtaining financial backing for a full year's study abroad. In Europe, particularly in Germany where there is a lack of naturally beautiful voices and a plethora of opera houses offering a ten-month season in almost every city of any size, he will then have much more of an opportunity to find engagements. Some of today's well-known stars such as Evelyn Lear, Thomas Stewart and Jess Thomas have made their fame and fortune via this road. Another American who has made her career almost entirely abroad is Teresa Stich-Randall. Indeed there are a number of Americans who have yet to be called back to their native land to sing professionally but are enjoying very respectable European careers.

In years past the young artist who aspired to the more subtle and musically demanding career of a lieder singer, would usually somehow raise the money to hire New York City's Town Hall, or the small recital auditorium in Carnegie Hall. London's equivalent is of course Wigmore Hall. They would have programs and tickets printed, pay for as much publicity as possible, paper the house and sing an afternoon or evening's concert of songs. On the strength of the (hopefully) favorable reviews, they would then attract the attention of one of the concert agents and obtain bookings in all parts of the country. Unhappily, the formula for launching a concert career has begun to change. Agents find increasing difficulty in selling recitals by even the top stars around the country, let alone unknowns. There seems to be altogether less demand for concerts of lieder, with the inevitable result that there are fewer and fewer artists proficient at the art. Nowadays would-be concert singers are advised to try to make some kind of name for themselves in opera, however much they may feel themselves unsuited to it; but with a background of operatic appearances agents feel that they can then obtain for them engagements in the musical field that they find more appealing.

Breaking into the world of church-singing is perhaps simpler than obtaining entrance to some of the other branches of the professional singing world. The young oratorio singer who manages to get a position with an important New York church virtually has it made, for these appearances will inevitably lead to calls from other parts of the country for his services in performances of oratorios and other religious musical works. Like aspiring young opera singers, it is important that the church soloist know the standard repertory such as *Messiah* or *Elijah* and have worked with a coach who specializes in this type of music. Another way for a church singer to get his break is to be taken on by a church agent who will help him to get engagements.

So far we have considered only the training and subsequent struggles to gain notice of the singer of so-called classical music. What about the huge flock of hopeful pop singers?

With the age of the microphone the actual vocal training of a pop singer is far less necessary, providing the voice possesses some kind of appealing or arresting quality. The training of a pop singer consists much more in developing a definite style, a "way" with the words and music of his songs, which, however, most of the great entertainers seem to possess naturally. I have read somewhere the earnest declaration that singing off the beat can be taught— but if this essential timing that is the pulse of any good pop singer's interpretations has to be painstakingly learned, it seems to me that the would-be Frank Sinatra or Ella Fitzgerald had better call the whole thing off.

Ideally the hopeful pop star should have musical training and be able to read music at sight. Many in this hectic age never do, but they are the ones who though they may come on strong for a moment or two, vanish with equal rapidity. To make a career that does not burn itself out overnight a pop singer should have coached extensively with a professional who will concentrate on his timing, his expression and teach him an all-important microphone technique to bring out the best in his voice. The pop singer also needs an accompanist with whom he has rapport and an arranger who understands and suits his style. Arrangements are a big expense for a pop singer. In addition to the mandatory photographs and résumés of his appearances, he must also circulate among the powers who control the pop vocal world tapes or demonstration records of his singing and his songs.

We have seen too many movies about the struggles of the un-recognized pop singer to break into "show biz." Unfortunately the difficulties are all too true. It is a big, highly competitive, unfair and very often corrupt business requiring the utmost toughness and determination from the singer hopeful of becoming a star. For example, nothing is more pathetic and awful than the "open" call for the casting of the chorus (perhaps twelve male and twelve female singers) in a Broadway musical. Among the several hundred or more who show up, there will be every kind of singer from opera to pop all seeking the same two things: the security of a good salary for singing eight times a week, and possible recognition. With such a multitude to be heard the auditionist is not permitted to sing through a whole number, though many hopefuls do not know this and look surprised and pained when they are cut off halfway through their song. The experienced auditionist usually begins with the return of the refrain of his number in order to include a top note that he wishes to show off. Sometimes at these auditions which frequently require a whole morning or afternoon's wait on the part of the hopeful singer, high notes or indeed any kind of notes don't seem really to be on the mind of the producer or casting director at all. Even the men may be asked to strip to their waists and judged on the strength of their less than vocal "cheese cake."

Through whatever avenues the break into a professional career is made, the initial start centers on an audition. With one aria or song, not even five minutes in length, a singer soars or is grounded. If the voice at that particular moment fails to respond there will only be a chilling "thank you" and that is the end of it. Unless a sensitive listener happens to hear the potential of a voice through the cloudiness that nervousness has laid on it, rarely does a singer have a second chance. (Not so with Thomas Stewart, now a leading Wagnerian baritone, who declared on a recent Metropolitan broadcast, "I've never sung a good audition in my life.") Perhaps even more than an actual performance auditions put a singer's nerves to their severest test.

Tremors and Terrors. "I have never been nervous in all my life and I have no patience with people who are," declares Mary Garden in her autobiography. Caruso's opinion then cannot have been very high of her (their careers coincided, but they did not sing together) for he is on record as saying, "The artist who boasts he is never nervous is not an artist—he is a liar or a fool." Singers obviously vary in their capacity for nervousness, just as people do.

Petite, thin Lily Pons suffered agonies before each of the many performances of her long career, and her voice always wavered noticeably at her entrance until she gained assurance. Rosa Ponselle was another hyper-jittery singer. As she tells the story, she faced her debut as Leonora in *Forza del Destino* opposite Caruso with perfect equanimity. On the day before it, however, she happened to notice a review of a tenor named Giulio Crimi who had made his debut the previous evening as Radames in *Aida*. The review was not at all favorable and the totally inexperienced soprano who had sung in vaudeville but never in an opera house suddenly realized the enormity of what she was about to undertake. Not the pleadings nor prayers of her family, their hands rattling with rosaries, could make her agree to go out on the stage— only the intercession of Caruso himself. According to her story she knew nothing of what she was doing throughout the whole performance and was amazed when she discovered that she had made a wonderfully successful debut.

Other less remarkable vocalists might not have been able to triumph so readily over their nerves, for the plain fact of the matter is that when it comes to nervousness nature sets a cruel and cunning trap for a singer. Anyone who has ever undergone an "attack of nerves" knows that the two immediate reactions of the body are a shortness of breath and trembling both of which immediately affect the quality of the voice. In addition, nervousness inhibits the glands that lubricate the mouth with saliva, so much so that the tongue can stick to the roof of the mouth. The larynx also needs its lubrication of mucus and this too dries up under conditions of fear. Any or all these reactions can and do have a disastrous effect on the singing voice.

Nor does the plight of the nervous singer end there. As a British laryngologist points out: "The larynx to the singer is what the hands are to the surgeon, limbs to the dancer or eyes to the marksman. But unlike the latter, the singer's throat is subject to a multitude of strange sensations which he usually tries to analyse, often with the handicap of very erroneous ideas of structure, function and what he calls 'voice production.' Almost assuredly he becomes obsessed with such notions, which serve only to increase his anxiety and may lead to injurious habits or treatments."

In short the nervous student singer or professional is trapped by a vicious circle. One or two lessons, or performances, when the voice has not come out with a free and ringing tone but sounds labored and of poor quality will set him to worrying. Something has gone wrong with his vocal technique he decides (particularly if he does not possess a particularly secure one). In this state of worry he works to correct what is wrong and by his anxiety only makes matters worse.

The ordinary tensions and problems of everyday living can also affect the voice. A teacher with a promising pupil who suddenly goes into a slump will do well in his role as counselor and confessor to inquire gently into the circumstances of the student's life. He may not at all be surprised to discover the damaging presence of an unhappy love affair, or perhaps extreme worry over finances. Heightened emotions also affect the voice so that it trembles and becomes distorted. For this reason during a performance singers must never lose themselves completely say, in the tragedy of Violetta's plight or the angers of Otello, lest the quality of the voice be too much affected. Singers must sometimes sing over the griefs of real life. The day after the dress rehearsal of the Vienna première of *Arabella* Lotte Lehmann's mother died. There was no cover for the part, so, in her own words:

". . . I sang at the première . . . There were moments when I forgot the sorrow I bore, whose magnitude only those can realize who have been attached to their mother as I was to mine . . . I was no longer Lotte Lehmann, a daughter bowed down with grief. I was Arabella . . .

"Immeasurable boon of being an artist!

"Only when I got home did I break down and weep."

With the approach of each performance the same unconscious

questions begin to mobilize: "Am I in voice?" "Am I sure of my words? my music?" "How will the audience react to me?" To make a singing career is to have to undergo the exactions of nervous tension until the last note is uttered.

Debut.   As has been said it is the fantasy of many young singers struggling to gain recognition that they will be "discovered" under dramatic conditions and gain stardom in one night. The last such happening of this kind that took place, at the Metropolitan anyway, occurred in November, 1950 when a twenty-year-old soprano was thrust into the part of Zerlina on five hours' notice and with no orchestra rehearsal. She had worked the part thoroughly with the stage director, Herbert Graf, the previous autumn, but she had never before set foot on an operatic stage. This was Roberta Peters who instantly proved that she was born to it. On the other hand if she had made her debut as scheduled there is no doubt that she would have gained equal, though less sensational recognition of her vocal and histrionic talent. Her real break was in 1) making a successful audition at the Metropolitan and 2) that the company in this season was giving a number of student performances of *Zauberflöte* and needed an exceptional soprano voice such as Peters possessed to sing the Queen of the Night as well as to cover the regular performances of Erna Berger, the reigning coloratura at the Metropolitan of the time.

For most singers a debut will be inconspicuous in America, at best, with the New York City Opera; in England, at Sadler's Wells. Both companies have proved to be an accommodating stepping stone to the larger New York and London houses for a number of singers. In America a debut can also be made with little local companies, which however present only a few performances (sometimes only one) and therefore provide only limited experience for young artists anxious to sing as many times as possible. This, as I have already pointed out, is the advantage of going to a country such as Germany, with its numerous opera houses, to gain a start. The pay in the various theaters is mostly not much and very often young singers find themselves called upon to sing in unknown operas such as *Der Liebestrank* or *Der Bajazzo*—until they discover that these are none other than the familiar *L'Elisir d'Amore* and *Pagliacci* as performed in German. The pervasive and disciplined musicianship of the Teuton, above all the experience of singing evening after evening before the public returns ample rewards and also offers total immersion in at least one language vital to a singer. Of late, Germany, with fewer good native voices (presumably because the harshness of the language does not permit them to form naturally), has been more welcoming to foreign singers, particularly Americans, than Italy with its many opera companies but with a more abundant native talent on which to draw.

In Europe the young singer need fear far less the rut of *comprimario* roles than he might at the Metropolitan. The soprano who sings Violetta's maid one night may quickly make her way to Musetta the next, and perhaps Mimi six months later. Thus, some small European opera house is probably the best and most likely place for the debut to be made—quietly, undramatically and probably with no stupendous response from the public. The extraordinary, long-lived baritone Sir Charles Santley as far back as 1857 made his debut in the tiny role of the Doctor in *Traviata* at Pavia. Giglio Nordica, as she called herself in 1879, made her debut with an inferior opera company at Milan singing Donna Elvira in *Don Giovanni* which at that time was considered a secondary role. The nervous debutante was the only one of the Don's pursued and pursuing ladies not to be hissed. Melba made no great splash in her debut role of Gilda at La Monnaie, the theater in Brussels, while Louise Homer first tried out the experience of singing and acting on stage with a full orchestra in the pit at Vichy. Of the great English-speaking singers in that era only one, as she puts it, seems to have gone on stage "a nobody" and found herself "the next day the talk of two continents." This

was Emma Eames who made her first appearance in a theater anywhere at the Paris Opéra, 14 March, 1889 as Gounod's Juliette,
having been coached by the composer himself. Two other Marchesi pupils, Suzanne Adams and Bessie Abott, also debuted in
this role at the Opéra but neither achieved the glowing stardom
of Eames, though judging from their phonograph records their
voices were lovely. Geraldine Farrar offered a contract to sing
small parts at the Metropolitan turned it down for European
training and experience, confident that one day she would sweep
back across the Atlantic as a reigning prima donna which of
course she did.

It was really not until 1918 in her triumphant debut at the New
York Metropolitan Opera House that Rosa Ponselle proved that
it wasn't absolutely essential for English-speaking singers to undergo European training and experience, but she of course was a
phenomenon, one who must almost be classified as a miracle.
Nevertheless she broke the shibboleth, and gradually singers entirely trained in America who had never soaked up the atmosphere of Europe began to trickle into the Metropolitan, including Lawrence Tibbett, Gladys Swarthout, Helen Jepson and
Helen Traubel, to enumerate some of the stars of the late nine-
teen-twenties and thirties.

Since extra strain accompanies a debut certain roles are often
favored to introduce new singers. Mimi is a graceful, untaxing
part in which to introduce the lyric or *spinto* soprano. Heavier
voiced sopranos often make their bows as Sieglinde, while the
leggiero or coloratura may be heard first in the relatively undemanding part of Gilda. Gilda's Duke and Mimi's Rodolfo are
popular tenor debut roles, while a new baritone may appear for
the first time singing the smooth, non-arduous music of the elder
Germont in *Traviata*.

Whatever the part and wherever it is sung, the debut, even if
it earns splendid critical acclaim, is just that—a first appearance,

a beginning. Now the singer is faced with yet another challenge, that of establishing himself.

Drop-Outs. "The following season [after her debut] Miss Ponselle slipped slowly backward. When she sang with Caruso in the memorable revival of *La Juive,* we said: 'Miss Ponselle did not fulfill the promise of last season. Her voice sounded much more constrained and less noble in tone, while her action was primitive indeed . . .'

"Miss Ponselle continued her descent for a considerable period . . ."

These were comments in retrospect by an astute vocal critic, W. J. Henderson, on the career of one of the world's greatest singers. What happened to Ponselle, thrust totally inexperienced before the public in a leading opera house and expected to fulfill all that her debut had promised, is, on a less flamboyant level, the experience of many singers after their initially successful debut. Until that moment the singer has led a life in the studio, protected and encouraged by his teacher and his coach, his faults scolded but forgiven, his virtues touted. Now he is out in a chilling world, facing audiences that may be sympathetic but who after all have paid their admission prices and expect a reasonable degree of professionalism from the fledgling singer. In the studio a faulted note, a muffed entrance can be repeated—not so in performance. And should mistakes occur during rehearsals there is the far from tolerant conductor to deal with besides the weary scorn of the other, more experienced singers, who do not relish having to repeat duets or ensembles because of the rawness of their new colleague.

The first professional years, the ones after the debut, then, require tremendous physical and psychological adjustments on the part of the singer launched on a career. For the first time he realizes that he no longer quite owns himself: one part now belongs to the opera house that holds him under contract, and another belongs to the public itself. His life is partly planned by the General Manager as to what days he must sing, or to stand by covering other performers in case of an indisposition. There are also rehearsals and even if he does not participate in them he may be required to sit out front and watch the blocking of the part currently being performed by an older leading artist, a role, naturally, to which the young singer aspires. Of the two, the junior singer will probably think bitterly and often rightly that he possesses the fresher voice, but he finds that maddeningly, the management will not scrap older, experienced artists no longer in their prime, but who have served the company faithfully and well, in favor of raw youth. So he must sit there fuming, prevented from appearing for lack of experience, but having no other means of obtaining it.

In these first arduous professional years, the young singer's voice is also subject to far rougher treatment than in the days of its training when his various masters handled it with sympathetic care. Now he may be asked to learn a role that does not lie well for him but which he dares not refuse. Singing the whole time with orchestra, too, is quite different from letting the voice soar over a single piano. He may be called upon to rehearse the day before or after the evening of a performance or sometimes on the very day itself. In these years he learns how to husband his voice, to sing through a rehearsal *piano,* and "mark" his high notes, which means to sing them an octave down. (Melba never sang her high notes while practicing or in rehearsal, believing like a penurious miser that she only had so many and when one was spent it was gone forever.) Because of this extra strain singers who reveal fresh, lovely voices at their debuts frequently go "off" in the years that immediately follow. Due to over-singing and the strain of numerous public appearances in a competition-ridden opera house, the quality may become shrill or coarse and the voice sound strained and fatigued.

There have also been young singers who have made it to the

top, but finding the grind and discipline not rewarding enough have turned to show business or night club work. In former times both Fritzi Scheff and Lina Abarbanell sang at the Metropolitan but left it for fame and stardom in operetta. More recently during the season of 1943-44 Christine Johnson, a young American with a luscious, beautifully trained contralto voice made her debut at the Metropolitan as Erda in *Das Rheingold*. The reviews were very favorable and much was expected of her. Offered an attractive part the following year in Rodgers and Hammerstein's new musical, *Carousel*, Miss Johnson became the first of many to give out the joyous "June is bustin' out all over." But after the run of the musical she was never heard at the Metropolitan again and her career simply dissolved.

The reaction of her teacher, one of the most distinguished and conscientious in the field, can be imagined.

Sometimes young singers burst upon the musical scene—a "meteor" is usually the image conjured up in connection with them—and after a few years before the public burn themselves out. One of these whose memory is still revered was the great French singing actress, Marie Cornélie Falcon who made a sensational debut in 1832 when not quite nineteen at the Paris Opéra and thereafter attracted an adoring public every time she sang. Five years after her debut, she was appearing opposite the tenor, Nourrit, in an opera based on the life of Alessandro Stradella when at the end of the first act she opened her mouth to sing and nothing came out but a kind of strangled cry. The soprano went white and Nourrit is said to have gripped her by her shoulders in order to hold her up until the curtain could be rung down. Falcon went to Italy in an attempt to retrain her voice but it had been irreparably damaged by singing too much with a faulty vocal technique, as a single reappearance in 1840 gave sad testimony.

Another in more recent times who came and went amid the most tremendous publicity was the young coloratura soprano, Marion Talley, who made her debut at the Metropolitan in

February, 1926 at the age of nineteen—one for which she was
patently not ready. Though youthful and attractive in voice and
appearance, her technique was faulty and her musicianship insecure. Talley lasted four seasons at the Met, each one with successively fewer appearances—and was not heard from again.

At this writing, one of course cannot be sure but I fear for the
voice of the dynamic young dramatic soprano Elena Suliotis from
the way that she abuses it to obtain effects, so that the unevenness
of her singing calls forth "bravas" from her audiences at one
moment and boos the next during the same performance.

V

> . . . . *And then the justice,*
> *In fair round belly with good capon lin'd,*
> *With eyes severe and beard of formal cut. . . .*
> . . . .
> *And so he plays his part.*

Routines. Once the precarious period of adjusting to the
strains of professional life is safely past, the existence of the singer
settles down into a more predictable pattern, but one which to
ordinary people would seem very strange and irregular. Now the
singer's life is completely dominated by the demands of his voice:
it is the master he must serve, the sometimes querulous mistress
that he must humor and cajole, the child that must be tended and
coddled and looked after with loving care. The entire being of
the dedicated singer is concentrated on his next performance, and
when it is finished the one after that. In between there is daily
practice which varies from singer to singer. Some spare their
voices and sing for themselves as little as possible; others believe
it efficacious to vocalize regularly up to an hour a day or even
more. (A coloratura soprano or mezzo for the length of her singing career is a slave to exercises; not so other singers.) Then there

At the Rehearsal. Cavalieri and Scotti by Caruso.

are rehearsals * and sessions with coaches at the opera house or work with the singer's own coach and accompanist. Scores already committed to memory have to be reviewed and new ones learned. Nowadays, costumes are usually part of an overall operatic production and supplied by the opera company, as in former days they were not, but expressed, exclusively, the singer and his tastes. In any case costumes have to be tried on and fitted. Women singers also require flattering dresses for their concert appearances. Interviews and public appearances have never been thought harmful to a singer's career; letters must be answered, photographs autographed and managers and agents dealt with, particularly if the artist is a big star. All of these activities come together in a kind of lump which provides a routine for a singer—albeit a knobby, irregular

---

* In former times stars often avoided rehearsals to spare their voices. It is said that Patti never went to a rehearsal in her whole career.

one—but a routine that requires a very strict kind of discipline.

If the singer should try to forget all these impositions on his life by say, going to a party, it is not easy to relax totally. Among a large group may be some traitor with a cold. Drink, a usually reliable provider of relaxation, has to be taken judiciously and rich food regarded with suspicion. A full night's sleep, naturally, is essential to a singer's vocal health.

From these pressures feelings, of not really belonging to themselves, there is no surcease for the man or woman who has chosen to become a serious, dedicated singer. On the one hand he is owned by his voice; on the other he is possessed by his public who are free to applaud or withhold their approval as they see fit. Only a decision to take a month or two off and totally "forget" can provide a singer with temporary relief from this unusual human condition in which he has worked so hard to embroil himself. But even then, relaxing somewhere in the country and not singing at all (a hiatus, by the way, that can have a most salubrious effect on the voice of a hard-working artist), the thought of next season cannot be totally forgotten: new roles . . . perhaps an engagement in a different, more important opera house . . . an increased number of recital dates . . .

On Stage! The day of the performance finds the singer transformed into a monastic figure, refusing human contact as much as he possibly can. Mrs. Caruso describes grippingly how the famous tenor passed the slow, attenuated hours before an appearance: "On the day of a performance there was no music in the house and Enrico rarely spoke. Through the silent hours he played solitaire, drew caricatures and sorted the rare collection of gold coins he had begun in 1907 . . . The only occupations that relaxed and amused him were those in which he could use his hands . . ."

Many artists do not sing or even speak on the day they are to appear, contenting themselves with a few scales in the morning to confirm that the voice is "there." Two noted Wagnerian sopranos made an exception to this routine of silence. Frida Leider would get her voice up early in the day with soft arpeggios, then study her role of the evening silently, after which, as she says in her autobiography, "I would sing the most difficult parts. The arduous training in the morning made me feel secure for the evening performance, *if I was in good form*" [italics mine]—that conditional clause which inevitably qualifies the performance of every singer. Helen Traubel, even more astonishingly, says she would go over the whole long Wagnerian role that she was to sing in the evening at full volume—a practice that would appall most singers. Wildest of all pre-performance routines is one attributed to the mercurial Maria Malibran who thought nothing of staying up the entire night before a performance dancing at a ball. Then she would sleep to noon and ride horseback all afternoon.

The problem of what to eat is also a vexing one. A singer needs his strength; on the other hand a full stomach restricts deep breathing, while any kind of digestive disorder will of course disrupt song entirely. Usually then, singers on the day of a performance will restrict themselves to a light, simple meal in the middle of the day, and perhaps a cup of tea or broth at the end of the afternoon. Again, the redoubtable Traubel describes how she shocked a fellow singer by devouring a bag of peanuts and an ice cream cone not long before a Hollywood Bowl concert. Even she, however, imposed on herself the recluselike standards to which most singers resort, refusing to see anyone or talk on the telephone.

Finally the time for departure to the theater is reached. Many singers like to get to the dressing room early to make sure that their costumes are perfectly in order, to warm up their voices and commune with or propitiate whatever gods they feel have control over the quality of the night's performance. Much has been written of the dressing room rivalries on evenings when an opera such as *Don Giovanni* is presented, involving three prima donnas and perhaps a single star dressing room. At the old Met, Geraldine Farrar obviated any competition by having her own dressing room fitted up for her. It was little larger than a cubicle but it was hers and she kept it padlocked when not using it. At the old Met too, Rosa Ponselle used to cause consternation among the other singers, ever fearful of catching cold, by demanding that the steam heat which she disliked intensely be shut off.

Caruso as Don José in Carmen, *by Caruso.*

Within the dressing room the final, sometimes very odd, routines are accomplished. Caruso, for example, on seeing his wife, who came later when his make-up was already in place, would become calm and ask "for a cigarette which he smoked slowly in a long black holder . . .

"When he had finished the cigarette he went to the washstand and filled his mouth with salt water, which he inhaled—or seemed to inhale—into his lungs, then spat out before he strangled. Mario (his valet) held out a box of Swedish snuff from which he took a pinch to clear his nostrils; then he took a wineglass of whisky, next a glass of charged water and finally a quarter of an apple. Into the pockets that were placed in every costume exactly where his hands dropped, he slipped two bottles of warm salt water, in case he had to wash his throat on the stage. When all was ready Mario handed him his charms—a twisted coral horn, holy medals and old coins, all linked together on a fat little chain . . . Just before he left the dressing room he called upon his dead mother for help, since the thought of her gave him courage. No one ever wished him luck because, he said, that was sure to bring disaster."

With all their training and experience during these last moments before their entrance many singers lapse back into faith in spells and superstitions. All has become totally fatalistic. Tetrazzini's barometer was a dagger that she used in *Lucia di Lammermoor* and which one night when she was singing at her best had fallen from her hand and stuck upright in the floor. Thereafter the tormenting test had to be made before each performance: if the dagger landed flat—*downfall!* Some singers rely on fetish objects such as a doll or a toy animal to bring them luck. These have to be touched before leaving the dressing room or else worn or carried during the performance. Others spread out photographs of their families and solemnly kiss the faces of the loved ones before going off to perform the night's vocal work. An amusing story of a singer's superstition is told by George Marek in his collection of little pieces called *A Front Seat at the Opera:*

"Selma Kurz, the Viennese coloratura, believed that she would sing well if she saw a chimney-sweep before the performance. Her manager used to hire one to saunter accidentally past the stage door. On one occasion, seeing the sooted man, she called him over, reached into her purse, and gave him a tip; whereupon the honest fellow said, 'Not necessary, Madame. I have already been paid.' "

As the time of the performance approaches most singers now try out their voices at full volume in a series of whoops and howls that have been much mocked over the ages. Each artist will have his own pet way of warming up—scales, arpeggios, hummed notes or singing odd-sounding syllables—"oh Oh! OH; Tee-Tee-Tee" sounded on different pitches. Others may sing snatches of a song or even a bit of the role they are about to perform. This process of warming up as with an athlete loosens and tones up muscles connected with the vocal process and brings blood into the throat, increasing the resonance and ring of the singing voice.

Certain operatic roles give the singer no opportunity to get the feel of his voice onstage before the performer must launch into a famous and difficult aria. The tenor cast as Radames leads off with the recitative of "Celeste Aida" having sung a bare fifteen measures before the aria. The mezzo portraying Azucena doesn't even have that: she simply begins "Stride la Vampa" without any vocal introduction of any kind. This same mezzo must also begin her entrance as Carmen with the tricky melodic pattern of the "Habanera" made even more difficult by the fact that she is usually positioned up a flight of steps far back on the stage so that it is difficult to hear the orchestra. On these nights when the singer must jump into a famous aria "cold," extra warming up may take place in the dressing room. Pity the poor soprano who sings the *Siegfried* Brünnhilde; no matter how much preliminary vocalizing she may have done, she still has to lie for many long minutes silent on her rock, while her hero accomplishes her rescue and puzzles over the fact that she is not a man.

Finally the moment of the entrance is at hand. In a concert or recital naturally it will be applauded—not so in every opera house. If a star has come to rely upon a burst of applause to bolster his confidence, he will be very upset in a theater such as Covent Garden to be greeted by silence. It is the reverent custom in that theater usually not to interrupt the music and many singers appearing there for the first time have been seriously shaken by this cold lack of greeting.

Once out on the stage and actually performing, the singer, if he is an artist as well, loses himself in the role he is portraying—or the song he is singing—but only a portion of himself. Another vigilant part of his artistic being must stand off watching, listening, alert to any mistakes and critical of lapses in musical and dramatic taste. In an operatic performance time is the despot; everything must be performed to cues in the music moved on relentlessly by the conductor. Yet among the most faithful opera goers who can ever remember a performance, however complicated, being stopped because a singer has lost his way? It seems remarkable that it almost never happens. A singer, terrifyingly, may make a wrong entrance, skip a number of measures of his role, get out of time with the orchestra, but somehow with the help of the conductor and the prompter, he will right himself again and very often few in the audience are even aware of the mistake. The singer knows, however.

Occasionally in recitals I have heard an artist get out with his accompanist and make a false entrance. If worst comes to worst the error can be glossed over with a charming smile, a word of explanation and recommencement of the song. Popular vocalists have been known to muddle the words of a number or fail to mesh with their accompanying band in some way, but again these mistakes can be glossed over or the song begun again. The only time I have ever read of an operatic performance coming to a halt in a major opera house is this incident related by Blanche Marchesi of a performance of *Walküre* at the Paris Opéra:

"with Paul Viardot, son of the great Pauline, as conductor. In the first act, Sieglinde got out of control, and Viardot had to stop the orchestra. After a deadly silence in which the audience dared not breathe, he had to restart the scene. Such an incident is so terrifying that it can never be forgotten," she continues in true operatic style; "dying in front of a cannon seems a joke compared with it. That night Paul Viardot could not continue his conducting, being too ill, and Monsieur Mangin, accompanist of my mother's opera class, a person for whom music had no secrets, took his place without ever having rehearsed the opera, and carried it through without a hitch."

Act after act the opera progresses. The physical as well as the nervous strain can be tremendous. Sweat from the tension, the heat of the lights and the heavy costumes flows freely. A tenor performing the prostrate, dying Tristan was once temporarily blinded by perspiration pouring off the faithful Kurvenal leaning over to tend him. Another potential source of moisture, particularly in German opera, is a pointedly enunciated interchange between singers involving such spit-spraying words as "Mutter" or "Freude." Opera singers also run the risk of being gassed by garlic or onions when playing an intimate scene with a fellow artist.

In between the acts the voice must be rested, but the excitement and energy generated in the performance kept at the highest possible peak. Singers at Glyndebourne, the tiny English opera house set so unexpectedly among the downs of East Sussex, find that amid ideal rehearsal conditions and a satisfying repetition of an opera with the same cast, there is one drawback to performing there. The operas are usually given with a single interval of seventy-five minutes duration, which means that a singer with his voice warmed up and energy mobilized for the first part of the opera must repeat the whole process for the second time in one evening.

When the final curtain falls there is a burst of applause. This is the moment for which every singer, however selfless and artistic, waits, whether in an opera house or before a television audience. Applause for all singers becomes like a habit-forming drug, lifegiving, stimulating, essential. In the opera house I am always amused by the various styles of taking a solo curtain call as practiced by singers. There is the exultant approach, when the singer strides quickly out onto the stage, arms raised, sweeping the audience with the proud, happy gaze of a warrior who has conquered.

"Signorina . . . acknowledges applause" by Gerald Hoffnung.

Then there is the "modest" style, in which the singer glances
shyly, almost timidly around the theater with an expression of
dawning awareness as the applause continues—for me?—all this
for ME? which is followed by a girlish curtsey or a boyish bow.
Still another type of curtain call might be entitled, "Over-
whelmed." Here the star, delaying fractionally the moment when
the excited audience expects to glimpse the singer, moves gravely
before the curtain, exhausted, drained, still in a trance from the
role that has been interpreted. Clutching at the edge of the curtain for support the artist scarcely seems to see the audience until
the roars of approval and the sound of beating hands breaks
through to conscious awareness. Completely overcome, the singer
sinks down in a long deferential curtsey or bow while the applause
washes over this humble figure. Just the opposite is the jaunty,
casual—"Aw, anyone could have done it"—style of accepting the
acclaim of the audience, accompanied by a grin and perhaps a
little wave of the hand. Any of these approaches is more than ac-

ceptable, particularly if the singer puts them over with apparent sincerity. It must never be forgotten that mixed in with all the necessary ingredients for becoming a great star is the final one of a certain innate showmanship.

With the last bow made, all the excited energy generated by the performance must be allayed. Some singers will go out with friends and wolf down a large meal, having had little to eat that day; others fearing not to sleep on a full stomach will try to calm themselves down in other ways. Olive Fremstad was so keyed up after a performance, according to her one-time secretary, that she had to cool off before she could even eat a bite of supper prepared by "a cross and sleepy cook." After the meal the young Mary Watkins Cushing had to read aloud to the diva "a rubbishy detective story, usually, so that her mind could relax . . . If insomnia plagued Madame, as it often did, she would call me an hour or two later to come and talk to her."

Willa Cather in her novel *The Song of the Lark,* which is supposed to be based on the character and career of Olive Fremstad, gives an episode in which the prima donna heroine, Thea Kronborg, keyed up but desperate for sleep, agitates over whether or not to have a hot bath (sometimes the effect is a rousing one), decides to, and having soaked for half an hour gets into bed. There, in order to calm herself still more, she re-enters in her mind the old house in Moonstone, her midwestern home town, passing from room to room until she climbs the back stairs to her own bedroom under the roof. After which she sleeps ten hours.

"My poor Willa," was Fremstad's comment on *The Song of the Lark.* "It wasn't really much like that. But after all, what can you know about me? Nothing!"

Indisposed. How often has it happened in opera houses around the world that audiences gather expectantly to hear a favorite singer, only to have, as the time of the performance is at hand, a figure inevitably bowed with guilt step before the curtain to announce that Madame X or Signor Y "is indisposed. The part will be sung instead by . . ." The groans that go up! The sighs of desperation! (Occasionally though, such a situation provides a young singer with a chance to appear in an important leading role before the public.) On rarer occasions audiences have arrived at the opera house and because of a plague of indispositions heard an entirely different work than the one they expected. Sometimes another kind of announcement is made: "Though suffering from a cold Madame X or Signor Y has graciously consented to appear in tonight's performance."

(There have been occasions when a star not wanting to sing a performance or wishing release from a contract may feign indisposition. The management, if suspicious, usually has the right to require a doctor's certificate as proof.)

Bugaboo of all mankind, the common cold is the singer's particular nightmare. He lives in constant dread of it, fleeing from rain, drafts, cold—indeed, it sometimes seems, in constant flight from all weather. Obviously for a singer the worst type of cold is the sore throat which strikes at the very core of his vocal apparatus. Under examination the vocal cords, normally a pearly white (though in some singers, because of so much use, they sometimes show up a pale pink), will appear a brilliant red. In other cases, the top surfaces of the cords, the only ones visible to the laryngoscope, may look perfectly normal, but the degree of the singer's hoarseness will lead the doctor to suspect that the underneath surfaces which cannot be glimpsed may be acutely inflamed. Should a singer against the advice of a physician or plain common sense attempt to perform when suffering from such an acute inflammation (and singers under pressure or out of inexperience have been known to do so) the result, as one distinguished laryngologist thunders, "may entail weeks or months away from the stage and has been known to ruin a larynx permanently." * When in the

* This is supposed to have been the case with Ljuba Welitsch, whose career terminated prematurely.

grip of such an affliction, that most distasteful of all conditions to a singer, silence is the best recourse.

Curiously enough a head cold may actually add resonance to a singer's voice and many a student singer has thought he has at last won through to his teacher's method with a sudden enrichment of tone, only to discover the next day what he has really acquired is a stuffed-up nose. If no evidence of any inflammation of the larynx exists, it is also possible for a vocalist to "sing over" a head cold. This however is not possible if the inflammation sinks to the chest causing the lungs to throw up a glutinous coating of phlegm over the vocal cords, making the voice soft and weak.

Even when in perfect health a sudden surge of phlegm into the throat, familiar to us all, is the bane of the singer's existence, causing imperfections or even the breaking of tones. "How often it happens that one comes to a concert in splendid trim only to be met by a cool wind at the very first entrance," writes Lilli Lehmann in *How to Sing*. "The difference in temperature between the artists' room and hall very often with the first inhalation causes a clearing of the throat, loosening small particles of phlegm which in the constantly out-flowing breath move to and fro completely spoiling one's pleasure in the concert . . . If they are happily situated they are sometimes quite loosened with the first number" (hence the veiled or uncertain sounds that some singers make on their first appearance) "very often, however, not for half, or even all the evening . . . Sometimes even a single little thread lying across the vocal cords may spoil everything . . . One can't clear or cough it away, neither during the concert, nor during the singing."

Small wonder then if an evening's performance can be affected by a simple temperature change that a singer must be highly self-centered or at least self-protective. On the morning of a day when he is to appear, one basic question will absorb his mind: am I in voice? As with any ordinary human being, supine through hours of sleep, phlegm will have collected in his throat. But will it be gone by curtain time? "You never can tell early in the day how you are going to feel in the evening," Lilli Lehmann writes with the intent to comfort—but the sentence can be read another way as well. It's interesting how many speak of "the voice" as something outside themselves, a capricious, willful creature whose whims are innumerable and not simple to satisfy. Yet this is understandable given the invisibility of the vocal apparatus and the number of outside factors—dust, humidity, temperature—that can affect it. One would think that a brisk walk with a friend on a crisp winter's day would relax and divert a singer facing a performance that evening. In fact nothing could be more ruinous than cold, dry air being taken into the throat while conversing, and some doctors advise their vocalist patients always to wrap a scarf around their mouths when going out in the wintertime.

And what about those vices, drinking and smoking, much beloved by most of the world? Certainly great singers have been drinkers. Caruso never drank wine, writes Dorothy Caruso, but he always took a wineglass full of whisky before going onstage. I have been told on good authority that Flagstad would knock back a martini before her entrance. Jussi Bjoerling is said to have been a heavy drinker but not the slightest alcoholic vapor ever seemed to cloud the purity of his voice. Most laryngologists and teachers agree, however, that alcohol, particularly spirits, can in the long run be injurious to the voice and should be taken with great moderation.

As to the use of tobacco, certainly on the face of it hot smoke drying out the secretions of the mouth and larynx and ultimately (as we are now certain) limiting the smoker's lung capacity, would scarcely be thought to bestow any benefits on a singer. Yet many vocalists find tobacco a relaxation and support to the nerves and have smoked throughout their entire careers. The suave, handsome nineteenth-century tenor, Giovanni Mario, frequently laid down his cigar to go out and sing before an adoring public, and took it up again as soon as he re-entered the wings. Another famous teno, Enrico Caruso, smoked two packs a day while the great pop singer, Billie Holliday, who took her addictions seriously, got through almost a carton a day. So, as with human beings in general, there can be no set rule against smoking for singers, though common sense declares that they will do well to avoid the habit if they possibly can.

Formerly, singers traveling about to fulfill engagements were forced because of slow transportation to rest their voices. Today a singer can appear one night in London, the next in Milan, and perhaps rush to New York on the following evening to substitute for an ailing colleague. In addition there is the call of the recording studio with repeated takes during sessions. Goaded by ambition and the desire for fees, many a young singer of today is threatened by the annihilating gust of the jet. In general the public thinks that singers spend hours and hours of the day bellowing out scales and whooping up and down arpeggios. In fact singers, teachers (the intelligent ones) and doctors all warn against the dangers of over-singing. The vocal cords, though muscles, are not like those of an athlete which must be worked out to keep their elasticity. Precisely the opposite: tired or overworked or strained because they are not correctly manipulated, these extraordinary ligaments that singers call on to make lightning changes in length and tension lose their ability to do so. Sensing this, the singer forces them on, bringing their two delicate edges together violently while attacking a note. Loss of brilliance, flexibility and the ability to stay on pitch—these are the first warnings of an over-used voice. The next consequence may be hoarseness, and then, most dreaded of all, the eruption of a node or nodule on the vocal cord.

Tiny, pimple-like protuberances, they are sometimes called "screamers' nodes" because when they develop, a singer can no longer properly diminish his tone nor sing softly, particularly his high notes, but must shout or scream them. This causes the cords to fly together still more violently, exacerbating the nodes (usually there are two, exactly opposite one another) until the cords are prevented from approximating, leaving a space through which air rushes, creating breathiness or hoarseness. Nodes, which often develop in the throats of people who put a heavy strain on their voices such as clergymen, schoolteachers, or even ebullient children, can usually be seen with the aid of a laryngoscope by throat doctors, who refer to them as chorditis nodosa. Recognized early enough, they give warning to student singers of imperfections in the technique that they are acquiring, and to professionals of over-singing, or performing music too exacting for their voices. Rest, refraining from singing and a correction of the abuses that caused the nodes will usually cure them. In more serious cases surgery is sometimes advised, but this is a tremendous decision for a singer to take, since the slightest nick of the delicate ligaments by the scalpel will permanently scar the voice. Even a perfect operation may leave the vocal cords less malleable than they once were. Blanche Marchesi says that because Caruso, the possessor of an essentially lyric voice, invaded the dramatic repertory and at the same time sang as many as five times a week at the Metropolitan, he developed a node on one of his vocal cords, which he had removed. This operation was a complete success. But when a second nodule occurred and had to be excised he never was able to sing a lovely high pianissimo as before.

The high voices, particularly those of sopranos, are most prone to nodes; indeed, laryngologists have found tiny chronic protuberances on the cords of professional women singers, which because they are so minute, have not impaired their careers. Melba, who kept at least a semblance of a voice for nigh on forty years, was aware of the danger of high notes sung loudly, and reserved them only for performances. Yet even she, because she once invaded the dramatic repertory to sing the *Siegfried* Brünnhilde with her light, silvery voice, developed a node and had to cancel all her appearances for a year. Fortunately her voice was restored to her and when she returned to the lyric parts for which it was suited, nodes never afflicted her again.

After three seasons of charming audiences at the Metropolitan, Lucrezia Bori was forced to retire and undergo surgery for the removal of nodes on her vocal cords by a specialist in Milan. Terrified of the experience, she later discovered that Caruso had gone to the same doctor, a fact that might have provided her with some comfort, only by that time it was too late. For two years thereafter, Bori lived the existence of a mute hermit in the mountains of her native Spain. Eventually she gained courage to try her voice and found that it still existed. Her first reappearance in opera was at Monte Carlo: the strain and nervous tension can be imagined. In January, 1921, after an absence in all of five seasons, she was joyfully welcomed back to the Metropolitan. Her most astute critics, however, always declared that her voice was never quite what it had been.

Of the vocal cords, Blanche Marchesi has written: "One can pinch, burn, pull or cut them, but they have never been known to tear." Small comfort this, to the singer, considering all the additional scourges to which they are prey. Indeed it leaves one amazed that fine singing exists at all.

The Human Condition. Around those formidable shoals that comprise the demands of a singer's career, must run his personal life, the ordinary ingredients of existence—love, sex, meaningful relationships, raising a family, which most of us consider difficult enough to manage without all the extra strains and complexities that a professional singer has to endure. It won't come as any surprise to the reader then that many singers at least resolve (though life being what life is that resolution can be undermined) never to marry nor attempt to mix a family life with their careers. For obvious reasons this is more true of women singers than men. One who kept firmly to this vow was the glamorous Mary Garden.

The defenses of another beautiful singer in that era proved less redoubtable and Geraldine Farrar succumbed to her cost to the attractions of an actor, Lou Tellegen. Two fine vocal artists at the turn of the century and afterwards, Ernestine Schumann-Heink and Louise Homer, managed to be both mothers and mezzos as well, but they were exceptions. The beauteous Emma Eames tried marriage twice, first with the attractive painter Julian Story and later with the baritone, Emilio de Gorgoza. Neither was a success. Handsome Lillian Nordica, who was evidently naïve and too trusting of men, chalked up a score of three unsuccessful marriages. She is generally considered to be the original for the prima donna heroine Willa Cather called Cressida Garnett, the much-worked "Diamond Mine" which is the name Miss Cather gave to her short story. In all such marriages a great female star obviously cannot make the usual wifely subordinations expected of a woman. Equally, the husband, unless he is an out-and-out gold-digger happy to live off his wife's large earnings, finds himself in the somewhat humiliating position of being Mr. Emma Eames or Mr. Lillian Nordica. But if he shares his wife's career in some way, either as another singer, or an authoritative musician such as conductor or coach, or acts on her behalf as agent or manager, the marriage would appear to have a better chance of survival.

MARRIAGES BETWEEN SINGERS

Not surprisingly, marriages sometimes occur between singers, enabling them to share the peculiar problems of the life that they lead. They may also share the operatic stage and concert platform, as currently do Christa Ludwig and Walter Berry and Evelyn Lear and Thomas Stewart. However, the tensions and jealousies inherent in a singing career can also contribute to the failure of these unions. In the following list an asterisk indicates some of those which did not survive.

Wanda Achsel (soprano)
Ada Adini (soprano)
Pierette Alarie (soprano)
Aurora d'Alessio (contralto)
Sari Barabas (soprano)
Jane Bathori (soprano)
Gemma Bellincioni (soprano and first Santuzza)
Sophie Bischoff-David (soprano)
Joyce Blackham (mezzo)
Inge Borkh (soprano)
Gemma Bosini (soprano)
Geori Boué (soprano)
Helena Braun (soprano)
Clara Butt (contralto)
Monserrat Caballé (soprano)
Lina Cavalieri (soprano)
Augusta Concato (soprano)
Fiorenza Cossotto (mezzo)
Toti Dal Monte (soprano)
Pauline Donalda (soprano)
Elen Dosia (soprano)
Maria Duchêne (mezzo)
Emma Eames (soprano)
Florence Easton (soprano)
Marta Eggerth (soprano)
Lucia Evangelista (soprano)
Malfada Favero (soprano)
Malvina Garrigus (soprano and first Isolde)
Maria Gay (contralto)
Ada Giacchetti (soprano)
Christine Görner (soprano)
Marie de Goulsin (contralto)

Hans Clemens (tenor)
Antonio Aramburo (tenor) *
Leopold Simoneau (tenor)
Roberto d'Alessio (tenor)
Franz Klarwein (tenor)
Emile Engel (tenor)
Roberto Stagno (tenor and first Turiddu)
Johannes Bischoff (baritone)
Peter Glossop (baritone)
Alexander Welitsch (baritone)
Mariano Stabile (baritone)
Roger Bourdin (baritone)
Ferdinand Franz (baritone)
Kennerley Rumford (baritone)
Bernardé Marté (tenor)
Lucien Muratore (tenor) *
Nino Piccaluga (tenor) *
Ivo Vinco (bass)
Enzo de Muro Lomanto (tenor) *
Paul Seveilhac (baritone)
André Burdino (tenor)
Léon Rothier (bass) *
Emilio de Gogorza (baritone) *
Francis Maclennan (tenor) *
Jan Kiepura (tenor)
Jerome Hines (bass)
Alessandro Ziliani (tenor) *
Ludwig Schnorr von Carolsfield (tenor and first Tristan)
Giovanni Zenatello (tenor)
Enrico Caruso (tenor) * [1]
Benno Kusche (baritone)
Jean de Reszke (tenor)

[1] Caruso and Giacchetti were not legally married but she was the mother of his two sons. When she ran away from him he was heartbroken.

Mathilde Graumann (mezzo)
Giulia Grisi (soprano)
Winifred Heidt (mezzo)
Dagmar Hermann (contralto)
Maria Ivogün (soprano)
Mathilde Jonas (soprano)
Sena Jurinac (soprano)
Hermine Kittel (contralto)
Adrienne von Kraus-Osborne
  (contralto)
Evelyn Lear (soprano)
Lilli Lehmann (soprano)
Adele Leigh (soprano)
Gabrielle Lejeune (soprano)
Loretta di Lelio (soprano)
Mary Lewis (soprano)
Ilva Ligabue (soprano)
Lydia Lipkowska (soprano)
Liselotte Losch (soprano)
Christa Ludwig (mezzo)
Marguerite Matzenauer (mezzo)
Mariette Mazarin (soprano)
Tatiana Menotti (soprano)
Ruth Miller (soprano)
Patricia Moore (soprano)
Lillian Nordica (soprano)
Maria Olszewska (mezzo)
Lina Pagliughi (soprano)
Adelina Patti (soprano)
Luisa Perrick (soprano)
Roberta Peters (soprano)
Clara Perry (soprano)
Leontyne Price (soprano)
Rosa Raisa (soprano)
Marie Rappold (soprano)
Hilde Reggiani (soprano)

Salvatore Marchesi (bass)
Giovanni Mario (tenor)
Eugene Conley (tenor)
Hans Braun (baritone) *
Karl Erb (tenor) *
Harry de Garmo (baritone)
Sesto Bruscantini (baritone)
Alexander Haydter (baritone)
Felix von Kraus (bass)

Thomas Stewart (baritone)
Paul Kalisch (tenor) *
James Pease (baritone)
Charles Gilibert (baritone)
Franco Corelli (tenor)
Michael Bohnen (bass) *
Paolo Pesani (bass)
George Baklanoff (baritone)
Josef Metternich (baritone)
Walter Berry (baritone)
Edoardo Ferrari-Fontana (tenor) *
Léon Rothier (bass) *
Juan Oncina (tenor)
Mario Chamlee (tenor)
Dino Borgioli (tenor)
Zoltan Döme (tenor) *
Emil Schipper (baritone) *
Primo Montanari (tenor)
Ernesto Nicolini (tenor) *
Miguel Fleta (tenor) *
Robert Merrill (baritone) *
Ben Davies (tenor)
William Warfield (baritone) *
Giacomo Rimini (baritone)
Rudolf Berger (tenor)
Bruno Landi (tenor)

Delia Reinhardt (soprano)

Caroline Raitt (mezzo)

Elisabeth Rethberg (soprano)

Bidu Sayão (soprano)

Grete Stückgold (soprano)

Maureen Springer-Dickie (soprano)

Adelina Stehle (soprano and first Nanetta in *Falstaff*)

Gladys Swarthout (mezzo)

Pia Tassinari (soprano)

Sandra Warfield (mezzo)

Claire Watson (soprano)

Virginia Zeani (soprano)

Lore Wissman (soprano)

Gustav Schützendorf (baritone) *

Hans Kaart (tenor)

George Cehanovsky (baritone)

Giuseppe Danise (baritone)

Gustav Schützendorf (baritone)

Murray Dickie (tenor)

Edoardo Garbini (tenor and first Fenton in *Falstaff*)

Frank Chapman (baritone)

Ferrucio Tagliavini (tenor) *

James McCracken (tenor)

David Thaw (tenor)

Nicola Rossi-Lemeni (bass)

Wolfgang Windgassen (tenor)

A male singer married to a non-professional wife has an easier time achieving the condition of a normal head of a family. His hours are a bit peculiar and irregular and he may be away from home for periods at a time, but probably no more than any hard-working salesman or ambitious junior executive. As I have already remarked, singers on the whole seem to be more than usually highly sexed and so the wife who kisses her husband goodbye and sends him off with a cheery wave to the intrigues and passions of the backstage world in which she does not mingle may be pos-sibly exchanging peace of mind for a false illusion of fidelity. Singing as they do of heightened passions it is not surprising that male singers seek, sometimes tirelessly, to give expression to these emotions in a fundamental way. Marjorie Lawrence tells in her autobiography of her amazement following a joint recital with Ezio Pinza, when the magnetic *basso* declared his love for her: she was, she gathered, one more to be added to his list, like that of the Don whom he sang so marvelously. Handsome and ener-getic Giovanni Martinelli is another whose activities were said to be unfailing till the end of his days in his eighties. And of course the Sinatra legends top them all. His biographer declares that Sinatra's friends say when he arrived on the MGM lot to make the musical *Anchors Aweigh,* the singer tacked up a list of "desirable females on his dressing room door. As the shooting proceeded, pencil lines were drawn through various names."

Since sex and the singing voice seem to have such a close connection, this raises the question whether sexual over-indulgence will not put a strain on the vocal apparatus. Some teachers warn against the perils of sexual excess to which, according to Madame Ida Franca anyway, sopranos and tenors are most prone. The prima donna heroine of Marcia Davenport's enormously enjoyable novel *Of Lena Geyer* sings an "off" performance of Donna Anna after having spent the night with her lover, Louis, Duc de Chartres, at whom she bursts out bitterly after the performance: " 'You and your love. I never want to see you again. I never want you to touch me. I ought to have known better than to make a mess of my life because of you.' "

Later when the nobleman succeeds in calming down the tall, wide-shouldered diva, she warms to the subject.

" 'Other women may be able to combine love and their art, if they have one,' " she continued, 'I cannot. We've talked of this before. In holiday time, perhaps, I could make love and not suffer from it. But not when I'm working.

". . . 'When I practice on a day after you have stayed with me, do you think I don't feel the difference, the let-down, the lack of resilience? Of course I do and I have been worrying about it . . . Do you know where I think the voice comes from?'

"I knew indeed and nodded.

" 'Exactly. I once heard a teacher give a girl a terrible scolding for having a love affair, and I'll never forget what he said to her . . . It is not pretty . . . He said it could not come out in two places at once. It comes out either in bed or on the stage and she could take her choice.' "

Whether this would be true of all singers is a fact defiant of proof, * but it is nevertheless something they have to consider in their personal relationships, another extra imposition, to which we ordinary mortals need pay no mind.

The consequences of sex, a family, is also something that singers must consider carefully. During the period of training when the financial drain is so enormous, it would be most unwise for a student singer to take on the additional burden of raising children, apart from the physical strain and sleeplessness that the tyrannical infant imposes upon his parents. Once enough funds are coming in to support full-time help the rearing of a family becomes more feasible, though a female singer ought to be prepared to take at least six months from her career for the birth of a baby. After the fifth month of pregnancy she will find that her breathing capacity is inhibited by the size of the child she is carrying. After the birth she has to allow an adequate period of time to re-build her strength for the taxing strain of singing before the public. In the years of growing up, a certain amount of separation is, of necessity, inherent in the singer-parent and child relationship, but many artists have managed to rear families, sometimes surprisingly large ones, with great success.

The Force of Destiny. And so pass the arduous, exacting years of appearing before the public with its daily diet of tension, its nightly dose of applause. How long and how brilliant that career depends on many of the factors already mentioned—plus one other: quite simply, luck. During the years that Caruso reigned at the Metropolitan, for example, a number of gifted tenors who had to all intents and purposes "made it"—the American Riccardo Martin is a good example—sang at the famous theater but did not achieve careers of long endurance. During more or less the same seasons, Louise Homer dominated the mezzo repertory and none could depose her. One who tried was another American,

---

* There are tales of singers having sex in their dressing room just before a performance as a necessary stimulus.

Edyth Walker, a fine artist who eventually became a dramatic soprano. But not at the Metropolitan. She returned to Europe and made a distinguished career there mainly in Germany.

Another soprano who did not feel called to compete against such potential rivals as Nordica, Eames, Fremstad and Gadski was the San Francisco-born Maude Fay, who made a very fine it not international career, again almost entirely in Germany where she was dubbed "Königliche Bayerische Hopofersangerin" by the Prince Regent of Bavaria. A singing actress of great magnetism she is said to have been the model for the improbable novel about a Wagnerian soprano called *Tower of Ivory* by Gertrude Atherton.

Thus fate definitely plays a hand in careers. The Second World War dried up any possibility of obtaining European-trained artists and undoubtedly gave many inexperienced American singers the chance to show what they could do, which they might not otherwise have had. During that period the Met's leading lyric soprano was Licia Albanese, a most convincing performer, but one who lacked any bottom tones to her range and was incapable of singing high pianissimi.

When Rudolf Bing took over the management of the Metropolitan he announced for the opening night of the season the debut of the Bulgarian bass Boris Christoff as King Philip in a revival of Verdi's *Don Carlo*. But passport difficulties prevented this singer from coming to America and Bing imported Cesare Siepi instead, thus launching a distinguished and enduring international career for the Italian that might not have flourished so abundantly had Christoff made it to the United States.

Today at the New York State Opera, Patricia Brooks, a fine coloratura soprano, suffers from the overwhelming presence of Beverly Sills on the roster. Miss Sills, on the other hand, has had to build her career during the time of a star of even greater magnitude—Joan Sutherland.

Since there are just so many operas in the repertory and just so many roles in these operas, the jockeying for leading parts can well be imagined, also the feelings between rival singers who after all are not people of exactly inhibited emotions. Fremstad and Gadski who sang more or less the same repertory appeared together one night in *Walküre* during which Gadski managed to draw literally the blood of the other diva. Fremstad's clever retaliation during the curtain calls was to put her arm around the German soprano, thus calling the attention and sympathy of the audience to her wound besides thoroughly staining her colleague's costume. Was it Gadski then who sent Fremstad a note containing sneezing powder to her dressing room just before curtain time, knowing that one sneeze can loosen floods of unwanted phlegm and wreak general havoc to the singing voice for several hours? The teller of this tale does not say. Nor does Helen Traubel in her memoirs hint at the name of the person who mixed ground glass into a jar of cold cream which she was about to use to make up for her evening's performance.

The world of pop singing is not immune to unpleasantnesses either. Ethel Waters relates how when she appeared on the same bill with Bessie Smith she was prevented by the older star from performing her different, "non-shouting" style of blues singing. The audience clamored for it, however, and Bessie Smith had to relent. Later, after the engagement she called the younger singer to her and said, "You ain't so bad. It's only that I never dreamed that anyone would be able to do this to me in my own territory and with my own people. And you know damn well you can't sing worth a ******."

Ethel Waters doesn't seem to have been any more generous to upcoming rivals and bumped Billie Holiday from a show in Philadelphia because she auditioned "Underneath the Harlem Moon," a Waters specialty.

There is also another kind of luck that affects the careers of even the greatest singers. This pertains to the events of the time in which they live. Fremstad, frozen out of the Metropolitan by her rival Gadski, might have come back to sing when the German

soprano went back to her native country. But just at this time the
United States entered the First World War and Wagner, Fremstad's specialty, was entirely dropped from the repertory. The
Second World War affected the lives and careers of countless
singers, causing many, such as Lotte Lehmann, to emigrate from
Nazi-occupied countries. There was no greater martyr to that war
than Kirsten Flagstad, unjustly reviled and demonstrated against
in America, the very country that had been first to give full recognition to her peerless vocal and artistic qualities.

Finally there is the dark side of existence itself, the devils that
haunt many human beings, which can cast a shadow on the career
of a singer that should otherwise have been a source of unalloyed
satisfaction. Thus great artists such as Lillian Nordica seemed to
invite an unhappy love life. Jussi Bjoerling apparently could not
defeat a drink problem, though miraculously it did not affect the
quality of his voice. Presumably, however, the heart condition
that destroyed him at a comparatively early age was a result of it.
Nor was Billie Holiday able to lick the drugs that became her
downfall. But then these are the imponderables of living and
singers are no less vulnerable to them—indeed perhaps more so—
than other people.

CAREERS CUT SHORT

Perhaps in part due to the conditions under which they live, a
number of singers with beautiful voices worked their way to the
top only to have their careers tragically terminated for reasons of
health or outside circumstances.

Ettore Bastianini, baritone, died of throat cancer aged 44.
Gertrude Bindernagel, a highly successful German soprano was shot
    to death by her husband, jealous of her lover, as she was leaving
    the Berlin City Opera House following a performance.
Giuseppe Borgatti, a tenor, suddenly became blind on the stage of La
    Scala during a rehearsal of *Tristan*.

Armando Borgioli, baritone, was killed in an air raid traveling from Milan to Bologna in 1945.

Luca Botta, who it was believed would be a successor to Caruso, died of a brain tumor aged 35.

Lina Bruna-Rasa, a noted Italian soprano, developed schizophrenic symptoms after the death of her mother. In 1937 at the age of 30 she threw herself into the orchestra pit during a performance. Three years later she was confined to an institution though occasionally thereafter she was able to give concerts.

Madeleine Bugg, a French soprano who made a successful European career during the 1920's, disappeared after 1927 when she was 31. In 1936 a pathologist dissecting a body sent from a charity hospital recognized it as hers.

Maria Cebotari, a much-admired soprano, died of cancer aged 39.

Thomas Chalmers, an American baritone, was forced to end his singing career at the age of 38 because of a throat operation.

Buddy Clark, the pop baritone singer, was killed in an air crash.

Gervase Elwes, popular English tenor, died aged 32 from falling under a moving train in the Boston railroad station.

Saramae Endich, soprano, took her own life.

Kathleen Ferrier was struck down at the height of her career by cancer.

Amelita Galli-Curci developed a goiter which finally ended her career.

Judy Garland was another suicide.

John Garris, Metropolitan Opera tenor, was murdered while the company was on tour in Atlanta, Georgia.

Jeanne Gordon, a Canadian mezzo-soprano who sang at the Metropolitan for ten years, disappeared from the public at the age of 36, a victim of mental illness.

Trajan Grosavescu, a Roumanian tenor, ended his career abruptly at the age of 33. He was shot to death by his jealous wife.

Melitta Heim, Austrian coloratura, was the victim of a nervous disorder aged 34. Later, because she was Jewish, she had to flee to England where she earned a living scrubbing floors.

Zinaida Jurjewskaya, a Russian soprano, fled the 1917 Revolution to make a highly successful career with the Berlin State Opera. In a fit of melancholy while on holiday in Switzerland she took poison and threw herself into a mountain stream at the age of 31.

Aroldo Lindi, a Swedish-born tenor, died of a heart attack onstage in San Francisco during a performance of *Pagliacci* just after finishing "Vesti la Giubba."

Joseph Mann, an Austrian tenor, dropped dead on the stage of the Berlin State Opera in 1921 during a performance of *Aida*. He was 42.

Cléontine de Meo, a 26-year-old dramatic soprano well launched on her career at the Paris Opéra, shot herself in a fit of depression.

Grace Moore, the popular American soprano, died in a plane crash.

Augusto Scampini, an Italian tenor born in 1880, lost his leg in the first World War, ending his career.

Aksel Schiøtz, originally a tenor, developed a brain tumor at the age of 54. The resultant surgery forced him to re-educate his voice as a baritone but it was never the same.

Meta Seinemeyer, a German soprano, died at the age of 34 of a blood disease. On her deathbed she married the conductor, Frieder Weissmann.

Brian Sullivan, American tenor, killed himself.

Conchita Supervia, the fascinating Spanish mezzo-soprano, died aged 41 of complications following childbirth.

Anna Sutter, a soprano who sang mainly in Germany, came to an untimely end aged 39—was it because of poor musicianship?—shot by a conductor, Alois Obrist, who then committed suicide.

Milka Ternina, the celebrated Croatian soprano, was forced to give up her career because of a facial paralysis.

Genevieve Warner, a promising young American soprano, was beaten and raped in an Edinburgh alley. She never resumed her career.

Leonard Warren, baritone, dropped dead on the stage of the Metropolitan Opera House during a performance of *Forza del Destino*.

Walter Widdop, the English tenor, suffered a fatal heart attack following a London concert, while the audience was still applauding.

Fritz Wunderlich, the superb German tenor, died aged 36 as the result of a fall.

The Hourglass. So it is that when the top has been reached, the position must be zealously guarded and maintained. A moment's relaxation and it can be threatened by a newcomer. And yet the truth is that supremacy in the world of the singing voice is inexorably and continuously threatened by something over which the singer has no more control than a piece of wood bobbing on a current—the passage of time.

Indeed the singer has been fighting time throughout the making and maintenance of his career. As the years pass, though the voice may thicken, darken and grow larger, in doing so it will probably give up some of the bloom of youth that all the world worships. As the years pass too, the singer's art may become more refined and subtle together with a more perfect mastery of vocal technique that he did not possess when he was young. But now perhaps the high notes become more of an effort or are totally lacking, and he can no longer sustain long phrases, having to fall back on the device of "catch breaths" which he uses with great cunning. In the novel *Evensong,* with its merciless though otherwise foolish portrayal of Melba thinly disguised as "Irela," Beverley Nichols gives some harrowing descriptions of the soprano, whose secretary he was, fighting to maintain her career against the erosions of time.

" 'Do you realize why the orchestra plays *fortissimo* during the whole of the love scene in the first act of *Bohème,* whereas Puccini only marked *forte* in the score?' " he has a one-time admirer of Irela's voice say to her niece. " 'Because she can no longer take the high notes without using every ounce of her strength. Do you realize why she cut out nearly a quarter of an hour from the second act of *Faust?* Because she can't last the course. Have you ever listened to her singing the very first phrase in *Faust* . . . ? People used to come over from Paris in the height of the season merely to hear her sing that phrase. It was the loveliest thing in the world. It is still lovely . . . still, in some ways, incomparable, but it's no longer the same. She has to take four breaths where formerly she only took two. And the end of the phrase, with the low notes, is no longer like a 'cello . . . it's harsh . . . strained . . .

Jean de Reszke by Caruso.

she gets away with it . . . of course . . . with nearly everybody. But not with me.' "

Sometimes during the course of a career, illness or over-singing may force an artist to retire from public appearances for a time with the immediate rumors that the voice has been lost and the career finished, which loyal fans indignantly deny. Nothing, not even the debut, is more dramatic than the return of a much loved singer. Will he be the same? Is the old magic still there? Here are excerpts from a description by Clara Leiser of Jean de Reszke's return to the Metropolitan in *Lohengrin* on 31 December, 1900, after he had missed a season and his career was feared for.

" . . . as Lohengrin stepped from his bark a hush fell upon the audience. Out into the silence floated

"Nur sei bedankt, mein lieber Schwan!"

tender, beautiful, sweet as of old. The multiple sigh of relief was almost audible. Strangers smiled at each other. One enthusiast nudged another and whispered: 'Good as ever, old man! Good as ever!'

". . . That night Jean seemed to require less warming up than usual and when he uttered his soul's desire in the words, 'Elsa, Ich liebe dich!' his voice rang with such splendid power that the impression he had made on his entrance was intensified tenfold. 'Good as ever?' retorted the second enthusiast to the first. 'Better than ever!' "

After the performance "the audience was hysterical. Men shouted themselves hoarse and mopped their brows, and women wept. More than thirty years later a rather stolid businessman said to me: 'I remember every detail of that performance as though it had been last night. I don't know how I ever lived through it. I remember being afraid that I should take cold on the way home, because I was so excited; I perspired so that at the end of the opera my shirt, and even my collar and tie, were wringing wet.' "

Another such occasion at which the author was present was the return of Kirsten Flagstad to the Metropolitan, the opera house that had made her internationally famous, but from which she had then been excluded by one of the intolerant groups that America is so adept at hatching out. The opera was *Tristan* and when the curtain went up at the end of the Prelude revealing the familiar figure, her hair in a braid, reclining on a couch with her head sunk down on the back of her hand, the whole audience seemed to strain forward. The tension increased and became unbearable. As the Prelude died away to a buzzing of the strings it could no longer be endured. A single clap of hands like a shot sounded somewhere in the auditorium and a moment later had triggered the entire audience into an uncontrollable roar of applause that carried on through the Steersman's song. Irreverent of Wagner it may have been, but that ovation was essential to the feelings of everyone in the opera house. When at last the clapping died away a voice out of the darkness called, "Welcome back!"

And Madame Flagstad? What must she have felt at such a moment? Indeed one wonders how artists when the atmosphere trembles on the brink of tears can manage to keep control of themselves in order to sing at all.

These are reports of triumphant returns. Less is written about the much loved artist who lingers on. Melba's last appearances were not always unalloyed pleasure except to those whose loyalty stopped their ears to the aged sound of this once silvery, flawlessly produced voice. The singer who continues to cope with a vocal instrument from which time has rubbed its former lustrous beauty and effortlessness is a sad if plucky creature. In recent times it was regrettable that Giovanni Martinelli did not retire sooner, leaving audiences with more mellifluous memories of the voice of this great artist.

How long can a career be expected to last? The average one made in the opera house would seem to span about twenty to twenty-five years. Thereafter the wear and strain of singing takes its toll and a performance becomes too effortful for either artist or audience. The lighter voices usually make the career earlier and thus end it earlier. The dramatic soprano, as both Flagstad and Traubel illustrated, does not seem to attain full power and majesty till its possessor is close to forty. Thereafter it can be expected to stay in full vocal prime for perhaps ten years. (A few years of regularly singing Wagner noticeably took away the total effortlessness of Flagstad's high C's, which she had possessed when she first burst on the American scene.) As with individuals, some singers seem to age more successfully than others, holding on to their voices with surprising tenacity, when others will lose theirs completely.

OPERA SINGER ENDURANCE CHART

Name	Born	Opera Debut	Retired from Stage	Years Active	Died
Giovanni Battista Rubini	1795	1807	1844	37	1854
Luigi Lablache	1794	1812	1856	44	1856
Guiditta Pasta	1798	1816	1850	34	1865

OPERA SINGER ENDURANCE CHART (*Cont.*)

Name	Born	Opera Debut	Retired from Stage	Years Active	Died	
Henrietta Sontag	1805	1820	1854	34	1854	
Adolphe Nourrit	1802	1821	1839	18	1839†	
Wilhelmine Schröder-Devrient	1804	1821	1847	26	1860	
Maria Malibran	1808	1825	1836	11	1836†	
Giulia Grisi	1812	1829	1861	32	1869	
Rosina Stolz	1815	1832	1849	17	1903	
Joseph Tichatschek	1807	1837	1870	33	1885	
Pauline Viardot-Garcia	1821	1837	1870	33	1910	
Jenny Lind	1820	1838	1870	32	1887	
Enrico Tamberlik	1820	1841	1877	36	1889	
Julius Stockhausen	1826	1848	1870	22	1906	
Albert Niemann	1831	1849	1882	33	1917	
Jean-Baptiste Faure	1830	1852	1878*	26	1914	
Adelina Patti	1843	1859	1888	29	1919	*Patti's first New York farewell was in 1888*
			1914	55		
Christine Nilsson	1843	1864	1888*	24	1921	
Lilli Lehmann	1848	1868	1910*	42	1929	
Victor Maurel	1848	1868	1904	36	1923	
Minnie Hauk	1852	1866	1891	25	1929	
Emma (Marie) Albani	1847 or 1850	1870	1896*	26	1930	
Italo Campanini	1846	1871	1890	19	1896	*The longest known career*
Lucien Fugère	1848	1871	1932	61	1935	
Jean de Reszke	1850	1874§	1903	29	1925	
Edouard de Reszke	1855	1876	1906	30	1917	
Etelka Gerster	1856	1876	1890	14	1920	
Marcella Sembrich	1858	1877	1909	32	1935	
Pol Plançon	1854	1877	1908	31	1914	
Ernestine Schumann-Heink	1861	1878	1932	54	1936	
Mattia Battistini	1856	1878	1924	46	1928	
Lillian Nordica	1857	1879	1914	35	1914	
Emma Calvé	1858	1882	1920	38	1942	
Nellie Melba	1861	1887	1926	39	1931	
Milka Ternina	1863	1888	1906	18	1941	
Emma Eames	1865	1889	1912	23	1952	
Antonio Scotti	1866	1889	1933	44	1936	
Feodor Chaliapin	1873	1893	1937	44	1938	
Enrico Caruso	1873	1894	1920	26	1921†	
Leo Slezak	1873	1896	1934*	38	1946	
Giuseppe de Luca	1876	1897	1946	49	1950	
Titta Ruffo	1877	1898	1936	38	1953	
Emmy Destinn	1878	1898	1926	28	1930	
Geraldine Farrar	1882	1901	1922*	21	1967	
Lucrezia Bori	1887	1908	1936	28	1960	
Amelita Galli-Curci	1882	1909	1936	29	1963	
Maria Jeritza	1887	1910	1935*	25		

Lotte Lehmann	1888	1910	1945*	35	
Giovanni Martinelli	1885	1911	1946*	35	1969
Friedrich Schorr	1888	1911	1943	32	1953
Claudia Muzio	1889	1911	1936	25	1936†
Tito Schipa	1889	1911	1957?	46	1965
Edward Johnson	1878	1912‡	1935	23	1959
Lauritz Melchior	1890	1913§	1950*	37	
Kirsten Flagstad	1895	1913	1955	42	1962
Beniamino Gigli	1890	1914	1946*	32	1957
Elisabeth Rethberg	1894	1915	1942	27	
Rosa Ponselle	1897	1918	1936	18	
Lawrence Tibbett	1896	1923	1949	26	1960
Lily Pons	1904	1928	1962	34	
Zinka Milanov	1906	1928	1966	38	
Thelma Votipka	1906	1928	1962	34	

* Known to have continued concertizing after retiring from the stage
† Died at a young age
‡ Previously in operetta
§ As a baritone

Many opera singers have ended their careers in the opera house but prolonged them for a number of years by turning to the recital hall where there is no orchestra over which the voice must be projected, and music can be chosen to avoid the vocal deficiencies that come with age. Certain careers, however, have lasted an incredible length of time and in this matter baritones seem to endure particularly well. Lucien Fugère, the French artist, with an unforced, light voice sang before the public for sixty-one years. The Italians Mattia Battistini and Giuseppe de Luca were still performing while in their seventies. Recently I heard an energetic if not exactly youthful-sounding record of Sir Charles Santley singing "Non piu andrai" when he was sixty-nine, and one, less vital, but still authoritative made when he was seventy-nine. (This raises the question, in passing, whether all these singers were perhaps really tenors who, by not subjecting their voices to the strain of the very high notes, were thus able to endure.)

Popular entertainers have of course made fantastically long careers because thanks to the microphone they do not subject their voices to the tremendous strain of singing in large halls with equally large orchestras and without amplification.

The decision to retire is obviously an agonizing one to make. A few singers seem to lay away their careers with almost a feeling of relief, as if to say, "There! I'm free of you at last. Now I can live." The only trouble is the definition of the word "live" to a professional singer in his late forties or early fifties, after years of fame and adulation, who has frequently sacrificed the ordinary accretion of personal relationships to make his career. Where now goes all that formidable energy—that zest which has carried the singer to the top of his profession?

V I

> .... *The sixth age shifts*
> *Into the lean and slipper'd pantaloon*
> *With spectacles on nose and pouch on side,*
> *His youthful hose well sav'd, a world too wide*
> *For his shrunk shank; and his big manly voice*
> *Turning again toward childish treble, pipes*
> *And whistles in his sound.*

Coda.   At last the emotion-choked farewell is made. Sometimes the cries of the fans are piteous: "Don't go away. Don't leave us." A speech may be made, perhaps a commemorative trophy is presented by the opera company. Some great singers have simply slipped away without remark or ceremony, never to return to their adoring public.

"Not even in the theater, which is the only comparable world, is the inevitable tragedy of years so remorselessly imposed on the artist," writes Marcia Davenport, daughter of the lovely soprano, Alma Gluck. "In every other creative and interpretative avenue of life, age only richens and widens the artist's function and scope. In singing she must lose her means of expression when she is in the full flower of intelligence and experience with which to use it best. This is the reason for tears and sorrow at the thought of a singer's retirement; every sensitive person knows that the artist is condemned henceforward to prison."

How best for the retired singer to make that prison bearable? Some have managed well—and some scarcely at all. The most obvious way for a singing artist to extend his creative talent is by teaching and coaching. In this manner, like parents, they live on through their offspring pupils. And yet many great singers never teach, never impart the secrets of their art and technique to succeeding generations, some because they feel that they lack the ability to do so, others because they have no desire. Occasionally one hears of retired singers sponsoring a "protégé" whom they do not teach so much as help with psychological (and sometimes financial) encouragement, thus extending their own careers vicariously.

SOME VARIED WAYS IN WHICH SINGERS FINISHED OUT THEIR RETIREMENT YEARS

Suzanne Adams, the American soprano, operated a laundry in London.

André D'Arkor, a Belgian tenor, became director of the opera house at Liège.

Joel Berglund, Swedish baritone, became artistic director of the Stockholm Opera.

Michael Bohnen, the dynamic German bass-baritone, directed the Berlin City Opera.

Dino Borgioli, Italian tenor, founded the New London Opera Company just before the Second World War.

Carl Braun, a German bass, turned into a concert agent.

John Brownlee, the Australian baritone, became head of the Manhattan School of Music in New York City.

Victor Capoul, a French tenor, lost all his money through speculation and finished his years living in a peasant hut in southern France.

Florencio Constantino, Mexican tenor, lived in total poverty in Mexico City and died in a charity hospital.

Marie Delna, a much admired French contralto, ended her life in a poorhouse.

Louise Edvina, Canadian soprano, ran an antique shop on the Riviera.

Maria Galvany, Spanish coloratura, finished her days in total poverty.

Osie Hawkins, American bass, as stage manager for the Metropolitan Opera Company, never misses a performance.

Ottokar Mařák, for many years first tenor at the Prague Opera, was reduced to selling newspapers on the streets of Chicago in his retirement. A fund was raised in Czechoslovakia to enable him to return home.

Vanni Marcoux, a bass-baritone of French parents, managed the Opéra at Bordeaux.

Dorothy Maynor, the celebrated American soprano, runs the Harlem School of the Performing Arts.

José Mojica, Mexican tenor, in 1943 made a vow on his mother's deathbed to become a priest, which he did, entering a mission in Peru. He is said to be there still—totally deaf.

Jean Nadalovitch, the Roumanian tenor, trained as a doctor as well as a singer and retired in 1912 to open an Institute for the Physiology of the Voice in Vienna. In 1935 it was closed by the Nazis and he was thrown into a concentration camp at Theresienstadt in which he managed to survive through the Second World War.

Joseph Rogatschewsky, a Russian-born tenor who sang mainly in France and Belgium, directed the Brussels opera from 1953-59 after his retirement.

Thomas Salignac, French tenor, founded and edited a music magazine, *Lyrica*.

Susan Strong was another American soprano who went into the laundry business in London.

Erich Witte, German tenor, became chief stage director of the Frankfurt Opera.

A number of retired singers have involved themselves in the problems of managing an opera house. Herbert Witherspoon, a former Metropolitan bass, became "Artistic director" of the Chiago Opera in the season of 1931-32. In 1935 he was appointed general manager of the Metropolitan. When, a few weeks later, he died suddenly, another retired singer, the tenor Edward Johnson, took his place in a tenure that lasted until the coming of Rudolf Bing in 1950. Kirsten Flagstad was appointed general manager of

the Norwegian Opera, but filled the post for only a short time because of the onset of the cancer that eventually took her life. The
charming Lucrezia Bori continued to mingle in operatic affairs
after her retirement through her work with the Metropolitan
Opera Guild, and more recently Risë Stevens attempted to fill up
the days of her retirement by co-managing the Metropolitan National Opera Company, which however went down to a lamentable
financial defeat.

A few singers have appeared before the public in a different
guise after their singing days were over. Geraldine Farrar, in the
early years of the Metropolitan Opera broadcasts, was an inter-
mission commentator. Basil Ruysdael, a former Metropolitan
singer, became a radio announcer. Kathleen Howard, who sang
mainly character roles for twelve seasons at the Met, continued
in her retirement to play character parts in Hollywood films,
usually taking the part of a grumbling, comic domestic.

Adelina Patti, to whom singing came perhaps more naturally
than sleeping or breathing, managed not to forsake the stage by
building a tiny theater in her castle in Wales. On it she performed
excerpts from various operas for her house guests, and when her
voice no longer served her, assigned the guests parts in various
tableaux and pantomimes, thus enabling her still to face the footlights.

At this point in his life the singer's true existence is in the past:
he is all memory. Many then are persuaded to put down their re-
membrances in print, some by their own hand, but often "as told
to" others. Gossipy, inaccurate and of course totally self-absorbed,
a few of these memoirs give absorbing accounts of the struggles
involved in a singer's career, combined with amusing glimpses of
the social life at the time when the star was in the heavens.

For those singers who lack the resources or the spirit that would
involve them with a new generation of musicians, these gray,
empty years of retirement are no more than a period of waiting.
They may paint and garden and travel in order to while away the

hours. Some are fortunate enough to have husbands and children to fill in the vacuity of these years, though in many cases the exactions of the career have blighted the chances of making normal family relationships. Retired singers instead sometimes have the consolation of a connection with a well-loved coach or accompanist. A maid, who once served loyally in the opera house, will perhaps continue with equal loyalty at home. And there are always dogs. . . .

Living in the past this kind of retired singer finds little to admire in the present world of the singing voice. When asked to attend a performance of *Don Giovanni* at Glyndebourne after the Second World War, Emma Eames, who lived on for forty years after her retirement, divorced, neither teaching nor interesting herself in any activity, is said to have replied that in a *Don Giovanni* conducted by Gustav Mahler at the Metropolitan in January, 1907, Gadski was the Donna Elvira, Sembrich the Zerlina, Scotti the Don, Bonci the Ottavio, Chaliapin the Leporello and she herself, Donna Anna. What need had she to go to Glyndebourne? Her opposite in retirement, always to be seen alert, smiling, interested, in the corridors of the Metropolitan Opera House, was Giovanni Martinelli right up until the time of his death.

For those singers existing in the shroud of their remembered careers, there can be an occasional moment when life seems real again, all the more poignant because at the same time it is actually *not* real. This can be when they hear their own records. For singers of the era when the recording process was crude, this was not so true as for today's retired artists. Not long ago I sat with one of the Metropolitan Opera Company's most renowned artists, now retired, listening to records of some of her radio broadcasts. At times it seemed impossible to look at her face. . . .

VII

.................Last scene of all,
That ends this strange eventful history,
In second childishness and mere oblivion,
Sans teeth, sans eyes, sans taste, sans every-
thing.

As Emma Eames lay dying at the age of eighty-seven. the glories
of the singing voice no longer had any meaning for her. When a
member of the cloth called to give comfort she bade him strip
back the bed clothes to reveal her feet. Once she had sung a part
which required her to dance in her bare feet and they had been
much admired. She asked the church father if he did not think
they were lovely. . . .

WHITHER?

By Karl Trump, *President,*
National Association
of Teachers of Singing

In 1944, when a small group of farseeing voice teachers finally culminated their long months of planning with the organization of the National Association of Teachers of Singing, America was winning a war from which it would emerge relatively unscathed soon after. . . . As rapidly as bombed-out opera houses in Europe could be readied for performance, young American singers were hired to fill out the depleted rosters of these companies. It was a wonderful opportunity for our students and for us. Those of our pupils who were not quite ready for the exposure of performance abroad were often able to qualify for the Fulbright grants which were set up in 1946 to enable promising young Americans to study in Europe, to acquire fluency in foreign languages, to coach operatic roles with experts and to learn the great traditions of the celebrated European opera houses. It was a heady time for American voice teachers, for the products of our studios were admired and busy.

It was not just in Europe that they were finding employment. Opportunities abounded at home. Every American town large enough to have an auditorium supported a local concert series. A talented and dynamic young singer could accept sixty-five or seventy concert engagements a season if equipped with sufficient stamina and ambition. Or a promising young singer might turn to the musical theatre, where the team of Rogers and Hammerstein had started a trend, with a show called *Oklahoma,* toward a drama integrated with music which required trained singers in large quantities. For more than a decade the New York and Chicago and Los Angeles and touring national companies of such shows as *Brigadoon, Carousel, The King and I, South Pacific* and *My Fair Lady* would provide pay-checks and training for our students.

Further, all the most prestigious big network radio shows needed good singers for their programs, either in their choruses or for occasional or regular solo spots. The careers of many American singers, numbers of whom graduated from radio into concert and opera, were nurtured in the broadcasting studios: James Melton, Nelson Eddy, Vivian della Chiesa, Margaret Speaks, Jessica Dragonette, Igor Gorin, Richard Crooks, Lanny Ross, Allen Jones, Conrad Thibault, Helen Jepson and Eileen Farrell all developed their careers through the opportunity of radio. Male singing groups with names like "The Revelers," "The Vikings" and "The Pennsylvanians" were popular both on radio and on stage and, together with their less famous counterparts, provided jobs and training for some of our fine young baritones and tenors. Though at the time we took all this as the normal state of affairs, it appears in retrospect that this was a great period for singers and voice teachers in America.

What happened to all that opportunity? At the start of 1970, most of it has disappeared. European opera houses no longer welcome many young Americans; a new generation abroad has grown up healthy and well-trained for the positions their government-supported opera companies have to fill. Fulbright grants are scarce today, the sale of surplus U.S. property abroad having dwindled to a trickle. Community concert series are all but dead. Budding young artists, however talented, do not get on the rosters of the large managements which control such concert business as remains. Only the vocal luminaries get bookings and even they run the risk of singing to empty houses. I heard Marilyn Horne in a neighboring community recently sing a distinguished program to fewer than eighty people. Yet a few weeks earlier the same community—not mine, though it might have been—turned out an estimated three thousand people to hear a "musical ensemble" called "Blood, Sweat and Tears."

The day of the big, melodious musical drama seems over. A trained singing voice is not part of the equipment needed for work in Broadway shows like *Mame, Coco* or *Hello, Dolly!*; and it is an absolute detriment for the new-trend productions which feature "hard rock" music and have such names as "Stomp," "Hair" and "Salvation."

Radio long ago departed from the parlor. Colored television now stands in its place—and this is a medium that has shown itself to be stubbornly uninterested in good singing. Its viewpoint remains primarily visual. Though it may occasionally find a place on a variety program for a Birgit Nilsson, it has no confidence in her ability to hold the viewers with her art; it garbs her in exotic gowns and plumed headdresses and distracts our listening as it offers us a kaleidoscope of angle and distance shots that have no relationship to what she is singing. Or it dreams up some way to prove that artists are "just folks": I have not yet forgotten the disappointment I felt when I turned on the television one evening last winter and saw Eileen Farrell and Marilyn Horne disporting themselves with Carol Burnett as the Three Little Pigs!

GLOSSARY

Definitions of terms used in connection with singing, singers and vocal music that may be useful to the reader.

Appoggiatura—A leaning tone inserted between two notes usually for emphasis.

Arpeggio—A broken chord in which the notes are sounded successively.

Aria—A song, usually of some complexity as heard in the opera house.

Bis—Twice! Encore! Can sometimes sound like a cross between a hiss and a boo.

Brava! Bravo! Bravi!—The first an approving cry for a solo female singer; the second for a solo male singer; the third for a group. Often, however, used incorrectly.

Cabaletta—Now generally defined as the fast, second part of an aria.

Cadenza—An interpolated passage of music to show off the voice or other musical instruments.

Cantilena—A smooth-flowing line of melody.

Canzonetta—A "little song."

Cavatina—A short aria or air.

Comprimario—lit. "with the leading singer." A singer of supporting parts. See text p. 92.

Cover—A stand-by for another singer.

Embellishment—Ornamental notes or passages added to a given melody, designed to show off the singer's prowess.

Encore—In a recital this usually refers to an extra selection given by the singer, rather than a repetition of what was programmed. In the opera house it means literally "again."

Fioritura—From the Italian, "a flowering." A decorating of the melody with embellishments.

Gruppetto—An embellishment in the form of a turn.

Intonation—True adherence to the pitch of a note.

Legato—Flowing transition from one note to the next.

Mark—To sing high notes an octave down.

Messa di voce—A sustained note begun softly, swelled to full volume and diminished to its original softness.

Mezza voce—Half voice.

Partitura—Complete orchestra score.

Portamento—A gliding between notes without a break. This can lead to a "scoop" (q.v.).

Raccolto—lit. "collected." Used to describe a singer's high notes (particularly tenors') when they are intense and brilliant.

Recitative—A kind of speech-song often used for dialogue in operas and oratorios and to introduce arias.

Régisseur—Manager of a theater or opera house.

Répétiteur—A coach-accompanist and general musical drillmaster.

Scoop—To attack a note from below and slide into it unattractively.

Shake—Another word for "trill" (q.v.).

Sotto voce—lit. "under the voice." Barely audible.

Spartito—A piano-voice reduction of a full orchestra score.

Staccato—lit. "detached." A note not sustained and usually touched lightly.

Stretta—A kind of urgent closing to a scene or an aria.

Tessitura—lit. "texture." The average range in which a song or operatic role may lie.

Timbre—The tone quality of a voice.

Trill—Rapid alteration of notes a half or whole tone apart. See text p. 000.

Vocalise—A composition without words, frequently used in voice training, but occasionally heard as a song.

Throughout this book C refers to middle C; C′ an octave above it, C″ two octaves, etc. C͵ lies an octave below middle C, C͵͵ two octaves, etc.

REFERENCE NOTES

NOTE: Figures in parentheses refer to the bibliography, which is numbered

P. *xii*, l. 8-9. Cather, *My Mortal Enemy* (249): pp. 59-60

P. *xiv*, l. 8-9. Gene Lees, *High Fidelity* Magazine (234): July, 1968

P. *xiv*, l. 32-33; P. *xv*, l. 1-2. Charles Lamb, "A Chapter on Ears" from *The Essays of Elia*, London. Macmillan and Co., 1898

P. *xv*, l. 8-14. Quoted by Traubel (142): p. 199

P. *xvi*, l. 3-6. Quoted by Kay (32): p. 66

P. *xvi*, l. 18-19. Cather, *The Song of the Lark* (250): p. 420

P. 4, l. 11-20. Bowra (198): p. 1

P. 4, 5. Both poems quoted from Bowra (198): p. 213 and p. 267

P. 7, l. 23-31. Lang (204): p. 2

P. 8, l. 19-23. Wibberley (210): p. 33

P. 8, l. 28-34. Covent Garden Opera Program, June 12, 1969. Rex Warner from *The Stories of the Greeks*

P. 11, l. 17-24. Lang (204): pp. 33-34

P. 13, l. 12-13. Henderson, *Early History of Singing* (201): p. 22

P. 15-16. Poem (first stanza) in Henry Adams, *Mont-Saint-Michel and Chartres*, p. 222. Boston. Houghton Mifflin, 1913

P. 19, l. 9-23. Letter in *Stereo Review* (244): November, 1966

P. 21, l. 29-31. Tosi (67): p. 108

P. 22, l. 4-8. Mancini (39): p. 12

P. 22, l. 20-28. Quoted by E. Newman, *Wagner* etc. (274): V. I, p. 112

P. 24, l. 20-30. Mancini (39): p. 58

P. 25, l. 1-3. Kay (32): p. 22

P. 39, l. 10-13. B. Marchesi, *Singer's Pilgrimage* (41a): p. 223

P. 41, l. 29-30. Henderson, *Art of Singing* (27): p. 297

P. 54, l. 24-31. Quoted by Seltsam, *Annals of the Metropolitan Opera* (223): p. 184

P. 54, l. 33; P. 55, l. 1. Thompson (157): p. 234

P. 59, l. 24-32. Ferrier, Cardus (92): p. 235

P. 62, l. 15; P. 63, l. 1-3. Brown (5)

P. 64, l. 18-24, 31-34. Hardwick (100): p. 79

P. 65, l. 1-3. Ibid., p. 77

P. 70, l. 8-9. Caruso (83): Foreword, no page number

P. 71, l. 14-18. Kolodin (216): p. 281

P. 72, l. 19-21. Caruso (83): p. 76

P. 72, l. 24-25. Quoted by Newton (183): p. 199

P. 72, l. 31-34; P. 73, l. 1-5. Haggin (194) pp. 184-185

P. 98, l. f. Puritz (52): pp. 88-89 (footnote)

P. 99, l. 10-13. Poem from Plotz (270): p. 48 by Elizabeth Jennings in *A Way of Looking*

P. 99, l. 22-25. B. Marchesi, *Singer's Catechism* etc. (41): p. 121

P. 99, l. 27-29. Tosi (67): p. 83

P. 100, l. f. Ffrangcon-Davies (17): p. 119

P. 105, l. 16-20. Taubman (226): p. 14

P. 107, l. 25-28. Franca (20): Introduction, *xviii*

P. 107, l. 30-34. Ibid., p. 94 (footnote)

P. 122, l. 18-20. A. Shaw (138): p. 57

P. 125, l. 21-24. Quoted by R. Schauffler, (275): p. 157

P. 129, l. 4-14. Quoted by E. Newman, Wagner (274): V. II, p. 594

P. 130, l. 22-32. DeBovet (272): p. 20

P. 131, l. 2-6. Quoted by B. Marchesi, *Singer's Pilgrimage* (41a): p. 287

P. 131, l. 12-16. Curtiss (271): p. 110

P. 133, l. 31-34. DeHegermann-Lindencrone, *In the Courts* etc. (101): p. 70

P. 134, l. 1-7. Ibid., pp. 162-163

P. 134, l. 12-15, 17-19. *The Sunny Side* etc. (102): p. 160

P. 134, l. 26-29. James Joyce, *A Portrait of the Artist as a Young Man*, p. 163 N.Y. Viking (paperback), 1964

P. 135, l. 14-15. Quoted by Richard Ellmann: *James Joyce*, p. 612. N.Y., Oxford, 1959

P. 135, l. 16-17. Joyce (257): p. 272

P. 136, l. 3-9. Alda (76): p. 292

P. 145, l. 28-33. Kay (32): p. 83

P. 146, l. 14-16. Greene (23): p. 40

P. 148, l. 13-15. Franca (20): p. 11

P. 148, l. 17-20. Ibid., p. 11

P. 150, l. 18-19. Klein, *Bel Canto* (33): p. 22

P. 152, l. 17-19. Puritz (52): p. 15

P. 152, l. 19-22. Reid (53): p. 148

P. 155, l. 16-21. Henderson, *Art of Singing* (27): p. 39

P. 156, l. f. Garcia (22): p. 13 (footnote)

P. 157, l. 26-33; P. 158, l. 1-3. George Moore (261): p. 409

P. 158, l. 30-34; P. 159, l. 1-2. Curtis (9): p. 161

P. 159, l. 13-18. Seashore (59): p. 46

P. 159, l. 30-34. Ibid., p. 43

P. 161, l. 5-18. DeHegermann-Lindencrone, *In the Courts* etc. (101): p. 87

P. 162, l. 28-29. Reid (53): p. 135

P. 164, l. 33-34; P. 165, l. 1. Mancini (39): p. 20

P. 165, l. f. Fuchs (21): p. 90 (footnote)

P. 165, l. 14-16. Garcia (22): p. 8

P. 167, l. 9-10. Rose (56): p. 150

P. 167, l. 11-12. Marafioti (40): p. 51

P. 167, l. 13-16. Reid (53): p. 71

P. 167, l. 17-19. Fuchs (21): p. 64

P. 167, l. 20-21. Salvatore Marchesi. Quoted by Field-Hyde (18): p. 72

P. 167, l. 22. Browne, Behnke (7): p. 115

P. 167, l. 23-27. Lilli Lehmann (34): p. 112

P. 167, l. 28-29. Litante (36): p. 39

P. 167, l. 32-33; P. 168, l. 1-2. Punt (51): p. 27

P. 168, l. 7-8. Roma (55): p. 122

P. 168, l. 15-24. Shaw, *London Music in 1888-89* (185): p. 230

P. 172, l. 14-19. Calvé (82): p. 64

P. 172, l. 21-24. Martens (43): p. 40

P. 173, l. 7. Fuchs (21): p. 64

P. 173, l. 8-10. Mancini (39): p. 20

P. 179, l. 18-19; P. 180, l. 1. Moses (50): p. 16

P. 182, l. 20-33. Arditi (159): p. 81

P. 183, l. 7-9. Kellogg (112): p. 129

P. 186, l. 13-14. D. A. Weiss. Quoted by Greene (23): p. 78

P. 187, l. 3-4, 7-8. Voorhees (69): p. 8

P. 187, l. 20-26. Bashkirtseff, *Journal*, Quoted from Blom (268): p. 522

P. 190, l. 25-27; 34; P. 191, l. 1-14. DeMerlin (126): p. 9; also pp. 3-4

P. 192, l. 30-33. Ibid., p. 9

P. 194, l. 13-16. G. Sand (265): p. 37

P. 194, l. 20-22. Quoted by Fitzlyon (93): p. 52

P. 198-199. Material drawn from J. Kaplan: *Mr. Clemens and Mark Twain*, N.Y. Simon and Schuster, 1966

P. 200, l. 31-34; P. 201, l. 1-3. Litante (36): p. 20

P. 201, l. 25-31. Glackens (99): p. 340

P. 206, l. 22-25. *NATS Bulletin* (237), Feb. 1968 "Bookshelf"

P. 206, l. 30-34; P. 207, l. 1. *NATS Bulletin* (237), October, 1968 Editorial

P. 209, l. 9. DeHegermann-Lindencrone, *In the Courts* etc. (101): p. 15

P. 209, l. 30-31. B. Marchesi, *The Singer's Catechism* etc. (41): p. 142

P. 210, l. 9-12. Eames (89): p. 52

P. 210, l. 13-15, 19-21. Garden (96): p. 15

P. 210, l. 24. Alda (76): p. 45

P. 211, l. 12-23. Thursby (98): pp. 162-163

P. 214, l. 20-29. Homer (108): p. 60

P. 215, l. 3-15. DeHegermann-Lindencrone, *In the Courts* etc. (101): p. 77

P. 215, l. 26-34; P. 216, 1-2. DuMaurier (252): pp. 437-439

P. 217, l. 12. Holland etc. (107): V. I, p. 110. Also footnote

P. 219, l. 24-33; P. 220, l. 1. Brodnitz (4): p. 240

P. 220, l. 5-8. Caruso (83): p. 140

P. 220, l. f. Ferrier, Cardus (92): p. 237

P. 221, l. 10-20. Henderson, *Art of Singing* (27): p. 63

P. 222, l. 7-10. Witherspoon (72): p. 52

P. 222, l. 12-17. Ibid., (72): p. 52

P. 222, l. 20-26. Puritz (52): p. 50

P. 223, l. 9-17. Curtis (9): p. 160

P. 224, l. 3-5. Franca (20): p. 22

P. 224, l. 28-31. Caruso (83): p. 145

P. 225, l. 10-18. Lilli Lehmann (34): pp. 67-68

P. 225, l. 23-27. Kay (32): pp. 85-86

P. 227, l. 11-34; P. 228, l. 1-6. Rogers (134): pp. 250-251

P. 228, l. 21-24. Lilli Lehmann (34): pp. 65-66

P. 228, l. 25-28. Rose (56): p. 89

P. 228, l. 29-33. Herbert-Caesari (29): p. 165

P. 247, l. 27-28. Garden (96): p. 32

P. 247, l. 31-32. Caruso (83): p. 76

P. 248, l. 31-34; P. 249, l. 1-4. Punt (51): p. 4

P. 249, l. 27-34. Lotte Lehmann, *Wings of Song* (117): p. 214

P. 253, l. 3-10. Henderson, *Art of Singing* (27): 386-387

P. 258, l. 26-31. Caruso (83): p. 75

P. 259, l. 5-7. Leider (118): pp. 118-119

P. 260, l. 11-14; P. 261, l. 1-12. Caruso (83): p. 78

P. 261, l. 28-34. Marek (218): p. 296

P. 263, l. 29-34; P. 264, l. 1-5. B. Marchesi, *The Singer's Catechism* etc. (41): p. 111

P. 266, l. 13-16. Cushing (86): p. 244

P. 266, l. 27-29. Ibid., (86): p. 244

P. 268, l. 17-28. Lilli Lehmann (34): pp. 287-288

P. 272, l. 17-19. B. Marchesi, *The Singer's Catechism* etc. (41): p. 14

P. 277, l. 3-5. A. Shaw (138): p. 79

P. 277, l. 15-17, 20-33. Davenport (251): pp. 148-151

P. 280, l. 23-26. Waters (147): p. 92
P. 284, l. 21-34; P. 285, l. 1-2. Nichols (262): p. 93
P. 285, l. 12-16; P. 286, l. 1-16. Leiser (119): p. 228, p. 230
P. 290, l. 7-16. Davenport (251): p. 446

BIBLIOGRAPHY

The following is a list of books that I have looked into in connection with writing *The Singing Voice*. I have divided it roughly into categories with recommendations of books that I think most interesting, sensible or authoritative concerning the singer and his song.

How to Sing

The literature is vast. The idea that somehow one can learn a vocal technique from a manual seems to have captured the imaginations of publishers and public alike. Of the hundreds and hundreds of books written on "how to sing" I have listed what amounts to a mere handful.

To this reader's mind, most comprehensive and sensible—though not always easy to follow—is William Vennard's *Singing, The Mechanism and the Tecanic*, Mr. Vennard can also lay claim to being not merely a theorist: he is the teacher of one of the most remarkable singers of perhaps any epoch—Marilyn Horne. *Keep Your Voice Healthy* by Friedrich Brodnitz gives helpful and valuable information to the singer or layman and I also found *The Art of Singing and Voice Technique* by Viktor Fuchs interesting and instructive. From a totally physiological point of view Margaret C. L. Greene's *The Voice and its Disorders* belongs on the reference shelf of anyone interested in the singing voice as does *The Singer's and Actor's Throat* by Norman Punt. Finally, Blanche Marchesi's *The Singer's Catechism and Creed* strikes me as much more considered and less manic than many of the other volumes on this list. Victor A. Fields' *Training the Singing Voice* will give the reader an idea of the size and contrariness of this literature.

1. Aikin, W. A. *The Voice*. London: Longmans, Green & Company, 1920.
2. Bach, Alberto B. *On Musical Education and Vocal Culture*. London: William Blackwood and Sons, 1881.
3. Bowlly, Al. *Modern Style Singing ("Crooning")*. London: Henri Selmer & Company.
4. Brodnitz, Friedrich S. *Keep Your Voice Healthy*. New York: Harper & Row, 1953.
5. Brown, R. M. *The Singing Voice*. New York: The Macmillan Company, 1946.
6. Browne, Lennox. *Voice Use and Stimulants*. London: Sampson, Low, Marston, Searle & Rivington, 1885.
7. Browne, Lennox; Behnke, Emil. *Voice Song and Speech*. London: Sampson, Low Marston & Company.
8. Croker, Norris. *Handbook for Singers*. London: Augener Ltd.
9. Curtis, H. Holbrook. *Voice Building and Tone Placing*. London: D. Appleton and Company, 1909.

10. Davies, Clara Novello. *You Can Sing*. London: Selwyn & Blount, 1928.
11. Drew, W. S. *Singing, The Art and the Craft*. London: Oxford University Press, 1937.
12. Duval, J. H. *Svengali's Secrets and Memoirs of the Golden Age*. New York: Robert Speller & Sons, 1958.
13. Elkin, Robert. *A Career in Music*. London: Novello and Company, 1960.
14. Ellis, Alexander J. *Pronunciation for Singers*. London: J. Curwen & Sons, 1877.
15. Emil-Behnke, Kate. *The Technique of Singing*. London: Williams and Norgate, 1945.
16. Evetts, Edgar T.; Worthington, Robert A. *The Mechanics of Singing*. London: J. M. Dent and Sons, 1928.
17. Ffrangcon-Davies, David. *The Singing of the Future*. Champaign, Illinois: Pro Musica Press, 1968.
18. Field-Hyde, F. C. *The Art and Science of Voice Training*. London: Oxford University Press, 1950.
19. Fields, Victor Alexander. *Training the Singing Voice* (An Analysis of the Working Concepts Contained in Recent Contributions to Vocal Pedagogy). New York: King's Crown Press, 1947.
20. Franca, Ida. *Manual of Bel Canto*. New York: Coward McCann, 1953.
21. Fuchs, Viktor. *The Art of Singing and Voice Technique*. London: John Calder, 1963.
22. Garcia, Manuel. *Hints on Singing*. London: Ascherberg, Hopwood and Crew, 1894.
23. Greene, Margaret C. L. *The Voice and its Disorders*. London: Pitman Medical Publishing Company Ltd., 1957.
24. Guilbert, Yvette. *How to Sing a Song*. New York: The Macmillan Company, 1918.
25. Hahn, Reynaldo. *Du Chant*. Paris: P. LaFitte, 1920.
26. Hast, Harry Gregory. *The Singer's Art*. London: Methuen & Company, 1925.
27. Henderson, W. J. *The Art of Singing*. New York: The Dial Press, 1938.
28. Herbert-Caesari, E. *Tradition and Gigli*. London: Robert Hale & Company, 1958.
29. ———— *The Voice of the Mind*. London: Robert Hale & Company, 1951.
30. Jackson, C. and C. L. *Diseases and Injuries of the Larynx*. Temple U. Press, 1942.
31. Kagen, Sergius. *On Studying Singing*. New York: Dover Publications, 1950.
32. Kay, Elster. *Bel Canto and the Sixth Sense*. London: Dennis Dobson, 1963.
33. Klein, Hermann. *The Bel Canto*. London: Oxford University Press, 1923.
34. Lehmann, Lilli. *How to Sing*. New York: The Macmillan Company, 1960.
35. Levien, John Mewburn. *Some Notes for Singers*. London: Novello and Company, 1940.
36. Litante, Judith. *A Natural Approach to Singing*. London: Oxford University Press, 1962.
37. Mackenzie, Morell. *The Hygiene of the Vocal Organs*. London: Macmillan and Company, 1886.
38. MacKinlay, Sterling. *The Singing Voice and its Training*. London: G. Routledge & Sons, 1910.
39. Mancini, Giambattista (ed. Edward Foreman). *Practical Reflections on Figured Singing*. Champaign, Illinois: Pro Musica Press, 1967.
40. Marafioti, P. Mario. *Caruso's Method of Voice Production*. New York: D. Appleton and Company, 1922.
41. Marchesi, Blanche. *The Singer's Catechism and Creed*. London: J. M. Dent & Sons, 1932.
41a. ———— *Singer's Pilgrimage*. London: G. Richards, 1923.
42. Marchesi, Mathilde. *Ten Singing Lessons*. New York: The Macmillan Company, 1901.
43. Martens, Frederick H. *The Art of the Prima Donna and Concert Singer*. New York: D. Appleton and Company, 1923.
44. Martino, Alfredo. *Today's Singing*. New York: Executive Press.
45. Mayer, Frederick D.; Sacher, Jack. *The Changing Voice*. Minneapolis: Augsburg Publishing House.

46. McClosky, David Blair. *Your Voice at its Best*. Boston: Little Brown and Company, 1967.
47. McKenzie, Duncan. *Training the Boy's Changing Voice*. London: Faber and Faber, 1956.
48. Metzger, Zerline Mühlman. *Individual Voice Patterns*. New York: Carlton Press, 1966.
49. Miller, Frank E. *Vocal Art-Science and its Application*. New York: G. Schirmer, 1917.
50. Moses, Paul J. *The Voice of Neurosis*. New York: Grune & Stratton, 1954.
51. Punt, Norman A. *The Singer's and Actor's Throat*. London: William Heinemann Medical Books, 1952.
52. Puritz, Elizabeth. *The Teaching of Elisabeth Schumann*. London: Methuen & Company, 1956.
53. Reid, Cornelius. *Bel Canto*. New York: Coleman-Ross Company, 1950.
54. Rizzo, Raymond. *The Voice as an Instrument*. New York: Odyssey Press, 1969.
55. Roma, Lisa. *The Science and Art of Singing*. New York: G. Schirmer, 1956.
56. Rose, Arnold. *The Singer and the Voice*. London: Faber and Faber, 1962.
57. Russell, Louis Arthur. *The Commonplaces of Vocal Art*. Boston: Oliver Ditson Company, 1907.
58. Santley, Charles. *The Art of Singing and Vocal Declamation*. London: Macmillan and Company, 1908.
59. Seashore, Harold. *Psychology of Music*. New York: McGraw Hill Book Co., 1938.
60. Schiøtz, Aksel. *The Singer and his Art*. New York: Harper & Row, 1970.
61. Scott, Charles Kennedy. *The Fundamentals of Singing*. New York: Pitman, 1954.
62. Shakespeare, William. *The Art of Singing*. Boston: Oliver Ditson Company, 1898.
63. Sutro, Emil. *Duality of Voice and Speech*. London: Dryden House, 1904.
64. Taylor, David C. *The Psychology of Singing*. New York: The Macmillan Co. 1908.
65. Tetrazzini, Luisa. *How to Sing*. London: C. Arthur Peason, Ltd., 1923.
66. Thorpe, Clarence R. *Teach Yourself to Sing*. London: The English Universities Press, 1954. In paperback as *A Short Course in Singing*. New York: Funk and Wagnalls, 1968.
67. Tosi, Pier Francesco. *Observations on the Florid Song*. London: J. Wilcox, 1942.
68. Vennard, William. *Singing, The Mechanism and the Technic*. New York: Carl Fischer, Inc., 1967.
69. Voorhees, Irving Wilson. *Hygiene of the Voice*. New York: The Macmillan Company, 1923.
70. White, Ernest G. *Science and Singing*. London: J. M. Dent and Sons, 1909.
71. Whitlock, Weldon. *Bel Canto for the Twentieth Century*. Champaign, Illinois: Pro Musica Press, 1968.
72. Witherspoon, Herbert. *Singing*. New York: G. Schirmer, 1925.

Useful to any singer who has found a voice and is about to embark on a career are two paper bound booklets:

73. *Awards for Singers* Obtainable from the Central Opera Service, Lincoln Center Plaza, New York, 10023 50 cents.
74. Newsom, Frances. *A Guide for Young Singers*, William-Frederick Press, 55 East 86th Street, New York, 10028 $2.00.

Instructive not only to would-be accompanists but singers as well is the authoritative:

75. Moore, Gerald. *The Unashamed Accompanist*. New York: The Macmillan Company, 1946.

BOOKS BY OR ABOUT SINGERS

Here again the selection is large and checkered. Many great singers have, or caused to have had written their memoirs. These follow the usual pattern of struggle, debut, success, glamorous life at the top hob-nobbing with royalty et al until the final performance is sung. Of the books listed below, Mrs. Caruso's recollection of her husband including some of his comical, deeply moving letters to her is a must for anyone interested in the singing voice and the human spirit. Mary Watkins Cushing's *The Rainbow Bridge* is a vivid, absorbing account of a great artist, Olive Fremstad. The first book about a singer I ever bought (when I was ten) was Clara Leiser's *Jean de Reszke*. It seems as enjoyable now as it did then. Clara Louise Kellogg, one of America's first prima donnas gives an effective picture of the era in which she sang. The struggles of Ethel Waters and Billie Holiday in their careers are incredible and appalling.

76. Alda, Frances. *Men Women and Tenors.* Boston: Houghton Mifflin, 1937.
77. Anderson, Marian. *My Lord, What a Morning.* New York: The Viking Press, 1956.
78. Baez, Joan. *Daybreak.* New York: The Dial Press, 1968.
79. Bailey, Pearl. *The Rew Pearl.* New York: Harcourt, Brace & World, 1968.
80. Biancolli, Louis. *The Flagstad Manuscript.* New York: G. P. Putnam's Sons, 1952.
81. Bispham, David. *A Quaker Singer's Recollections.* New York: The Macmillan Co., 1921.
82. Calvé, Emma. *My Life.* New York: D. Appleton & Company, 1922.
83. Caruso, Dorothy. *Enrico Caruso, His Life and Death.* London: T. Werner Laurie, 1946.
84. Chaliapin, Fedor. *Man and Mask.* New York: Alfred A. Knopf, 1932.
85. Chaliapin *An Autobiography* (ed. Nina Froud and James Hanley). as told to Maxim Gorky. London: MacDonald, 1968.
86. Cushing, Mary Watkins. *The Rainbow Bridge.* New York: Putnam, 1954.
87. D'Alvarez, Marguerite. *Forsaken Altars.* London: Rupert Hart-Davis Ltd., 1954.
88. Dragonette, Jessica. *Faith is a Song.* New York: David McKay Company, 1951.
89. Eames, Emma. *Some Memories and Reflections.* New York: D. Appleton and Company, 1927.
90. Farrar, Geraldine. *The Story of an American Singer.* Boston: Houghton Mifflin, 1916.
91. ———— *Such Sweet Compulsion.* New York: The Greystone Press, 1938.
92. Ferrier, Winifred; Cardus, Neville. *Kathleen Ferrier.* London: Penguin Books, 1959.
93. Fitzlyon, April. *The Price of Genius. A Life of Pauline Viardot.* London: John Calder, 1964.
94. Flint, Mary H. *Impressions of Caruso and his Art.* New York: Privately printed, 1917.
95. Franklin, David. *Basso Cantante.* London: Gerald Duckworth, 1969.
96. Garden, Mary; Biancolli, Louis. *Mary Garden's Story.* New York: Simon and Schuster, 1951.
97. Gerhardt, Elena. *Recital.* London: Methuen & Company, 1953.
98. Gipson, Richard McCandless. *The Life of Emma Thursby.* New York: The New York Historical Society, 1940.
99. Glackens, Ira, Yanke, Diva. *Lillian Nordica and the Golden Days of Opera.* New York: Coleridge Press, 1963.
100. Hardwick, Michael and Mollie. *A Singularity of Voice.* London: Cassell and Company, Ltd., 1968.
101. De Hegermann-Lindencrone, L. *In the Courts of Memory.* New York: Harper & Brothers, 1912.
102. ———— *The Sunny Side of Diplomatic Life.* New York: Harper & Brothers, 1914.
103. Helm, MacKinley. *Angel Mo' and her Son, Roland Hayes.* Boston: Atlantic, Little, Brown, 1942.
104. Hetherington, John. *Melba.* London: Faber and Faber, 1967.
105. Hines, Jerome. *This is My Story. This is My Song.* Westwood, New Jersey: Fleming H. Revell Company, 1968.
106. Holiday, Billie Smith (with William Dufty). *Lady Sings the Blues.* New York: Doubleday, 1956.

107. Holland, Henry Scott; Rockstro, W. S. *Memoir of Jenny Lind-Goldschmidt.* London: John Murray Ltd., 1891.
108. Homer, Sidney. *My Wife and I.* New York: The Macmillan Company, 1939.
109. Howard, Kathleen. *Confessions of an Opera Singer.* New York: Alfred A. Knopf, 1918.
110. Hoyt, Edwin P. *Paul Robeson.* London: Cassell and Company, Ltd., 1967.
111. Kahn, E. J. Jr. *The Voice* (Frank Sinatra). New York: Harper & Brothers, 1946.
112. Kellogg, Clara Louise. *Memoirs of an American Prima Donna.* New York: G. P. Putnam's Sons, 1913.
113. Lawrence, Marjorie. *Interrupted Melody.* New York: Appleton-Century-Crofts, Inc., 1949.
114. Lawton, Mary. *Schumann-Heink, The Last of the Titans.* New York: The Macmillan Co., 1928.
115. Leblanc, Georgette. *Souvenirs.* New York: E. P. Dutton & Company, 1932.
116. Lehmann, Lotte. *Singing with Richard Strauss.* London: Hamish Hamilton Ltd., 1964.
117. —— *Wings of Song.* London: Kegan Paul, Trench, Trubner & Company, 1938.
118. Leider, Frida. *Playing My Part.* London: Calder and Boyars, 1966.
119. Leiser, Clara. *Jean de Reszke.* New York: Minton, Balch & Company, 1934.
120. Lethbridge, Peter. *Kathleen Ferrier.* London: Cassell and Company, Ltd., 1959.
121. Mackenzie-Grieve, Averil. *Clara Novello.* London: Geoffrey Bles Ltd., 1955.
122. Mackinlay, M. Sterling. *Antoinette Sterling and Other Celebrities.* London: Hutchinson & Company Ltd., 1906.
123. Martin, Sadie E. *The Life and Professional Career of Emma Abbott.* Minneapolis: L. Kimball Printing Company, 1891.
124. McArthur, Edwin. *Flagstad, A Personal Memoir.* New York: Alfred A. Knopf, 1965.
125. Melba, Nellie. *Melodies and Memoirs.* London: Thornton Butterworth, 1925.
126. de Merlin, Countess. *Memoirs of Madame Malibran.* London: Henry Colburn, 1840.
127. Merrill, Robert (with Sandford Dody). *Once More From the Beginning.* New York: The Macmillan Company, 1965.
128. Moore, Grace. *You're Only Human Once.* New York: Doubleday & Company, 1944.
129. Pearce, Charles E. *Madame Vestris and her Times.* New York: Brentano's, 1923.
130. —— *Sims Reeves, Fifty Years of Music in England.* London: Stanley Paul & Company, 1924.
131. Peters, Roberta (with Louis Biancolli). *A Debut at the Met.* New York: Meredith Press, 1967.
132. Piaf, Edith. *The Wheel of Fortune.* London: Peter Owen Ltd., 1965.
133. Robinson, Francis. *Caruso, His Life in Pictures.* New York: Bramhall House, 1957.
134. Rogers, Clara Kathleen. *Memories of a Musical Career.* Boston: Little, Brown, 1919.
135. Russell, Frank. *Queen of Song, the Life of Henrietta Sontag.* New York: Exposition Press, 1964.
136. Santley, Charles. *Reminiscences of my Life.* London: Isaac Pitman & Sons, Ltd., 1909.
137. —— *Student and Singer.* London: Edward Arnold, 1892.
138. Shaw, Arnold. *Sinatra.* London: W. H. Allen & Company, 1968.
139. Slezak, Leo. *Song of Motley.* London: William Hodge and Company, 1938.
140. Tetrazzini, Luisa. *My Life of Song.* London: Cassell and Company, Ltd., 1921.
141. Teyte, Maggie. *Star on the Door.* London: Putnam & Company, Ltd., 1958.
142. Traubel Helen (with Richard G. Hubler). *St. Louis Woman.* New York: Duell, Sloan and Pearce, 1959.
143. Truman, Margaret (with Margaret Cousins). *Souvenir.* New York: McGraw-Hill Book Company, 1965.
144. Tucker, Sophie. *Some of These Days.* New York: Doubleday Doran, 1945.

145. Wagenknecht, Edward. *Jenny Lind.* New York: Houghton Mifflin, 1931.
146. Ware, W. Porter; Lockard, Thaddeus C. Jr. *The Lost Letters of Jenny Lind.* London: Victor Gollancz, Ltd., 1966.
147. Waters, Ethel (with Charles Samuels). *His Eye is on the Sparrow.* New York: Doubleday & Company, 1951.
148. Waterston, R. C. *Adelaide Phillips, a Record.* Boston: A. Williams & Company, 1883.

COLLECTED SINGERS

149. Heriot, Angus. *The Castrati in Opera.* London: Secker & Warburg Ltd., 1956.
150. Klein, Hermann. *Great Women Singers of My Time.* New York: E. P. Dutton & Company, 1931.
151. Mackenzie, Barbara and Findlay. *Singers of Australia.* London: Newnes Books, 1968.
152. Marks, Edward B. (with Abbot J. Liebling). *They All Sang.* New York: The Viking Press, 1934.
153. Matz, Mary Jane. *Opera Stars in the Sun.* New York: Farrar, Straus and Company, 1955.
154. Pleasants, Henry. *The Great Singers.* New York: Simon and Schuster, 1966.
155. Sargeant, Winthrop. *Geniuses, Goddesses and People.* New York: E. P. Dutton & Company, 1949.
156. Strang, Lewis C. *Famous Prima Donnas.* Boston: L. C. Page & Company, 1900.
157. Thompson, Oscar. *The American Singer.* New York: The Dial Press, 1937.
158. Thurner, A. *Les Reines du Chant.* Paris: A. Hennuyer, 1883.

REMINISCENCES AND CRITICISMS OF SINGERS BY NON-SINGERS

G. B. Shaw, whose mother was a singer and teacher of singing, is wonderfully funny and astute about matters to do with the voice. Chorley, Cox, Hogarth and Mount-Edgcumbe all give detailed and carefully considered descriptions of singers before the days of recordings.

159. Arditi, Luigi (ed. Baroness von Zedlitz). *My Reminiscences.* London: Skiffington and Son Ltd., 1896.
160. Beecham, Sir Thomas. *A Mingled Chime.* London: Hutchinson & Company, Ltd., 1944.
161. Berlioz, Hector (ed. David Cairns). *Memoirs.* London: Victor Gollancz, Ltd., 1969.
162. Burney, Charles. *The Present State of Music in France and Italy.* London: T. Becket and Company, 1773.
163. Chorley, Henry F. *Thirty Years Musical Recollections.* London: Hurst and Blackett, 1862.
164. Cox, E. C. *Musical Recollections of the Last Half Century.* London: Tinsley Brothers, 1872.
165. Damrosch, Walter. *My Musical Life.* New York: C. Scribner's Sons, 1923.
166. Davison, J. W. *From Mendelssohn to Wagner.* London: William Reeves, 1912.
167. Diehl, Alice Mangold. *Musical Memories.* London: Richard Bentley and Son, 1897.
168. Gaisberg, F. W. *The Music Goes Round.* New York: The Macmillan Company, 1942.
169. Gollancz, Victor. *Journey Towards Music.* London: Victor Gollancz, Ltd., 1964.
170. Hanslick, Eduard (ed. Henry Pleasants). *Vienna's Golden Years of Music.* New York: Simon and Schuster, 1950.
171. Hogarth, George. *Memoirs of the Opera in Italy, France, Germany and England.* London: Richard Bentley, 1851.
172. Hughes, Spike. *Opening Bars.* London: Pilot Press, 1946.
173. Huneker, James Gibbons. *Letters.* New York: Charles Scribner's Sons, 1922.
174. Kelly, Michael. *Reminiscences.* London: Henry Colburg, 1826.
175. Klein, Hermann. *Thirty Years of Musical Life in London.* London: Willliam Heinemann Ltd., 1903.

176. Kuhe, Wilhelm. *My Musical Recollections.* London: Richard Bentley and Son, 1896.
177. Mapleson, J. H. (ed. Harold Rosenthal). *Memoirs.* London: Putnam & Company, Ltd., 1966.
178. Marchesi, Mathilde. *Marchesi and Music.* New York: Harper & Brothers, 1898.
179. Maretzek, Max. *Crochets and Quavers.* New York: Da Capo Press, 1966.
180. Moore, Gerald. *Am I Too Loud?* London: Hamish Hamilton, Ltd., 1962.
181. Moscheles, Ignatz. *Recent Music and Musicians.* New York: Henry Holt and Company, 1873.
182. Mount-Edgcumbe, Richard. *Musical Reminiscences of an Old Amateur.* London: W. Clarke, 1823.
183. Newton, Ivor. *At the Piano.* London: Hamish Hamilton, Ltd., 1966.
184. O'Connell, Charles. *The Other Side of the Record.* New York: Alfred A. Knopf, 1947.
185. Shaw, George Bernard. *London Music in 1888-89.* London: Constable and Company, Ltd., 1937.
186. Shaw, George Bernard (ed. Dan H. Laurence). *How to Become a Music Critic.* New York: Hill and Wang, 1961.
187. Sheean, Vincent. *First and Last Love.* New York: Random House, 1956.
188. Walker, Francis. *Letters of a Baritone.* London: William Heinemann Ltd., 1895.
189. Walter, Bruno. *Theme and Variations.* New York: Alfred A. Knopf, 1946.

OTHER CRITICAL WRITING

190. Arundell, Dennis. *The Critic at the Opera.* London: Ernest Benn, 1957.
191. Finck, Henry T. *Chopin and Other Musical Essays.* New York: Charles Scribner's Sons, 1904.
192. —— *Musical Progress.* Philadelphia: Theodore Presser Company, 1923.
193. Gardiner, William. *The Music of Nature.* London: Longman, Rees, Ormz, Brown, Green and Longman, 1832.
194. Haggin, B. H. *The Listener's Musical Companion.* New Brunswick, New Jersey: Rutgers University Press, 1956.
195. Newman, Ernest (ed. Felix Aprahamian). *From the World of Music.* London: John Calder, 1956.
196. Parker, H. T. *Eighth Notes.* New York: Dodd, Mead & Company, Inc., 1922.
197. Upton, George P. *Musical Pastels.* Chicago: A. C. McClurg & Company, 1902.

HISTORY

198. Bowra, C. M. *Primitive Song.* London: Weidenfeld & Nicholson, 1962.
199. Drinker, Sophie. *Music and Women.* New York: Coward McCann, 1948.
200. Grout, Donald Jay. *A History of Western Music.* New York: W. W. Norton & Company, 1960.
201. Henderson, W. J. *Early History of Singing.* New York: Longmans Green & Company, 1921.
202. Hurst, P. G. *The Age of Jean de Reszke.* London: Christoper Johnson, 1958.
203. —— *The Golden Age Recorded.* London: The Oakwood Press, 1963.
204. Lang, Paul H. *Music in Western Civilization.* London: J. M. Dent & Sons, Ltd., 1942.
205. Sendry, Alfred; Norton, Mildred. *David's Harp.* New York: New American Library, 1964.
206. Stevens, Dennis (ed.). *A History of Song.* London: Hutchinson & Company, Ltd., 1960.
207. Suetonius. *The Twelve Caesars.* London: Penguin Books, 1957.
208. Wallaschek, Richard. *Primitive Music.* London: Longmans Green, 1893.
209. Wellesz, Egon (ed.). *The New Oxford History of Music: Ancient and Oriental Music.* London: Oxford University Press, 1957.
210. Wibberley, Brian. *Music and Religion.* London: The Epworth Press, 1931.

211. Anonymous. *Twenty Years of New York Singing Teachers' Association, Inc.* Philadelphia: Theodore Presser Company, 1928.

OPERATIC HISTORY AND LORE

212. Cone, John Frederick. *Oscar Hammerstein's Manhattan Opera Company.* Norman, Oklahoma: University of Oklahoma Press, 1966.
213. Davis, Ronald L. *Opera in Chicago.* New York: Appleton-Century, 1966.
214. Eaton, Quaintance. *The Boston Opera Company.* New York: Appleton-Century, 1965.
215. Goldovsky, Boris; Peltz, Mary Ellis. *Accents on Opera.* New York: Farrar, Straus and Young, 1953.
216. Kolodin, Irving. *The Story of the Metropolitan Opera.* New York: Oxford University Press, 1953.
217. Lahee, Henry C. *Grand Opera in America.* Boston: L. C. Page & Company, 1902.
218. Marek, George R. *A Front Seat at the Opera.* New York: Allen, Towne & Heath, 1948.
219. Noble, Helen. *Life with the Met.* New York: G. P. Putnam's Sons, 1954.
220. Peltz, Mary Ellis (ed.). *Opera Lover's Companion.* New York: Ziff-Davis Publishing Company, 1948.
221. Rosenthal, Harold. *Two Centuries of Opera at Covent Garden.* London: Putnam & Company Ltd., 1958.
222. Rosenthal, Harold (ed.). *The Opera Bedside Book.* London: Victor Gollancz, Ltd., 1965.
223. Seltsam, William H. *Metropolitan Opera Annals.* New York: The H. W. Wilson Company, 1947.
224. ———— *First Supplement, 1947-1957.* New York: The H. W. Wilson Company, 1957.
225. ———— *Second Supplement, 1957-1966.* New York: The H. W. Wilson Company, 1968.
226. Taubman, H. Howard. *Opera Front and Back.* New York: Charles Scribner's Sons, 1938.
227. White, Eric Walter. *The Rise of English Opera.* London: John Lehmann, 1951.

OTHER REFERENCES

228. Davies, J. H. *Musicalia.* London: Pergamon Press, 1966.
229. Jacobs, Arthur. *A New Dictionary of Music.* London: Penguin Books, 1958.
230. Kutsch, K. J.; Riemens, Leo. *A Concise Biographical Dictionary of Singers.* Philadelphia: Chilton Book Company, 1969.
231. Newman, Ernest. *Stories of the Great Operas.* New York: Alfred A. Knopf, 1928.
232. ———— *More Stories of Famous Operas.* New York: Alfred A. Knopf, 1943.

PERIODICALS

233. *About the House.*
234. *High Fidelity.*
235. *London Times.*
236. *Metropolitan Opera Program.*
237. *NATS* (National Association of Teachers of Singing) *Bulletin.*
238. *The New York Times.*
239. *New Yorker.*
240. *Opera.*
241. *Opera News.*
242. *Records and Recordings.*
243. *Saturday Review of Literature.*
244. *Stereo Review.*
245. *Time.*

FICTION

Of the numbers of writers who have woven the singing voice into their fiction, outstanding is the incomparable Willa Cather. In his recent study, *Music in Willa Cather's Fiction* Richard Giannone points out how "singers and musical performances held a special fascination for her, though she herself was musically an amateur with no technical knowledge of the art." *The Song of the Lark* is Miss Cather's only full length novel dealing with the development of a successful opera singer, in which she relates the artistry of her heroine, Thea Kronborg, to the land from which she came. "It wasn't like that" said Olive Fremstad, the soprano on whom the author is supposed to have based her story. Nonetheless it is a very beautiful book about a great singer. Lillian Nordica, who made several unfortunate marriages, is supposed to have sat for *her* portrait in "The Diamond Mine", one of a number of stories about singers contained in *Youth and the Bright Medusa*. *My Mortal Enemy* and *Lucy Gayheart* also contain references to singing which capture exquisitely the spell of great vocal art.

James Joyce was another who had the power to evoke in words the effect of the singing voice. This is particularly true of "The Dead" in *Dubliners. Ulysses,* of course, is flooded with references to singing.

Of some of the others novels listed, the singing voice has called forth fantasies that seem mad or merely preposterous from their authors. Marcia Davenport's *Of Lena Geyer,* however, is a colorful and thoroughly enjoyable story of a prima donna's life. James M. Cain's *Serenade* graphically details some of the physical sensations of singing, while Martin Mayer's *A Voice that Fills the House* (with a plot that would have awed the librettist of *Trovatore)* contains authentic atmosphere of the opera house with shrewd comments on singing.

I have listed the Tolstoy for the lovely description of Natásha's singing, and the Thomas Mann for the chapter in which Hans Castorp listens to phonograph records of great singers.

246. Atherton, Gertrude. *Tower of Ivory*. New York: The Macmillan Company, 1910.
247. Cain, James M. *Serenade*. New York: Alfred A. Knopf, 1937.
248. Cather, Willa. *Lucy Gayheart*. New York: Alfred A. Knopf, 1935.
249. —— *My Mortal Enemy*. New York: Alfred A. Knopf, 1926.
250. —— *The Song of the Lark*. Boston: Houghton Mifflin, 1915.
250a. —— *Youth and the Bright Medusa*. New York: Alfred A. Knopf, 1920.
251. Davenport, Marcia. *Of Lena Leyer*. New York: Charles Scribner's Sons, 1936.
252. DuMaurier, George. *Trilby*. London: Osgood, McIlvaine & Company, 1896.
253. Eliot, George. *Daniel Deronda*. New York: Harper & Brothers, 1877.
254. Henderson, W. J. *The Soul of a Tenor*. New York: Henry Holt, 1912.
255. Huneker, James. *Painted Veils*. New York: Horace Liveright, 1928.
256. Joyce, James. *Dubliners*. London: Penguin Books, 1956.
257. —— *Ulysses*. New York: Random House, 1934.
258. Mann, Thomas. *The Magic Mountain*. (tr. H. T. Lowe-Porter). New York: Alfred A. Knopf, 1944. Chapter VII, pp. 635-653.
259. Mansfield, Katharine. *The Short Stories*. New York: Alfred A. Knopf, 1937. pp. 384-393.
260. Mayer, Martin. *A Voice that Fills the House*. New York: Simon and Schuster, 1959.
261. Moore, George. *Evelyn Innes*. New York: D. Appleton and Company, 1914.
262. Nichols, Beverly. *Evensong*. New York: Doubleday Doran and Co., 1932.
263. O'Brien, Kate. *As Music and Splendour*. London: Heinemann, 1958.
264. Sanborn, Pitts. *Prima Donna*. New York: Longmans Green and Company, 1929.
265. Sand, Georges. *Consuelo*. New York: A. L. Burt, 189?.
266. Tolstoy, Leo. *War and Peace* (tr. L. and A. Maude). New York: Simon and Schuster, 1942. Section 14, Book Four, Part One, pp. 367-370.

ANTHOLOGIES

267. Bishop, John (ed.). *Music and Sweet Poetry*. London: John Baker, 1968.
268. Blom, Eric (ed.). *The Music Lover's Miscellany*. London: Victor Gollancz, Ltd., 1935.
269. Cole, William. *The Fireside Book of Humorous Poetry*. New York: Simon and Schuster, 1959.
270. Plotz, Helen (ed.). *Untune the Sky*. New York: Thomas Y. Crowell Company, 1957.

BIOGRAPHIES

271. Curtiss, Minna. *Bizet and his World*. London: Secker and Warburg, 1959.
272. De Bovet, Marie-Anne. *Charles Gounod*. London: Sampson, Low, Marston, Searl and Rivington, 1891.
273. Martin, George. *Verdi: His Music, Life and Times*. New York: Dodd, Mead & Co., 1963.
274. Newman, Ernest. *The Life of Richard Wagner*. New York: Alfred Knopf, 1961.
275. Schauffler, Robert Haven. *Beethoven, The Man Who Freed Music*. Garden City, N.Y.: Doubleday, 1925.
276. Shaw, A. *Sinatra*. London: W. H. Allen, 1969.
277. Turner, W. J. *Mozart the Man and his Works*. London: Victor Gollancz Ltd., 1938.

INDEX

ABARBANELL, Lina (1879–1963) Soprano, 255
ABOTT, Bessie, born Pickens (1878–1919) Soprano, 252
Acis and Galatea (G. F. Handel), 66
"Acoustical Study of the Pitch of Infant Hunger Wails, An," 180
Adalgisa (Bellini: *Norma*), 50
ADAMS, Suzanne (1872–1953) Soprano, 252
Age of Pericles, 3, 7
AGUJARI, Lucrezia, "La Bastardella," (1743–1783) Soprano, 22, range, 31-32
"Ah, fuyez douce image" (Massent: *Manon*), 67
Aida (Verdi: *Aida*), 38, 40, 44; range, 55, 57, 204
Aida (G. Verdi), 42, 67, 83, 84, 87, 94, 248
ALBANESE, Licia (1913–) Soprano, 38, 41
Alcestis (C. W. Gluck), 195 f.
Alcindoro *(Bohème),* 88
ALDA, Frances (1883–1952) Soprano, 108, 135-136, 210, 211
Alfredo *(Traviata),* 66, 68, 75
Alisa, maid to Lucia (Donizetti: *Lucia di Lammermoor*), 95
"All es Vollbracht" (J. S. Bach), 115
"Alleluia" (Mozart: *Exsultate Jubilate*), 115
ALVA, Luigi (1927–) Tenor, 66
AMARA, Lucine (1927–) Soprano, 93
Amelia (Verdi: *Ballo in Maschera*), 40
American Theater Wing, 213, 214
Amneris (Verdi: *Aida*), 52, 55

Amonasro (Verdi: *Aida*), 83, 84
"Am stillen Herd" (Wagner: *Meistersinger*), 160
Anchors Aweigh (Film), 277
"Ancora un passo or via . . ." (Puccini: *Madama Butterfly*), 241
ANDERSON, Marian (1902–) Contralto, 58, 107, 117, 203
Andrea Chénier (U. Giordano), 38, 81, 95
Andrea Chénier (Giordano: *Andrea Chénier*), 67
ANDREWS, Julie, born Julia Elizabeth Wells (1935–) Soprano, 36
"Anges purs, anges radieux" (Gounod: *Faust*), 130
Anthropologie (I. Kant), 179
Apollo, father of Orpheus, 9
Arabella (Strauss: *Arabella*), 249
Arditi, Luigi (1822–1903) Conductor, composer, 182
Aridane auf Naxos (R. Strauss), 34
"Arie Antiche," 124, 226
Aristotle (384–322 B.C.) Philosopher, 142
Arlen, Harold (1905–) Pop Composer, 132
ARROYO, Martina, Soprano, 93
Arsace (G. Rossini: *Semiramide*), 50
Arturo Bucklaw (Donizetti: *Lucia di Lammermoor*), 94, 95
Astaire, Fred (1899–) Pop singer, movie actor, 123
Atherton, Gertrude Franklin, born Horn (1857–1948) Novelist, 279
Auber, Daniel-François-Esprit (1782–1871) Composer, 133, 134

Augustine, Saint (354–430) Doctor of the Church, 12, 14
Augustus, first Roman Emperor (63 B.C.–14 A.D.), 10
AUSTRAL, Florence, born Wilson (1894–1968) Soprano, 108
Azucena (Verdi: *Trovatore*), 52, 55, 262

BACCALONI, Salvatore (1900–) Bass, 87
Bach, Johann Sebastian (1685–1750) Composer, xv, 64, 115, 116, 156
BACQUIER, Gabriel, Baritone, 82 f.
BADA, Angelo (1875–1941) Tenor, 94
Bajazzo, Der (See *Pagliacci*), 251
BAKER, Janet (1933–) Mezzo-Soprano, 100
Balfe, Michael William (1808–1870) Composer, as singer, 127
Ballo in Maschera, Un (G. Verdi), 38, 40, 84
BAMPTON, Rose (1908 or 1909–) Mezzo-Soprano and Soprano, discussion, 55; 56, 208
Barber, Samuel (1910–) Composer, 132
Barbiere di Siviglia, Il (Rossini), 31, 66, 76, 86, 88, 127, 190, 209
Barnaba (Ponchielli: *Gioconda*), 84
Barnum, Phineas Taylor (1810–1891) Impresario, 182
Baron Ochs (Strauss: *Rosenkavalier*), 87
Bashkirtseff, Marie (1860–1884) Diarist, 187
BATTISTINI, Mattia (1856–1928) Baritone, 289
"Battle of New Orleans, The," 4
Bayreuth, 104, 197
BEATLES: George Harrison, John Lennon, Paul McCartney, Ringo Starr, Pop Singers, xiii, 120
"Be My Love," 74
Beecham, Sir Thomas, (1879–1961) Conductor, xvi
Beethoven, Ludwig van (1770–1827) Composer, 125, 192
Beggars Opera, The (John Gay), 34
Behnke, Emil (1836–1892) Voice Teacher, 165, 166
Bel Canto, 17, 20, discussion, 21-25; 99, 116, 124
Bel Canto, (Cornelius L. Reid), 162
Bel Canto and the Sixth Sense (E. Kay), 145, 225
Benoit (Puccini: *Bohème*), 88
Beppe (Leoncavallo: *Pagliacci*), 95
BERGANZA, Teresa (1934–) Mezzo-Soprano, 21, 50, 97
BERGER, Erna (1900–) Soprano, 33, 112, 250
BERGER, Rudolf (1874–1915) Tenor, 77
BERGONZI, Carlo (1926–) Tenor, 77

Berlin, Irving, born Isidore Balin, (1888–) Pop Composer, 124, 132
Berlin Opera Company, 94, 107
Berlioz, Hector (1803–1869) Composer, 58, 99, as singer, 127-128; 130
BERNAC, Pierre, born Pierre Bertin, (1899–) Baritone, 111, 123
"Bernoulli effect," 155
Bernstein, Leonard (1918–) Composer-Conductor, 73, 124, 132
Berry, Walter (1929–), 273
Bing, Rudolf (1902–) Impresario, xiii, 203, 279, 292
BISPHAM, David (1857–1921) Baritone, 106
Bizet, Adolphe Armand (1810–?) Singing Teacher, 131
Bizet, Georges (1838–1875) Composer, 51, 51, as singer, 131; 214
BJOERLING, family, 68
BJOERLING, Jussi (1907–1960) Tenor, xi, 23, discussion, 68-69; comparison with Caruso, 72-73; 97, 113, 269, 281
"Bless the Child" (B. Holiday), 132
Blondel de Nesle (late 12th Century), Troubadour, 15
Bohème, La (G. Puccini), 37, 64, 66, 82, 86, 88, 93, 94, 284
Bohemian Girl, The (M. Balfe), 127
Böhm, Karl (1894–) Conductor, 40
BOHNEN, Michael (1887–1965) Bass-Baritone, 104
Boïto, Arrigo (1842–1918) Composer-Librettist, 85
BONCI, Alessandro (1870–1940) Tenor, 66, 294
BORDONI *see* FAUSTINA
BORI, Lucrezia, born Lucrecia Borja y Gonzalez de Riancho (1887–1960) Soprano, 41, 208, 272, 293
Boris Godounov (Moussorgsky: *Boris Godounov*), 84, 86, 88
Boris Godounov (M. Moussorgsky), 93, 95
Bovet, Marie Anne de (1860–?) Author, 130
Bowra, Sir Cecil Maurice (1898–) Writer on Anthropology, 4
Branch, M. W., Poet, 75
BRANDT, Marianne, born Marie Bischoff (1842–1921) Mezzo-Soprano, 104
Brangäne *(Tristan und Isolde)*, 54
BRANZELL, Karin (1891–) Mezzo-Soprano, 55, 97
Breen, Bobby, born Bobby Borsuk (1928–) Child actor, 181
Brice, Fanny (1891–1951) Actress-Singer, 202
"Brindisi" (Verdi-*Otello*), 81
British Museum, 7

Britten, Benjamin (1913–) Composer, 65, 114, 117
Brodnitz, Friedrich S., Laryngologist, 219
BROOKS, Patricia, Soprano, 279
BROSCHI, Carlo "Farinelli" (1705–1782) Castrato, xiv, 20
Brown, Ralph Morse, Singing Teacher, 62
Browne, Lennox (1841–1902) Laryngologist, 166
Brünnhilde (Wagner: Götterdämmerung), 39, 40, 43, 55, 56, 99, 197
Brünnhilde (Wagner: Siegfried), 39, 40, 43, 55, 56, 197, 262, 271
Brünnhilde (Wagner: Walküre), 39, 40, 43, 55, 56, 161, 197
Bull, Ole Bornemann (1810–1880) Violinist, 182
Bülow, Hans von (1830–1894) Conductor-Pianist, 62 f.
BUMBRY, Grace (1937–) Mezzo-Soprano, 107
Burlington, Countess of, xii
BURROWS, Stuart, Tenor, 100
BUTT, Dame Clara (1873–1936) Contralto, 59, 63

CABALLÉ, Monserrat (1932?–) Soprano, 25, 97, 103, 156, 191
CAFFARELLI, Gaetano Majorano (1710–1783) Castrato, 233
CAHIER, Madame Charles, born Sara Jane Layton-Walker (1870–1951) Mezzo-Soprano, 78
Calaf (Puccini: Turandot), 69, 75
CALLAS, Maria, born Kalogeropoulos (1923–) Soprano, discussion, 25; 41, 51, 93, loss of weight, 201; 229
CALVÉ, Emma, born Rosa Emma Calvet (1858–1942) Soprano, 51, 172; fourth register, 207, 210
Campanini, Cleofonte (1860–1919) Conductor, 196
Canio (Leoncavallo: Pagliacci), 69
Carmen (G. Bizet), 37, 69, 84
Carmen (Carmen), discussion, 51-52; 84, 111, 262
Carnegie Hall, 36
"Caro mio Ben" (G. Giordani), 226
"Caro Nome" (Verdi: Rigoletto), 160 f.
Carousel (Rodgers and Hammerstein), 36, 255
Caruso, Dorothy (Mrs. Enrico) Writer, 70, 220, 258, 269
CARUSO, Enrico (1873–1921) Tenor, 42, 65 f., discussion, 69-73; 74, 83, 95, 159, 188, 189, 220 f., 224, on nerves, 247; 248, day of performance, 258; dressing

room routine, 260-261; 269, 270, 271, 278
Carvalho, Léon, born Carvaille (1825–1897) Impresario, 129
"Casta Diva" (Bellini: Norma), xii, 5, 42, 181, 182
CASTAGNA, Bruna (1908–) Mezzo-Soprano, 52
CATALANI, Angelica (1780–1849) Soprano, 195 f.
Cather, Willa Sibert (1873–1947) Author, xvi, 266, 273
Cavalleria Rusticana (P. Mascagni), 69
Cavaradossi (Puccini: Tosca), 67
CECCHI, Pietro (?–1897) Tenor, teacher of Melba, 210
CEHANOVSKY, George (1895?–) Baritone, 94
"Celeste Aida" (Verdi: Aida), 262
Celestial Voice (Verdi: Don Carlo), 93
Cenerentola (G. Rossini), 127
CHALIAPIN, Feodor (1873–1938) Bass, 113, 294
Charcot, Jean Martin (1825–1893) Neurologist, 199
Charlotte (Massenet: Werther), 50, 111
Charpentier, Gustave (1860–1956) Composer, 95
Chatauqua Opera, 242
Chaucer, Geoffrey (1340–1400?) Poet-Author, 187
Cherubino (Mozart: Nozze di Figaro), 20, 50
Chevalier, Maurice (1888–) Entertainer, 124
Chicago Opera Company, 68, 242
Chorley, Henry Fothergill, (1808–1872) Music Critic, 191, 193
Christian Church, attitude to singing, 13-15; to castrati, 18
CHRISTOFF, Boris (1918–) Bass, 86, 279
Cicero, Marcus Tullius (106–43 B.C.) Orator-Philosopher, 10
Cio-Cio-San (Puccini: Madama Butterfly), 37, 57, 240
CLEMENS, Clara (Gabrilowitsch) (1871–1962) Contralto, daughter of Mark Twain, 198, 199
Clemens, Samuel L. (Mark Twain) (1835–1910) Author, xv, 198, 199
Clemens, Susy, born Olivia Susan (1873–1895) Daughter of Mark Twain, discussion of health, 198-199
Clothilde (Bellini: Norma), 93
Cohan, George Michael (1878–1942) Singer-Actor-Composer, 117
COLLIER, Marie, Soprano, 108 f.
Colline (Puccini: Bohème), 86

"Come Scoglio" (Mozart: *Così fan Tutte*), 170

Commendatore (Mozart: *Don Giovanni*), 86

COMO, Perry (1913–) Pop Singer, 122

Comprimario Singers, discussion, 92-96

Constanze (Mozart: *Entführung*), 43

Consuelo (G. Sand), 194

Contes d'Hoffman, Les (J. Offenbach), 50, 95

Coq d'or, Le (Rimsky-Korsakov), 34

CORELLI, Franco (1923 or 1925–) Tenor, 77, 229

CORENA, Fernando (1916–) Bass, 87

Così fan Tutte (W. A. Mozart), 34, 50, 82, 170

Count Almaviva (Rossini: *Barbiere*), 66, 190

Count di Luna (Verdi: *Trovatore*), 78, 81, 82

Countess Almavia (Mozart:*Nozze*), 38, 43, 55

Coup de Glotte, Le, discussion, 155-156; 222

Covent Garden Opera House, 52, 54, 55, 60, 71, 82 f., 96, 100, 211, imaginary performance, 238-241; 242, 262

Crespel (Offenbach: *Hoffman*), 95

CRIMI, Giulio (1885–1939) Tenor, 248

CROOKS, Richard (Alexander) (1900–) Tenor, 107, 171

CROSBY, Bing (1903–) Pop singer, 121

Curtain calls, 264-266

CURTIS-VERNA, Mary (1927–) Soprano, 235

Curtis, Henry Holbrook (1856–1920) Laryngologist, 158, quotes de Reszke, 222-223

Cushing, Mary Watkins, Author, 266

CUZZONI, Francesca (1700–1770) Soprano, *xii-xiii*

Dafne (J. Peri), 124

"Daisy, Daisy, give me your answer, do.," 162

Daland (Wagner: *Holländer*), 87

Dalila (Saint-Saëns: *Samson*), 52

Dante, Alighieri (1265–1321) Poet, 103

Darwin, Charles R. (1809–1882) Naturalist, 3

Davenport, Marcia (1903–) Author, on retirement, 277; 290

David, King of Israel, *xiv*

Debut roles, 252

"Dein ist mein ganzes Herz" (Lehar: *Land of Smiles*), 75

Delacroix, Ferdinand Victor Eugène (1798–1863) Painter, 191

DELLA CHIESA, Vivian, Soprano, 36

DELLER, Alfred (1912–) Countertenor, 62, 64, 66

DE LOS ANGELES, Victoria, born Victoria Gomez Cima (1923–) Soprano, 42, 51, 97, 103, 112, 156

Delsarte, Françoise-Alexandre-Nicolos-Cheri (1811–1871 or 1878) Singing Teacher, 131, 214

DE PAOLIS, Alessio (1898–1964) Tenor, 95

Des Grieux (Massenet: *Manon*), 66, 67

Des Grieux (Puccini: *Manon Lescaut*), 72

Desdemona (Rossini: *Otello*), 126

Desdemona (Verdi: *Otello*), 38

Despina (Mozart: *Così*), 34

DESTINN, Emmy, born Kittl (1878–1930) Soprano, 104

"Diamond Mine, The" (Willa Cather), 273

Dido and Aeneas (H. Purcell), 125

DIETRICH, Marlene, born Maria Magdalene von Losch (1904–) Pop Singer, Actress, 123

Dionysus, cult of, 7-8

"Dite alle giovine" (Verdi: *Traviata*), 103

Doctor Bartolo (Mozart: *Nozze*), 88

Doctor Bartolo (Rossini: *Barbiere*), 88

Doctor Dulcamara (Donizetti: *L'Elisir*), 87

Doctor Grenville (Verdi: *Traviata*), 251

Don Basilio (Rossini: *Barbiere*), 86

Don Carlo (Verdi: *Don Carlo*), 160, 276

Don Carlo (Verdi), 38, 69, 84, 87, 93, 279, 294

Don Giovanni (Mozart: *Don Giovanni*), 81, 84, 86, 88

Don Giovanni (Mozart), 34, 66, 76, 82, 84, 86, 251, 259

Don José (Bizet: *Carmen*), 69, 74, 76

Don Ottavio (Mozart: *Don Giovanni*), 66, 68, 294

Don Pasquale (Donizetti: *Don Pasquale*), 87

Don Rodrigue (G. Bizet), 31

Donizetti, Gaetano (1797–1848) Composer, 25, 161, 191

Donna Anna (Mozart: *Don Giovanni*), 39, 40, 43, 55, 57

Donna Elvira (Mozart: *Don Giovanni*), 43, 57, 251

Dorabella (Mozart: *Così*), 50

DORIA, Clara, born Kathleen Rogers (1844–1931) Soprano, on voice training, 227-228

"Dover Beach" (S. Barber), 132

DOWD, Ronald, Tenor, 108 f., 242

DRAGONETTE, Jessica, Soprano, 36

DRAKE, Alfred (1914–) Baritone-Actor, 121

Drinker, Sophie, writer on anthropology, 5-6

Drinking, 269
Duke of Mantua (Verdi: *Rigletto*), 75, 252
Du Maurier, George, born Louis Pal-
mella Busson (1834–1896) Novelist, 195,
215
DUNNE, Irene (1904–) Soprano-Actress, 35
DURBIN, Deanna, born Edna Mae Durbin
(1922–) Soprano-Actress, 35
DYLAN, Bob (1941–) Folk Singer, 124

EAMES, Emma (1865–1952) Soprano, 23,
106, 150, 207, 209, on Marchesi, 210;
234, 252, 273, 279, 294; death, 295
Early History of Singing (W. J. Hender-
son), 13
Eboli (Verdi: *Don Carlo*), 52
EDDY, Nelson (1901–1967) Baritone, 121
Eleazar (Halévy: *La Juive*), 71
Elektra (Strauss: *Elektra*), 40
Elektra (R. Strauss), 39
Elijah (F. Mendelssohn), 116, 245
Elizabeth (Wagner: *Tannhäuser*), 39, 42,
55, 198
ELKINS, Margreta, Soprano, 108 f.
Elsa (Wagner: *Lohengrin*), 39, 40, 43, 55,
197, 198
Enrico Caruso, His Life and Death
(Dorothy Caruso), 70
Entführung aus dem Serail, Die (W. A.
Mozart), 43
ERB, Karl (1877–1958) Tenor, 113
Erda (Wagner: *Siegfried*), 58, 255
"Erlkönig" (F. Schubert), 113
Escamillo (Bizet: *Carmen*), 84
ETTING, Ruth, Pop Singer, 118
Eugen Onegin (Tchaikowsky: *Eugen
Onegin*), 84
Euridice (J. Peri), 17, 124
Eurydice, 9
Eva, (Wagner: *Meistersinger*), 39
EVANS, (Sir) Geraint (1922–) Bass-Bari-
tone, 84, 100
Evelyn Innes (George Moore), 157-158
Evensong (Beverly Nichols), 284
Exsultate Jubilate (W. A. Mozart), 115

Fafner (Wagner: *Rheingold*), 88
Fafner (Wagner: *Siegfried*), 85, 87, 88
FALCON, Marie-Cornélie (1814–1897) So-
prano, 255
Falstaff (G. Verdi), 66, 87, 93
Falstaff, Sir John (Verdi: *Falstaff*), 64,
84, 88, 107
FARINELLI (See BROSCHI, Carlo)
FARRAR, Geraldine (1882–1967) Soprano,
41, 42, 50, 51, 94, 106, 207, 211, 231,
252, 260, 273, 293
FARRELL, Eileen (1920–) Soprano, 36, 120
Fasolt (Wagner: *Rheingold*), 87

FAURE, Jean-Baptiste (1830–1914) Bari-
tone, 131
Faust (Gounod: *Faust*), 76
Faust (C. Gounod), 37, 81, 86, 284
FAUSTINA, born Bordoni (1700?–1781) So-
prano, *xii*
FAY, Maude (1878 or 1883–1964) Soprano,
279
Fenton (Verdi: *Falstaff*), 66
Ferrein, Antoine, Scientist, 142, 143
FERRIER, Kathleen (1912–1953) Contralto,
discussion, 59-60; 101, 111, 113, 220 f.
Ferrier, Winifred, 60
Ffrangcon-Davies, David, Singing
Teacher (1856–1918), 100 f.
Fidelio (L. van Beethoven), 39, 55, 75, 83
Figaro (Rossini: *Barbiere*), 76, 209
Figaro (Mozart: *Nozze*), 81, 84, 86
Fiordiligi (Mozart: *Cosi*), 43
FISCHER-DIESKAU, Dietrich (1925–) Bari-
tone, 104, 113
FITZGERALD, Ella (1918–) Pop Singer, *xi*,
25, 118, 119, 246
Fitzlyon, April, Biographer, 193
FLAGSTAD, Kirsten (1895–1962) Soprano,
23, 40, 41, 42, 78, 97, 105, 112, 123, 151,
161, 173, 197, 201, 202, 208, 234, 269,
281, return to Metropolitan, 286-287;
292
Fliegende Holländer, Der (Wagner), 39,
87
Florestan (Beethoven: *Fidelio*), 75, 76
Ford (Verdi: *Falstaff*), 93
Forza del Destino, La (Verdi), 38, 40, 43,
86, 88, 189, 248
Fra Melitone (Verdi: *Forza*), 88
Franca, Ida, Singing Teacher, 107, 277
FRANCHI, Sergio, Pop Tenor, 121
Frantz (Offenbach: *Hoffmann*), 95
Frederick II (the Great) (1712–1786) King
of Prussia, 103
FREMSTAD, Olive, born Olivia Rundquist
(1871–1951) Soprano, 51, discussion, 53-
55; 97, 207, 266, 279, 280
FRENI, Mirella (1935–) Soprano, 41
FRETWELL, Elizabeth, Soprano, 108 f.
Freud, Sigmund (1856–1939) Psychiatrist,
180
Fricka (Wagner: *Walküre*), 52, 54
FRIJSH, Povla (1881–1960) Soprano, 112,
123
Friml, Rudolf (1879 or 1881–) Com-
poser, 34
Froeschels, Emil (1884–) Laryngologist,
153
Front Seat at the Opera, A (George
Marek), 261
FUCHS, Marta (1898–) Mezzo-Soprano and
Soprano, 57

Fuchs, Viktor, Singing teacher, 165 f., 173
FUGÈRE, Lucien (1848–1935) Baritone, 289

Gabrilowitsch, Ossip (1878–1936) Pianist-Conductor, 198
GADSKI, Johanna (1872–1932) Soprano, 279, 280, 294
Galabert, Edmond, Composer-Student of G. Bizet, 131
Galen (130?–200?) Physician, 142
GALLI-CURCI, Amelita (1882–1963) Soprano, 36, 41, 159, 195, 229
GALLI-MARIÉ, Célestine (1840–1905) Mezzo-Soprano, 51
GARCIA, Manuel del Popolo Vicente (1775–1832) Tenor, Singing teacher, 190, 191, 192
Garcia, Manuel (Patricio Rodrigues) II (1805–1906) Singing teacher, 23, 133, invents laryngoscope, 143-144; 145, 149, 150, coup de glotte, 155-156; 165, 166, 188, 190, 192, 209, 211; on Lind, 217; 222, 226
GARDEN, Mary (1874 or 1877–1967) Soprano, 41, 51, 207, clash with Marchesi, 210; 234, 241, 247, 272
Gardner, Ava, Film actress, 123
GARLAND, Judy, born Frances Gumm (1922-1969) Pop Singer-Actress, 119
GAY, John (1685–1732) Playwright, 34
GAY, Maria (1879–1943) Mezzo-Soprano, 52
Gazette Médicale, 149
Gazza Ladra, La (G. Rossini), 127
GEDDA, Nicolai (1925–) Tenor, 77
George the Fourth (1762–1830) King of England, 126
Gèrard (Giordano: Andrea Chénier), 81
GERHARDT, Elena (1883–1961) Mezzo-Soprano, 111
Germont, Elder (Verdi: Traviata), 82, 84, 93, 252
Gershwin, George (1898–1937) Composer, 124
GERSTER, Etelka (1855–1920) Soprano, 209
GHIAUROV, Nicolai (1929–) Bass, 25, 82, 86
GIANNINI, Dusolina (1902–) Mezzo-Soprano and Soprano, 56
GIGLI, Beniamino (1890–1957) Tenor, 71, 73, 159
Gilbert, (Sir) William Schwenk (1836–1911) Playwright-Poet, 34, 59
Gilda (Verdi: Rigoletto), 37, 40, 251, 252
Gioconda, La (Ponchielli: La Gioconda), 38, 40, 55, 84
Gioconda, La (A. Ponchielli), 84, 115
Giordani, Giuseppe (1753?–1798) Composer, 226

Glagloitic Mass (J. Janáček), 116
GLOSSOP, Peter, Baritone, 83, 100, 113
Glottis, 143, 144, 155, 156, 157, 165, 166, 187, 222
GLUCK, Alma, born Reba Fiensohn (1884–1938) Soprano, 290
Gluck, Christoph Willibald (1714–1787) Composer, 58, 128, 195 f.
Glyndebourne Opera, 170, 264, 294
GOGORZA, Emilio de (1874–1949) Baritone, 202, 273
Got, Edmond, Comic actor, 130
Götterdämmerung, Die (Wagner), 40, 50, 99
Gottschalk, Louis Moreau (1829–1869) Pianist-composer, 182
GOULET, Robert (1933–) Baritone, 121
Gounod, Charles (1818–1893) Composer, 56, 85, as singer, 130-131; 133, 194, 252
Graf, Herbert (1904–) Opera Director, 250
Grand Inquisitor (Verdi: Don Carlo), 87
GRAYSON, Kathryn (1923–) Soprano-Actress, 35
Great Victor Herbert, The (film), 35
Gregory I (540–604) Doctor of the Church, 13
Grout, Donald Jay (1902–) Musicologist, 16
GRISI, Giulia (1811–1869) Soprano, 22
GRIST, Reri (1933?–) Soprano, 107
GUEDEN, Hilde (1917–) Soprano, 104
Guglielmo (Mozart: Così), 82
Guizar, Tito, Pop Tenor, 121
Gurnemanz (Wagner: Parsifal), 87

"Habanera" (Bizet: Carmen), 262
Hadrian (76–138) Emperor, 10
HAFLIGER, Ernst (1919–) Tenor, 113
Hagen (Wagner: Götterdämmerung), 87
Haggin, Bernard H. (1900–) Music critic, 72
Hahn, Reynaldo (1875–1947) Composer, 59, as singer, 131; 223
"Hail Bright Cecilia" (Purcell: Ode on St. Cecilia's Day), 125
"Hallelujah Chorus" (Handel: Messiah), 114
HAMAEKERS, Bernardine, Soprano, 160 f.
Hammerstein, Oscar 2nd (1895–1960) Lyricist, 255
Hamlet (Shakespeare: Hamlet), 88
HAMMOND, Joan (1912–) Soprano, 108 f., 208
Handel, George Frideric (1685–1759) Composer, 65, 100, 114, 156, 160
Hans Sachs (Wagner: Meistersinger), 87
Hänsel (Humperdinck: Hänsel und Gretel), 50

Hänsel und Gretel (E. Humperdinck), 50
HARPER, Heather, Soprano, 102
HARRELL, Mack (1909–1960) Baritone, 208
HARRISON, George (*see* Beatles)
Harrison, Rex (1908–) Actor, 124
HARSHAW, Margaret (1912–) Mezzo-Soprano and Soprano, discussion, 55-56; 208
HAYES, Roland (1887–) Tenor, discussion, 67
HAYMES, Dick, Pop Singer, 121
Hegermann-Lindencrone, Lillie de, born Greenough, first marriage Moulton (1844–1928), discussion, 133-134; trill, 160-161; on Delsarte, 215
Held, Anna (1873?–1918) Singer-Actress, 117
HEMPEL, Frieda (1885–1955) Soprano, 33
HENDERSON, Roy (1889–) Baritone, 59
Henderson, William James (1855–1937) Music critic, 13, 41, 155, 221, 253
Herald (Wagner: *Lohengrin*), 93
Herbert, Victor (1859–1924) Composer, 34
Herod (R. Strauss: *Salome*), 76
High Fidelity (Periodical), *xiii*
"High C," discussion 41-44
HINES, Jerome born Heinz (1918 or 1921–) Bass, 86, 87, 234
Hints to Singers (L. Nordica), 201
Hippolytus, Saint (217–235) Bishop, 14
HOFER, Josefa, born Weber (1758–1819) Soprano, 31
Hofmannsthal, Hugo von (1874–1929) Dramatist, 137
"Ho-jo-to-ho" (Wagner: *Walküre*), 161
HOLIDAY, Billie "Lady Day" (1915–1959) Pop singer, 118, 119, 123, 132, 203, 270, 281
Hollywood Bowl, 74
Homer (700 B.C.?) Poet, 7
HOMER, Louise, born Beatty (1871–1947) Mezzo-Soprano, 231, 251, 273, 278
Homer, Sidney, Composer, 214
HORNE, Marilyn (1929?–) Mezzo-Soprano, 25, 50
HOTTER, Hans (1909–) Bass-Baritone, 87
How to Sing (Lilli Lehmann), 225, 268
HOWARD, Kathleen (1880–1956) Contralto, 295
Howells, Mrs. William Dean, 199
Hunding (Wagner: *Walküre*), 87
Husson, Raoul Nicolas (1901–) Laryngologist-Singing teacher, 146

Iago (Verdi: *Otello*), 81, 82, 84
Iliad, The (Homer), 7
"Inflammatus" (Rossini: *Stabat Mater*), 58

Innkeeper (Moussorgsky: *Boris*), 95
Iolanthe (Gilbert and Sullivan), 34
Iphigénie en Aulide (C. W. Gluck), 128
Iphigénie en Tauride (C. W. Gluck), 128
Isolde (Wagner: *Tristan*), 39, 40, 54, 55, 115, 130, 198
IVOGÜN, Maria, born Ilse von Günther (1891–) Soprano, 33

Jackson, Chevalier and C. L., Professors of bronco-esophagology, 153, 154
James, Henry (1843–1916) Author, 195 f.
Janáček, Leoš (1854–1928) Composer, 116
JENKINS, Florence Foster (1868–1944) Soprano?, 136
JEPSON, Helen (1906–) Soprano, 252
JERITZA, Maria, born Jedlitzka (1887–) Soprano, 50, 51, 104
John, XXII (1244–1334) Pope, 16
JOHNSON, Christine, Contralto, 119, 255
JOHNSON, Edward (also Eduardo di Giovanni) (1878–1959) Tenor, 292
Jokanaan (R. Strauss: *Salome*), 83
JONES, Gwyneth (1936–) Soprano, 39, 50, 57, 100
Joyce, James (1882–1941) Author, as singer, 134-135
Juilliard School of Music (New York City), 208, 212
Juive, La (J. F. Halévy), 71
Juliette (Gounod: *Roméo*), 252
"June is bustin' out all over" (Rodgers and Hammerstein: *Carousel*), 255

Kahn, Otto (Hermann) (1867–1934), 135
Kalergis, Countess Marie von, born Mouchanoff (1823–1874), 130
Kant, Immanuel (1724–1804) Philosopher, 179
KAPPEL, Gertrude (1884–) Mezzo-Soprano and Soprano, 56
Karajan, Herbert von (1908–) Conductor, 56
Katisha (Gilbert and Sullivan: *Mikado*), 59
Kay, Elster, Music Writer, 145, 225
Keep Your Voice Healthy (Friedrich S. Brodnitz), 219
Kelly, Gene (1912–) Pop Singer-Film Actor, 123
KEMBLE, Adelaide (1816–1879) Soprano, 188
KEMBLE, Fanny (Frances Anne) (1809–1893) Actress-Writer, 195 f.
Kent, Duchess of (Maria Louisa Victoria) (1786–1861) Mother of Queen Victoria, 133
Kern, Jerome (David) (1885–1945) Composer, 35, 124

Kimball, Florence Page, Singing teacher, 211

King of Fools (Charpentier: *Louise*), 96

King's Theater (London), *xii*, 125

KIPNIS, Alexander (1891–) Bass, 111, 113

KIRSTEN, Dorothy (1917 or 1919–) Soprano, 38

Kismet (Robert Wright and George Forrest), 121

Kiss me Kate (Cole Porter), 36, 121

Klein, Hermann (1856–1934) Music writer, 150, 159, 182

Kolodin, Irving, (1908–) Music writer, 71

KONETZNI, Anny (1902–1968) Mezzo-Soprano and Soprano, 56

KOSHETZ, Nina (1894–1965) Soprano, 105

Koussevitsky, Serge (Alexandrovitch) (1874–1951) Conductor, 73

KRAUSS, Gabrielle (1842–1906) Soprano, 209

Krehebiel, Henry (1854–1923) Music Critic, 195

Kundry (Wagner: *Parsifal*), 39, 54, 55, 56, 197

Kurvenal (Wagner: *Tristan*), 83, 264

KURZ, Selma (1874–1933) Soprano, 33, 261

LABLACHE, Luigi (1794–1858) Bass, 22, 133, 187

Lady Jane (Gilbert and Sullivan: *Patience*), 59

Lady Macbeth (Verdi: *Macbeth*), 30

Lamb, Charles (1775–1834) Essayist, *xv*

Lamperti, Giovanni Battista (1839–1910) Singing teacher, 150

LANCE, Albert, born Ingram (1925–) Tenor, 108 f.

Landgrave, Hermann (Wagner: *Tannhäuser*), 87

Lang, Paul Henry (1900 or 1901–) Musicologist, 7, 11

LANZA, Mario, born Alfredo Cocozza (1912–1959) Tenor, discussion, 73-74; 121

Laryngoscope, invention, 144; 145, 146, 156, 267

Larynx, 63, 101, 102, 106, 141, 142, 143, 144, 146, 152, uses of, 153-154; 156, 163, 164, 173, 174, 186, 220, 221, 225, 228, 248, 267, 268, 269

Laura (Ponchielli: *Gioconda*), 55

LAWRENCE, Marjorie (1909–) Soprano, 78, 108, 276

LEAR, Evelyn (1931?–) Soprano, 244, 273

LEE, Peggy, born Norma Egstrom (1920–) Pop Singer, *xiv*, 119

LEHANE, Maureen, Mezzo-Soprano, 102

Lehar, Franz (1870–1948) Composer, 34

LEHMANN, Lilli (1848–1929) Soprano, 39, 40, 41, 51, 54, 104, 151, 155, 207, sensations, 225; 268, 269

LEHMANN, Lotte (1888–) Soprano, 72, 104, 111, 112, 148 f., 208, 249, 281

LEIDER, Frida (1888–) Soprano, 78, 104, 259

Leiser, Clara, Author, 285

L'Elisir D'Amore (G. Donizetti), 66, 87, 251

LENNON, John (*see* Beatles)

Leonardo da Vinci (1452–1519) Artist, Scientist, 142

Leonora (Verdi: *Forza*), 38, 40, 189, 248

Leonora (Verdi: *Trovatore*), 38, 40, 57, 84

Leonore (Beethoven: *Fidelio*), 39, 55

Leporello (W. A. Mozart: *Don Giovanni*), 84, 88, 294

Liebestrank, Der (see *L'Elisir D'Amore*), 251

L'Incoronazione di Poppea (C. Monteverdi), 17

LIND, Jenny (-Goldschmidt) (1820–1887) Soprano, 117, 134, 161, 217

LIPKOWSKA, Lydia (1882 or 1884–1955) Soprano, 105

Liszt, Franz (Ferencz) (1811–1886) Composer-Pianist, 134, 193

Litante, Judith, Singing Teacher, 200

Liu (Puccini: *Turandot*), 37

Lockhart, Rupert Bruce, 149

Lohengrin (*Lohengrin*), 75, 76, 285

Lohengrin (Wagner), *xv*, 39, 43, 71, 93, 198, 285

LONDON, George, born George Burnstein (1919 or 1920–) Bass-Baritone, 82, 84

LORENZ, Max (1901 or 1902–) Tenor, 78

Louise (Charpentier: *Louise*), 234

Louise (G. Charpentier), 95, 241

"Love Letters", 119

LOVITZKY (Moussorgsky: *Boris*), 93

LUCA, Giuseppe de (1876–1950) Baritone, 289

Lucia di Lammermoor (G. Donizetti), 172, 261

Lucia di Lammermoor (Donizetti: *Lucia di Lammermoor*), 37, 94, 95

LUDWIG, Christa (1928–) Mezzo-Soprano, 56, 104, 113, 273

Luisa Miller (Verdi), 69

"Lullaby of Birdland" (Shearing-Forster), 119

Mabel (Gilbert and Sullivan: *Pirates of Penzance*), 34

MACDONALD, Jeanette (1907–1965) Soprano-Actress, 35

"Mad Scene" (Donizetti: *Lucia di Lammermoor*), 172
Macama Butterfly (*see* Cio-Cio San)
Madama Butterfly (G. Puccini), 73
Maenads, Bacchic women, 9
Maddalena (Giordano: *Chénier*), 38
Madelon, blind mother (Giordano: *Chénier*), 95
Magnolia (Kern: *Showboat*), 35
Mahler, Gustav (1860–1911) Composer-Conductor, 54, 294
MALIBRAN, Maria (Felicità) born Garcia (1808–1836) Soprano, 22, 25, 56, 127, 153, 189, discussion, 190-192; 193, 259
Mancini, Giovanni Battista (1716–1800) Singing teacher, 22, 24, 164, 165, 167, 221
Manon (Massenet: *Manon*), 37
Manon Lescaut (Puccini: *Manon Lescaut*), 38
Manon Lescaut (G. Puccini), 72
Manrico (Verdi: *Trovatore*), 69
Mansfield, Katharine, born Beauchamp (1888–1923) Writer, 235
MANSKI, Dorothee (1891 or 1895–1967) Soprano, 208
Manual of Bel Canto, Ida Franca, 107
Manzoni, Alessandro (1785–1873) Author, 103
Marcello (Puccini: *Bohème*), 64, 82
MARCHESI, Blanche (1863–1940) Soprano-Teacher, 39, 99, 151, on Susy Clemens, 198-199; 209, 221, 263, 271, 272
Marchesi de Castrone, Mathilde, born Graumann (1821–1913) Singing teacher, 145, 198, discussion, 209-211; 226, 234
Marek, George Richard (1902–) Music writer, 261
Marguerite (Gounod: *Faust*), 37, 38, 130
Maria Stuarda (Donizetti: *Maria Stuarda*), 191
Maria-Theresa, Empress (1717–1780) Hapsburg Empire, 133
MARIO, Giovanni, born Mario Calvaliere di Candia (1810–1883) Tenor, 269
MARIO, Queena, born Tillotson (1896–1951) Soprano, 208
Marke, King (Wagner: *Tristan*), 87
Marschallin (Strauss: *Rosenkavalier*), 40, 43, 204
Martial, born Marcus Valerius Martialis (40?–104?), writer, 11
MARTIN, Dean (1917–) Pop Singer, 122
Martin, George Whitney (1926–) Author, 128
MARTIN, Mary (Virginia) (1913–) Pop Singer, 35, 88
MARTIN, Riccardo, born Hugh Whitfield Martin (1874–1952) Tenor, 278

MARTINELLI, Giovanni (1885–1969) Tenor, 74, 159, 208, 287, 294
MARTINI, Nino (1905–) Tenor, 121
Marullo (Verdi: *Rigoletto*), 93
Masetto (Mozart: *Don Giovanni*), 82
Massenet, Jules Émile-Fréderic (1842–1912) Composer, 37, 66, 133, 134
MATERNA, Amalie (1844–1918) Soprano, 104
MATHIS, Johnny (1935–) Pop Singer, 121
MATZENAUER, Marguerite (1881–1963) Mezzo-Soprano, 55
MAYNOR, Dorothy (1910–) Soprano, 107
MCCARTNEY, Paul (*see* Beatles)
MCCORMACK, John (1884 or 1894–1945) Tenor, 67, 101, 161
McCormick, Harold, Financier, 135
MCCRACKEN, James (1927–) Tenor, 78, 94
Meistersinger von Nurenberg, Die (Wagner), 16, 39, 71, 87, 93, 160
MELBA, Nellie, born Helen Porter Mitchell (1861–1931) Soprano, xiii f., 23, 36, 41, 108, 150, attack, 155; 158, 209, 210, 234, 253, 284, 287
MELCHIOR, Lauritz, born Lebrecht Hommel (1890–) Tenor, 23, 77, discussion, 78
Men, Women and Tenors (Frances Alda), 136
Mendelssohn, Felix, born Jacob Ludwig Felix Mendelssohn-Bartholdy (1809–1847) Composer, 115, 116
Méphistophélès (Gounod: *Faust*), 84, 86, 88
MERCER, Mabel (1900–) Pop Singer, 123
Merlin, Countess Maria de Las Mercedes, born Jaruco (1789–1852) Writer of memoirs, on Garcia sisters, 190-192
MERMAN, Ethel (1909–) Pop Singer-Actress, 119
MERRILL, Robert (1917 or 1919–) Baritone, 82, 93
Mesopotamians, 7
Messenger (Verdi: *Aida*), 94
Messiah (G. F. Handel), 66, 115, 245
Metropolitan Opera Auditions, 93, 203, 242
Metropolitan Opera Broadcasts, 106, 293
Metropolitan Opera Company, 38, 50, 52, 54, 55, 56, 57, 69, 71, 73, 74, 81, 82, 83, 87, 93, 94, 119, 153, 158, 159, 171, 189, 197, 208, 209, 211, 216, 238, 242, 250, 251, 252, 255, 256, 260, 271, 272, 280, 286, 292, 293, 294
Metropolitan Opera Guild, 293
Micaela (Bizet: *Carmen*), 37, 38
Midsummer Night's Dream, A (B. Britten), 65
Mignon (Thomas: *Mignon*), 50, 111

Mignon (A. Thomas), 50
Mikado, The (Gilbert and Sullivan), 34, 59
MILANOV, Zinka (1906–) born Kunc, Soprano, 39, 104
MILLER, Mildred (1924–) Mezzo-Soprano. 148 f.
MILNES, Sherrill (1935?–) Baritone, 25, 106
Mimi (Puccini: *Bohème*), 37, 38, 40, 251, 252
"Mira, O Norma" (Bellini: *Norma*), 133
"Mr. Reginald Peacock's Day" (Katharine Mansfield), 235
Mistress Ford (Verdi: *Falstaff*), 64
Monnaie, Théâtre de la (Brussels), 251
Monterone (Verdi: *Rigoletto*), 86
Monteverdi, Claudio Giovanni Antonio (1567–1643) Composer, 17
"Moon and I, The" (Gilbert and Sullivan: *Mikado*), 34
Moore, George (1852–1933) Novelist, 157
MOORE, Grace (1901–1947) Soprano, 35
MORGAN, Helen, Singer-Actress, 118
MORISON, Elsie (1924–) Soprano, 108 f.
Moscow Imperial Opera, 105
Moses, Paul J., Laryngologist, 179
Moses and Aaron (A. Schoenberg), 96
Most Happy Fella (F. Loesser), 36
Moulton, Lillie, *see* de Hegermann-Lindencrone
Mozart, Wolfgang A. (1756–1791) Composer, 30, 43, 60, 81, 82, 86, 112, 115, 125, 156, on vibrato, 158; 230
MURSKA, Ilma di (1836–1889) Soprano, 209
Musetta (Puccini: *Bohème*), 88, 251
Music in Western Civilization (Paul Henry Lang), 7
Musset, Alfred de (1810–1857) Poet, 194
MUSTAFÀ, Domenico (1829–1912) Castrato, 172
MUZIO, Claudia, born Claudina (1889 or 1892–1936) Soprano, 41
My Fair Lady (Lerner-Loewe), 124
"My Heart Belongs to Daddy," 35

Nanetta (Verdi: *Falstaff*), 107
National Association of Teachers of Singing, discussion, 205-207
National Metropolitan Opera Company, 238
Natural Approach to Singing, A (J. Litante), 200
Nedda (R. Leoncavallo: *Pagliacci*), 37, 40
Nemorino (Donizetti: *L'Elisir d'Amore*), 66

Nero, Claudius Caesar (37–68) Emperor, as singer, 10-11
Nerves, 200; discussion, 247-250
"Nessun Dorma" (Puccini: *Turandot*), 242
NEVADA, Emma, born Wixom (1859 or 1862–1940) Soprano, 209
New Republic, The (Periodical), 122
New York City Opera, 238, 242, 250, 279
New York Singing Teachers' Association, 205
New Yorker, The (Periodical), 40
Nichols, Beverly (1899–) Author, 284
Nicklausse (Offenbach: *Hoffmann*), 50
NIEMANN, Albert (1831–1917) Tenor, 104
NILSSON, Birgit (1918 or 1922–) Soprano, 25, 40, 42, 97, 105
NILSSON, Christine, born Kristina (1843–1921) Soprano, 41, 97
"Nina," 226
Nodes, 181, 270-272
"Non più Andrai" (Mozart: *Nozze*), 289
"NORDICA Giglio" (See Lillian Nordica), 251
NORDICA, Lillian, born Norton (1857–1914) Soprano, 23, 40, 41, 150, 197, discussion, 201; 215, 221, 273
Norma (*Norma*), 5, 39, 40, 50, 56, 93, 195
Norma (Bellini), 42, 181, 183
NOURRIT, Adolphe (1802–1839) Tenor, 255
NOVELLO, Clara Anastasia (1818–1908) Soprano, 117
Nozze di Figaro, Le (W. A. Mozart), 34, 50, 55, 88

"O Erbarme Dich" (Bach), 115
"O for the Wings of a Dove" (Mendelssohn: *St. Paul*), 181
"O Paradiso" (Meyerbeer: *L'Africaine*), 72
"O Patria Mia" (Verdi: *Aida*), 44
"O Rest in the Lord" (Mendelssohn: *St. Paul*), 115
"O Ruddier than the Cherry" (Handel: *Acis and Galatea*), 66
Oberon (C. M. von Weber), 161
Oberon (Britten: *A Midsummer Night's Dream*), 65
Observations on the Florid Song (P. F. Tosi), 21
Octavian (Strauss: *Rosenkavalier*), 20, 50
Odyssey, The (Homer), 7
Of Lena Geyer (Marcia Davenport), 277
Offenbach, Jacques (1819–1880) Composer, 34
Oklahoma! (Rodgers and Hammerstein), 121
Olympia (Offenbach: *Hoffmann*), 34

"On Dramatic Song" (Richard Wagner), 103
Once More from the Beginning (Robert Merrill), 93
ONEGIN, Sigrid, born Elisabeth Elfriede Emilie Sigrid (also known as Lilly Hoffmann) (1889–1943) Mezzo Soprano, 113, 218
Opera (Periodical), 149
Opéra, Paris, 102, 252, 263
Opéra-Comique (Paris), 102
Opera News (Periodical), 106
Orfeo (Gluck: *Orfeo*), 58, 60
Orfeo ed Eurydice (C. W. Gluck), 58, 128
Orpheus, legend of, 8-9, 141
Ortrud (Wagner: *Lohengrin*), 43, 52
Otello (G. Rossini), 126
Otello (Verdi: *Otello*), 249
Otello (G. Verdi), 82, 83, 94
Oxford Dictionary of English, The, 162
"Ozean zu Ungeheur" (Weber: *Oberon*), 161

PACCHIEROTTI, Gasparo (1740–1821) Castrato, 22
Padre Guardino (Verdi: *Forza*), 86
Pagliacci (R. Leoncavallo), 38, 69, 81, 82, 95, 251
Paleolithic Age (c. 30,000-15,000 B.C.), 4
"Palms, The" (*see* "Les Rameaux")
PANZÉRA, Charles (1896–) Baritone, 82
Papageno (Mozart: *Zauberflöte*), 82
Parpignol (Puccini: *Bohème*), 94
Parsifal (Wagner: *Parsifal*), 76
Parsifal (R. Wagner), 87, 197
PASKALIS, Kostas, Baritone, 82 f.
Passion According to St. John (J. S. Bach), 116
PASTA, Giuditta, born Negri (1798–1865) Soprano, 22, 25, 195
Patience (Gilbert and Sullivan), 59
PATTI, Adelina, born Adela Juana Maria (1843–1919) Soprano, 23, 36, 41, 51, 179, discussion, 181-183; 189, 195 f., 207, 257 f., 293
PATTI, Carlotta (1835–1889) Soprano, 183
PATZAK, Julius (1898–) Tenor, 113
Paul, Saint (?-67?), 11
PEERCE, Jan, born Jacob Pincus Perelmuth (1904–) Tenor, 96, 115
Pelléas (Debussy: *Pelléas*), 82
Pelléas et Melisande (C. Debussy), 96
Penderecki, Krzystof (1933–) Composer, 114
"Per me giunto" (Verdi: *Don Carlo*), 160
Pergolesi, Giovanni Battista (1710–1736) Composer, 226

Peri, Jacopo (1561–1633?) Composer, 17, 124
Peter Grimes (Britten: *Peter Grimes*), 242
Peter Grimes (Benjamin Britten), 75, 242
PETERS, Roberta (1930–) Soprano, 34, Metropolitan debut, 250
Petrarch, born Francesco Petrarca (1304–1374) Poet, 103
Pharynx, 101, 102, 146, 174, 220
Philip II, King (Verdi: *Don Carlo*), 87, 279
Philip V, King of Spain (1683–1746), *xiv*
Phillips, Ambrose (1675–1749) Poet, *xiii*
Phyllis (Gilbert and Sullivan: *Iolanthe*), 34
PIAF, Edith (1916?–1963) Pop Singer, *xi*, 132, 202
Pinkerton, B. F. (Puccini: *Madama Butterfly*), 240
PINZA, Ezio, (Fortunio) (1892–1957) Bass, *xi*, 81, 82, 86, 88, 104, 196, 276
Pirates of Penzance, The (Gilbert and Sullivan), 34
Pizarro (Beethoven: *Fidelio*), 83, 84
PLANÇON, Pol (Henri) (1851–1914) Bass, 150
Plato (427?–347? B.C.) Philosopher, 8
Pogner (Wagner: *Meistersinger*), 87
Polly Peachum (Gay: *Beggar's Opera*), 34
Polyeucte (Gounod: *Polyeucte*), 130
PONS, Lily (Alice-Joséphine) (1904–) Soprano, 23, 33, 35, 41, 171, 197, 208, 248
PONSELLE, Rosa, born Ponzillo (1897–) Soprano, *xii*, 39, 41, 42, 51, 188, 189, 208, 229, Metropolitan debut, 248; 252, after debut, 253; 260
"Poor Wandering One" (Gilbert and Sullivan: *Pirates of Penzance*), 34
Porpora, Niccolò (1686–1767) Singer-Teacher, 233
Portrait of the Artist as a Young Man, A (J. Joyce), 134
Poulenc, Francis (1899–1963) Composer, 131
POWELL, Jane (1929–) Soprano-Actress, 35
Practical Reflections on Figured Singing (1774) (G. Mancini), 24
Premier Jour du Bonheur, Le (D. F. Auber), 134
PREVEDI, Bruno (1928–) Tenor, 77
PREY, Hermann (1929–) Baritone, 82, 104, 113, as potential tenor, 218-219
PRICE, Leontyne (1927 or 1929–) Soprano, 25, 32, 38, 44, 52, 107, 119, 120, 163, 197, 211, 231
Pride and Prejudice (J. Austen), 133
Primitive Song (C. M. Bowra), 4

Prodigal Son, The (A. Sullivan), 135
"Prologue" (Leoncavallo: *Pagliacci*), 81
Puccini, Giacomo (1858–1924) Composer, 52, 64, 72, 284
Purcell, Henry (1659?–1695) Composer, 64, 125
Puritz, Elizabeth, Singing teacher, 98 f.

Quantz, Johann (1697–1773) Flautist, 20
Queen of Shemakha (Rimsky-Korsakov), 34
Queen of the Night (Mozart: *Zauber-flöte*), 30, 31, 33, 34, 37, 40, 250
Quintilian, born Marcus Fabius Quintilianus (35?–95?); rhetorician, 11

Radames (Verdi: *Aida*), 67, 74, 75, 76, 248, 262
Radio City Music Hall, 96
Rainbow Bridge, The (Mary Watkins Cushing), 266
"Rameaux, Les" (J. B. Faure), 131
Ramfis (Verdi: *Aida*), 87
"Recondita Armonia (Puccini: *Tosca*), 107
Records of a Girlhood (Fanny Kemble), 195 f.
Reid, Cornelius L., Singing teacher, 162
Registers, 42, 58, 63, 64, 65, 107, women's chest, 118; discussion, 163-173; 181
"Rejoice Greatly" (Handel: *Messiah*), 115
Renato (Verdi: *Ballo*), 84
Requiem (B. Britten), 117
Requiem Mass (G. Verdi), 38, 115, 117
RESNIK, Regina (1922 or 1923–) Mezzo-Soprano and Soprano, discussion, 57
Resonators, 146, 147, discussion, 173-175
RESZKE, Edouard de (1853 or 1855–1917) Bass, 23, 104, 150
RESZKE, Jean de (Jan Mieczisiaw) (1850–1925) Baritone and Tenor, 23, discussion, 76-77; 104, 150, 195, 207, 221, on the nose, 222-223; return, 285-286
RETHBERG, Elisabeth, born Sattler (1894–) Soprano, 104
"Rêve, Le" (Massenet: *Manon*), 67
Rheingold, Das (R. Wagner), 255
Richard I (Coeur de Lion) (1157–1199) King of England, 15
Ries, Ferdinand (1784–1838) Pianist-Composer, 125
Rigoletto (Verdi: *Rigoletto*), 81, 82, 84
Rigoletto (G. Verdi) 37, 75, 86, 93
Rimsky-Korsakov, Nicolai A. (1844–1908) Composer, 34
ROBESON, Paul (1898–) Bass, 89, 107
ROBIN, Mado (1918–1960) Soprano, 33
Robinson, Francis, Writer, 71
Rodgers, Richard (1902–) Composer, 255

Rodolfo (Puccini: *Bohème*), 66, 68, 252
Rodrigo (Verdi: *Don Carlo*), 84, 160
Rogers, Clara Doria *see* Doria
Roman Empire (31 B.C.–476 A.D.), 9-11
Romberg, Sigmund (1887–1951) Composer, 34
Roméo (Gounod: *Roméo*), 76
Rosenkavalier, Der (R. Strauss), 34, 50, 87
Rosina (Rossini: *Barbiere*), 31, 37
ROSSI, Tino, Pop Tenor, 121
Rossini, Gioacchino (1792–1868) Composer, 25, 30, 49, 58, 81, 112, 115, 124, as singer, 125-127; 133, 160, 161, 188, 190, 195
Royal Zoological Society, xvi
ROZE, Marie (–Hippolyte) born Rose-Ponsin (1846–1926) Soprano, 51
RUBINI, Giovanni-Battista (1794 or 1795–1854) Tenor, 22
RUDERSDORFF, Ermine (1822–1882) Soprano, 211
RUFFO, Titta, born Giovanni Titta (1876 or 1877–1953) Baritone, 83
Ruslan and Ludmilla (M. Glinka), 105
Russell, Lillian (1861–1922) Singer-Actress, 117
RUYSDAEL, Basil, born Basil Spaulding Millspaugh, Bass, 293

SACK, Erna, born Erna Weber (1903 or 1906–) Contralto and Soprano, 33, 57
Sacristan (Puccini: *Tosca*), 88
Sadler's Wells Opera, 250
St. Paul (F. Mendelssohn), 115
Saint-Saëns, Camille (1835–1921) Composer, 193
Salome (Strauss: *Salome*), 54
Salome (R. Strauss), 83, 96
Samson (Saint-Saëns: *Samson*), 71
San Francisco Opera Company, 242
Sand, Georges, born Aurore Dupin, Baronne Dudebant (1804–1876) Author, 194
SANDERSON, Julia, Singer-Actress, 117
SANDERSON, Sibyl, also sang as Ada Palmer (1865–1903) Soprano, 209
Santa Fe Opera, 242
SANTLEY, (Sir) Charles (1834–1922) Baritone, 251
Sapho (C. Gounod), 130
Sarastro (Mozart: *Zauberflöte*), 86, 88
Saul, King of Israel, xiv
SAYÃO, Bidu (1902–) Soprano, 23, 41, 208, 223 f.
Sbriglia, Giovanni (1832–1916) (Tenor and singing teacher), 221
Scala Opera House, La, 74, 127

Scarpia (Puccini: *Tosca*), 82, 83, 84, 95
Schaunard (Puccini: *Bohème*), 93
SCHEFF, Fritzi (1879–1954) Soprano, 255
SCHIØTZ, Aksel (1906–) Tenor and Baritone, 113
SCHIPA, Tito, born Raffaele Attilio Amedeo (1889–1956) Tenor, 66, 67
"Schmalztenor" (M. W. Branch), 75
SCHMIDT, Joseph (1904–1942) Tenor, 77, 202
Schoenberg, Arnold (1874–1951) Composer, 96
Schola Cantorum, 13
SCHRÖDER-DEVRIENT, Wilhelmine (1804–1860) Soprano, 104
Schubert, Franz (1797–1828) Composer, 58, 113
SCHUMANN, Elisabeth (1885–1952) Soprano, 112, 222
SCHUMANN-HEINK, Ernestine, born Rossler (1861–1936) Mezzo-Soprano, 104, 113, 273
SCHWARZKOPF, Elisabeth (1915–) Soprano, 98, 104, 111, 112
Schwertleite (Wagner: *Walküre*), 55
Science and Singing (Ernest G. White), 145
SCOTTI, Antonio (1866–1936) Baritone, 81, 93, 294
Seashore, Harold, Psychologist, 159, 162
SEEFRIED, Irmgard (1919–) Soprano, 104
SEMBRICH, Marcella, born Praxede Marcelline Kochánska (1858–1935) Soprano, 41, 104, breathing, 150; 197, 207, 221, 294
Semiramide (G. Rossini), 50
Seneca, Lucius Annaeus (3 B.C.?–65 A.D.) Philosopher-Statesman,
Senta (Wagner: *Holländer*), 39, 104
Shakespeare, William (1564–1616) Dramatist-Writer, 76, 158, 168
SHAW, John (1921–) Baritone, 108 f.
Sheldon, W. H., Physiologist, on body types, 200-201
SHERIDAN, Margaret (1889–1958) Soprano, 101
SHIRLEY, George (1934–) Tenor, 242
SHORE, Dinah, born Frances Rose (1920–) Pop Singer, 25
Short Course in Singing, A (C. R. Thorne), 228
Showboat (J. Kern), 35
Shuisky, Prince (Moussorgsky: *Boris*), 95
"Si per Ciel" (Verdi: *Otello*), 83
Siegfried (Wagner: *Götterdämmerung*), 76, 78, 99
Siegfried (Wagner: *Siegfried*), 75, 76, 78, 99

Siegfried (R. Wagner), 54, 58, 161, 262, 271
Sieglinde (Wagner: *Walküre*), 39, 54, 55, 57, 99, 263
Siegmund (Wagner: *Walküre*), 75, 76, 99
SIEPE, Cesare (1923–) Bass, 82, 86, 279
SILLS, Beverly (1930–) Soprano, 25, 279
Silvio (Leoncavallo: *Pagliacci*), 82
SIMIONATO, Giulietta (1910–) Mezzo-Soprano, 201
SINATRA, Frank (1915–) Pop Singer, 9, 119, discussion, 122-123; 189, 246, 277
Singer's Pilgrimage, A (Blanche Marchesi), 221
Singers, beginnings, 231-233
Singers, careers abruptly terminated, 282-283
Singers, families of, 183-184
Singers, length of careers, 288-289
Singers, marriages between, 273-276
Singers, marriages with musicians, 235-237
Singers, name changes, 243-244
Singers, retirement activities, 291-292
Singing of the Future, The (D. Ffrangcon-Davies), 100
Singularity of Voice, A (Hardwick), 64
SLEZAK, Leo (1873–1946) Tenor, 78
SMITH, Bessie (1904–1937) Jazz singer, 203, 280
Smoking, 270
Sonata, Piano (Opus 57) (Beethoven), 125
Song of the Lark, The (Willa Cather) xvi, Fremstad's comment, 266
Sonnambula, La (V. Bellini), 182
SONTAG, Henrietta, born Gertrude Walburga Sonntag (1804 or 1806–1854) Soprano, 22
Sophie (Strauss: *Rosenkavalier*), 34, 40
SOUEZ, Ina, born Rains (1908–) Soprano, 170
South Pacific (Rodgers and Hammerstein), 88
SOUZAY, Gérard (1918–) Baritone, 82, 113
SPEAKS, Margaret, Soprano, 36
Spoletta (Puccini: *Tosca*), 95
Spontini, Gasparo (1774–1851) Composer, 128, 229
Stabat Mater (G. Rossini), 58, 115
"Ständchen" (R. Strauss), 112
STARR, Ringo (see Beatles)
STEBER, Eleanor (1916–) Soprano, 40
Steersman (Wagner: *Tristan*), 286
STEFANO, Giuseppe di (1921–) Tenor, 71
Stereo Review, (Periodical) xiii, 19
STEVENS, Risë (1913–) Mezzo-Soprano, 35, 293

STEWART, Thomas (1923–) Baritone, 244, 247, 279
STICH-RANDALL, Teresa (1927–) Soprano, 107, 244
STOJANOVIC, Milka, Soprano, 104 f.
Story, Julian (1857–?) Painter, 273
Stradella, Alessandro (1642–1682) Composer, 255
"Strange Fruit" (Allen-Holiday), 132
STRATAS, Teresa (1938 or 1939–) Soprano, 50
Strauss, Richard (1864–1949) Composer, 34, 43, 112, 230
STREICH, Rita (1920 or 1926–) Soprano, 33
STREISAND, Barbra (1942–) Entertainer, xiii
"Stride la Vampa" (Verdi: Trovatore), 262
Suetonius, Caius (69–140) Biographer, 10
SULIOTIS, Elena (1943–) Soprano, 256
Sullivan, Sir Arthur (1842–1900) Composer, 34, 59, 135
SUMAC, Yma, born Emperatriz Chavarri (1927 or 1928–), 33
SUPERVIA, Conchita (1895–1936) Mezzo-Soprano, 52
Susanna (Mozart: Nosse), 34, 38
SUTHAUS, Ludwig (1906–) Tenor, 78
SUTHERLAND, Joan (1926–) Soprano, 20, 21, 25, 32, 36, 37, 38, 41, 93, 100, 108, 220, 279
Suzuki (Puccini: Madama Butterfly), 240
SVANHOLM, Set (1904–1964) Tenor, 76, 77, 78
SWARTHOUT, Gladys (1904–1969) Mezzo-Soprano, 35, 252

TADOLINI, Eugenia (1809–?) Soprano, 30
TAGLIAVINI, Ferruccio (1913–) Tenor, 71
TALLEY, Marion (1906 or 1907–) Soprano, 255-256
Tamino (Mozart: Zauberflöte), 68
Tanglewood Music Center, 73
Tannhäuser (Wagner: Tannhäuser), 71
Tannhäuser (R. Wagner) 39, 42, 84, 87, 129, 198
TAUBER, Richard, born Ernst Seiffert (1892–1948) Tenor, 75
Taubman Howard (1907–) Music Critic, 105
Taylor, Bernard U., Singing Teacher, 206
Teachers' hierarchies, 212
Teaching of Elizabeth Schumann, The (E. Puritz), 98 f.
TEBALDI, Renata (1922–) Soprano, 32, 38, 40, 41, 42
Tellegen, Lou, Actor, 273

Telramund (Wagner: Lohengrin), 83, 84
Temple, Shirley (Jane) (1929–) Actress, 181
TERNINA, Milka (1863–1941) Soprano, 104
TETRAZZINI, Eva (1862–1938) Soprano, 196
TETRAZZINI, Luisa (1871–1940) Soprano, 36, 41, 105, 185, 196, 202, 234, 261
TEYTE, Maggie, born Tate (1888 or 1889–) Soprano, 123
Thomas, Ambroise (1811–1896) Composer, 50
THOMAS, Jess (1927 or 1928–) Tenor, 74, 75, 106, 244
THOMAS, John Charles (1891–1960) Baritone, 106
THORBORG, Kerstin (1896–1970) Mezzo-Soprano, 23
Thorne, Clarence R. Voice Teacher, 228
THURSBY, Emma (1845–1931) Soprano, 211
TIBBETT, Lawrence, born Tibbet (1896–1960) Baritone, 23, 93, 106, 252
TIETJENS, Therese (Johanne Alexandra) (1831–1877) Soprano, 202
TIGELLIUS, Roman singer, 10-11
Times (London), 19, 122
TINY TIM, Pop Singer, 65, 117
Tippett, Michael (1905–) Composer, quote, 64-65
" 'Tis Nature's Voice" (H. Purcell), 125
"Tod und das Mädchen, Der" (F. Schubert), 58, 113
Tonio (Leoncavallo: Pagliacci), 81
Tosca, La (G. Puccini), 83, 88, 95, 107
Tosca (Puccini: Tosca), 38, 40, 55, 82, 84, 204
Toscanini, Arturo (1867–1957) Conductor, 55, 71, 94, 107
Tosi, Pietro Francesco (1650?–1730 or 1732) Singing teacher, 21, 24, 99
Tower of Ivory (G. Atherton), 279
Town Hall (New York City), 245
TOZZI, Giorgio (1923–) Bass, 86, 87
Trachea, 142
Tramp Abroad, A (Mark Twain), xv
TRAUBEL, Helen (1899–) Soprano, 23, 42, 78, 120, 197, 234, 252, 259, 280, 287
"Traum" (Elsa's) (Wagner: Lohengrin), 39
Traviata, La (G. Verdi), 38, 41, 82, 251, 252
Tremolo, discussion, 162-163
Trilby (George du Maurier), 195, quote, 215-216
Trill, 22, discussion, 160-161
Tristan (Wagner: Tristan), 74, 75, 76, 78, 130, 264
Tristan und Isolde (R. Wagner), 83, 130

Trovatore, Il (G. Verdi), 38, 40, 43, 57, 69, 78, 81, 82, 84, 238, 239
Troubadours, 15-16
Truman, Margaret (1922–) Pres. Harry Truman's daughter, 135
"Tu che invoco (Spontini: *La Vestale*), 229
TUCKER, Richard (1913 or 1914–) Tenor, 69, 73, 75, 115
TUCKER, Sophie (1894–1966) Pop Singer, 118, 124
Turandot (G. Puccini), 37, 69, 75, 242
Turgenev, Ivan Sergeyevich (1818–1883) Author, 193
Turiddu (Mascagni: *Cavalleria Rusticana*), 67, 69, 70
Twain, Mark (*see* Samuel L. Clemens)
TYLER, Veronica, Soprano, 211

Ulrica (Verdi: *Ballo*), 52, 55
Ulysses (J. Joyce), 135
"Un bel di" (Puccini: *Madama Butterfly*), 239
"Underneath the Harlem Moon," 280

Valentin (Gounod: *Faust*), 81, 93
VALLEE, Rudy, born Hubert Prior, Pop Singer, 120, 121
VALLETTI, Cesare (1921–) Tenor, 66
Varlaam (Moussorgsky: *Boris*), 88
VARNAY, Astrid (1918–) Soprano, 235
VAUGHAN, Sarah (Lois) (1924–) Pop Singer, 117, 119
Veaco, J. C., Writer on voice production, 150
VEASEY, Josephine (1931–) Mezzo-Soprano, 100, 242
"Veilchen, Das" (W. A. Mozart), 112
Velluti, Giovanni-Battista (1781–1861) Castrato, 19
Vennard, William, Voice Teacher, 162
Venus (Wagner: *Tannhäuser*), 52, 54, 104
Verdi, Giuseppe (1813–1901) Composer, 30, 43, 44, 64, 66, 81, 82, 83, 84, 115, 117, as singer, 128; 160, 179
VERRETT (Carter) Shirley (1933 or 1938–) Mezzo-Soprano, 243
Vestale, La (G. Spontini), 128, 229
Vetta-Karst, Mme., Singing Teacher, 234
Viardot, Paul (1857–1941) Violinist-Conductor, Son of Pauline, 263-264
VIARDOT, Pauline, born Garcia (1821–1910) Mezzo-Soprano, 56, 58, 130, 133, 145, 189, 190, discussion, 192-195
Vibrato, 98, 115, 122, discussion, 157-162; 163
VICKERS, Jon (1926–) Tenor, 74, 242
Victor, RCA (Victor Talking Machine Company), 73, 74

Victoria, Princess (1819–1901) later Queen of England, 133
"Vie en Rose, La" (E. Piaf), 132
VINAY, Ramon (1914–) Baritone and Tenor, 77
Violetta (Verdi: *Traviata*), 38, discussion, 41; 51, 103, 251
VISHNEVSKAYA, Galena (1926–) Soprano, 105
Voice Building and Tone Placing (H. Holbrook Curtis), 223
Voice, Song and Speech (Behnke and Browne), 166
Voorhees, Irving Wilson (1878–?) Laryngologist, 187
VOTIPKA, Thelma (1906–) Soprano, 202
VYVYAN, Jennifer (1924?–) Mezzo-Soprano and Soprano, 57

Wagner, Cosima (1837–1930) Wife of Richard Wagner, 197
Wagner, Minna Planer (1809–1866) Wife of Richard Wagner, 103
Wagner, Wilhelm Richard (1813–1883) Composer, 16, 22, 43, 77, 103, 104, as singer, 128-130; 131, 287
WALKER, Edyth (1870–1950) Mezzo-Soprano and Soprano, 56
Walküre, Die (R. Wagner), 39, 43, 55, 87, 96, 161, 263, 280
Walpole, Sir Robert (1676–1745) Statesman, *xii*
Walska, Ganna, Amateur Singer, 135-136
Walter, Bruno, born B. W. Schlessinger (1876–1962) Conductor, 60
Walther von Stolzing (Wagner: *Meistersinger*), 71, 76, 160
War and Peace (L. Tolstoy), 133
War Requiem (B. Britten), 117
WARD, David (1925–) Bass, 87
WARREN, Leonard, born Warenoff (1911–1960) Baritone, 82, 96, 113
WATERS, Ethel (1900–) Pop Singer, 118, 203, 280
Weigert, Hermann (1890–1955) Singing Teacher, 235
Weiss, Deso A., Laryngologist, 219
WELITSCH, Ljuba, born Velitchkova (1913–) Soprano, 152, 267 f.
Wellington, Duke of, born Arthur Wellesley (1759–1862), 126
Werther (J. Massenet), 111
"Where Have All the Flowers Gone?," 123
White, Ernest G., Singing teacher, 145
Why Abdominal Breathing is Fatal to Bel Canto, (J. C. Veaco), 150

"Why do the Nations" (Handel: *Messiah*), 66, 116
Wigmore Hall (London), 245
Wilson, Margaret (Pres. Woodrow Wilson's daughter), 135
WINDGASSEN, Wolfgang (1914–) Tenor, 76, 78
WITHERSPOON, Herbert (1873–1935) Bass, 153, 292
Wolfram (Wagner: *Tannhäuser*), 84
Wotan (Wagner: *Rheingold*), 83
Wotan ("Der Wanderer") (Wagner: *Siegfried*), 83
Wotan (Wagner: *Walküre*), 83, 84, 87
Wozzeck (A. Berg), 64
Wozzeck (Berg: *Wozzeck*), 84

WUNDERLICH, Fritz (1930–1966) Tenor, 104, 113

"You'll Never Walk Alone" (Rodgers and Hammerstein: *Carousel*), 119
Young, Loretta (Gretchen) (1913–) Film Actress, 122
Yum-Yum (Gilbert and Sullivan: *Mikado*), 34

Zauberflöte, Die (W. A. Mozart), 30, 82, 86, 88
Zerbinetta (Strauss: *Ariadne*), 34
Zerlina (Mozart: *Don Giovanni*), 34, 38, 250, 294
Zeus, supreme god, 9